BLACK MAGIC

BLACK

A Pictorial History of the

Langston Hughes

MAGIC

Negro in American Entertainment

Milton Meltzer

PRENTICE-HALL, INC., ENGLEWOOD CLIFFS, NEW JERSEY

Second printing......July, 1968

BLACK MAGIC: *A Pictorial History of the Negro in American Entertainment* by Langston Hughes and Milton Meltzer © 1967 by Langston Hughes and Milton Meltzer All rights reserved. No part of this book may be reproduced in any form or by any means, except for the inclusion of brief quotations in a review, without permission in writing from the publisher. Library of Congress Catalog Card Number: 67-22993 Printed in the United States of America T 07757 Prentice-Hall International, Inc., London Prentice-Hall of Australia, Pty. Ltd., Sydney Prentice-Hall of Canada, Ltd., Toronto Prentice-Hall of India Private Ltd., New Delhi Prentice-Hall of Japan, Inc., Tokyo

This book was to have had no dedication.
The authors felt there were so many distinguished people in the world of entertainment it would be impossible to select any one man or woman to pay tribute to.

On May 22, 1967, shortly after work on the book was completed, and before it could be published, Langston Hughes died.

I think, now, that the artists who played and sang and danced in the many works he created for them, and the audiences to whom he gave such joy, would want to see the book dedicated

To Langston, with love

Milton Meltzer

The authors are indebted to many individuals and institutions for their assistance in the preparation of this book. We should like especially to express our gratitude to the following for their generous help in obtaining pictures or information:

Abby Aldrich Rockefeller Folk Art Collection; American Shakespeare Festival Theatre and Academy of Stratford, Connecticut; Sidney Bernstein; Columbia Television Network Division; Chicago Historical Society; Columbia Records; Culver Service; Merle Debuskey; Art D'Lugoff of the Village Gate; *Ebony; Esquire;* Fisk University Library; Theatre Collection of the Harvard College Library; Al Hirschfeld; Stella Holt; Sol Hurok; *Jet;* Metro-Goldwyn-Mayer; Metropolitan Opera Association; Museum of the City of New York; Museum of Modern Art Film Library; National Broadcasting Company; Robert Nemiroff; the Dance, Music, Picture, Schomburg and Theatre Collections of the New York Public Library; New York Shakespeare Festival; North Carolina Museum of Art; *Phylon;* RCA Victor Records; Lloyd Richards; Norman Rosten; Edward Steichen; Philip Sterling; Suffolk Museum; Twentieth Century Fox; Valentine Museum; Warner Bros.; Eric Weber, and the James Weldon Johnson Collection of the Yale University Library.

We owe special thanks to Raoul Abdul and Lindsay Patterson for research assistance, to Bernard Cole for photography, to Mrs. Molly Gallon for typing, and to Mr. and Mrs. Emerson Harper for living memories.

LANGSTON HUGHES
MILTON MELTZER

CONTENTS

THE BIG BEAT

*Terra cotta heads from Ife, Nigeria,
perhaps 13th century.*

The Indian tom-toms of the Mohawks and Seminoles proved no match for the basic beat which the Africans brought with them over three hundred years ago on their enforced migrations to American shores. Now Negroes (as Africans were called by the Spaniards) have been music makers and entertainers in the New World for more than three centuries. The first stage for the captive Africans was the open deck of a slave ship. There on the way to the Americas, blacks in chains, when herded up on deck for exercise, were forced to sing and dance in the open air for the amusement of the crew. The log of the English slave ship *Hannibal* in the year 1664 recorded that the Africans linked together aboard that vessel were made to "jump and dance for an hour or two" every day when weather permitted them out of the hole.

"If they go about it reluctantly or do not move with agility, they are flogged," states an account of the slave trade published in England in 1788. "Their musik upon these occasions consists of a

2

Old engraving of an African family.

Captives are escorted from interior of Africa to the coastal barracoons where they were kept until the slave ships called.

An artist of the 1790s depicts "remarkably as though it were a dance" the landing in North America of a group of Africans to be sold as slaves.

drum, sometimes with only one head, and when it is worn out . . . they make use of the bottom." The white sailors on the Middle Passage found these Africans and their rhythms highly entertaining, as did the planters ashore who purchased these black imports to work on their American plantations.

The syncopated beat which the captive Africans brought with them—and which perhaps lightened a little the burden of their servitude—quickly took root in the New World. Now that beat has been for generations a basic part of American musical entertainment. In Colonial days in New Orleans under the Spanish and the French (and later the Americans), black rhythms delighted Creole ears. The basic beat then went up the Mississippi, spreading East and West, and travelled wherever the Union spread from Virginia to the Sacramento Valley. Over the years Negro rhythms made fortunes for impresarios (the first of whom were slave masters), booking agents, A. & R. Men (Artists & Repertory), radio and television stations, and Broadway music publishers. In the twentieth century they launched *Porgy and Bess*, clothed Josephine Baker in gowns by the great Parisian fashion houses, initiated rock and roll, and started the Beatles on their million dollar way—not to mention building careers for innumerable black-

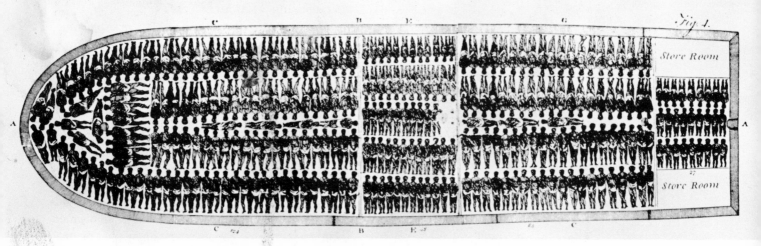

By the early 1500s the slave trade was an essential and highly profitable part of Europe's business. This plan of a slave ship shows the stowage for the dreaded crossing of the Atlantic. The branded slaves were packed like so many non-human commodities.

face minstrels from Dan Emmett before the Civil War to Al Jolson of the first talking picture, *The Jazz Singer,* in which he was made up as a Negro.

So this implantation of the basic beat in America began with the hand-clapping, feet-stomping, drum-beating rhythms (related, of course, to the rhythms of the human heart) that Africa exported

A 19th century artist sketched a Balunda playing the marimba and a few of the many drums, harps and pipes of the West African musicians.

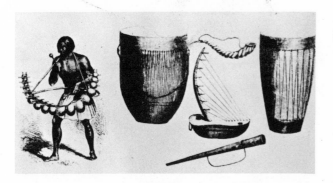

to our shores in the fifteenth century. Perhaps this basic beat arrived in the Americas even before that, since there were Negroes like Estabanico who, as explorers, antedated the first slaves. There were black men with Magellan at the Straits and even one, Pedro Alonzo Nino, who was said to be a pilot with Columbus. Probably long ago those black explorers possessed the same rhythm that Duke Ellington has today in "It don't mean a thing if it ain't got that swing."

Long before the Civil War the first Negro professional entertainers came into being. These were slaves under the management of their masters, whose services other whites might engage. In the *Richmond Daily Inquirer* for June 27, 1853, two slave brokers, Toler and Cook, advertised:

FOR HIRE, either for the remainder of the year or by the month, week, or job, the celebrated musician and fiddler, GEORGE WALKER . . . admitted by common consent to be the best leader of a band in all eastern and middle Virginia.

5

Walker's fees, unless by special arrangement, were to be paid to Toler and Cook.

"My master often received letters, sometimes from a distance of ten miles, requesting him to send me to play at a ball or festival of the whites," wrote a slave, Solomon Northup, in his published memoirs of a Louisiana plantation. "He received his compensation," he said of his master. "But, usually I also returned with many picayunes jingling in my pockets."

The most famous of all slave musicians was a Georgia-born child prodigy, Blind Tom, whose master, Colonel Bethune, made him into a national attraction. Tom's concert career continued long after Emancipation since he was a pianist-composer of real talent. Other black musicians who had developed their talents in slavery, became in freedom minstrel men who during the postwar Reconstruction added to the joys of popular entertainment with bones and banjoes, song and dance —usually as individual performers since the early minstrel companies, being white, did not permit Negroes on the stage. Carnivals and medicine shows, however, employed colored performers.

African musician.

Musicians and dancers on a West Indies plantation.

PLANTATION DAYS

In de evening by de moonlight,
You could hear de darkies singing . . .

So ran the refrain of a song by a Negro composer, James Bland, born before the Civil War. And in truth, on the more opulent plantations, it was not uncommon for slave masters to summon their Negroes to sing for them as they rocked away balmy summer nights on their wide verandas. Sometimes, too, on Sunday mornings, curious whites invaded Negro "praise meetings" to listen to what they called the "little spiritual songs" of the blacks.

"When you hear them," wrote one listener in 1846, "you are half inclined to laugh at their queerness, and yet cannot but be affected at the sincerity." Another listener on a plantation in

"The Banjo Player," painted in 1856 by William Sidney Mount.

The Bone Player *was painted by William Sidney Mount in the 1850s.*

One of America's great genre painters, the Long Islander William Sidney Mount, did the oil of the fiddler in Right and Left.

10

Georgia wrote, "I wish I was musician enough to write down the melodies; they are worth preserving." But before the Civil War, little effort was made to annotate the slave songs, religious or secular—possibly because to whites, as British actress Fanny Kemble wrote, these songs seemed "almost impossible to imitate." In her famous *Journal* of life on a Georgia plantation in 1838, Miss Kemble wrote of the slaves, "They always keep exquisite time and tune, and no words seem too hard for them to adapt to their tunes, so that they can sing a long-metre hymn to a short-metre tune without any difficulty . . . with the most perfect time and rarely with any discord." In other words, these Negro singers never missed a beat.

Early in the slave period, however, white Baptists and Methodists began to object to the religious singing of the slaves as being "too lively," and their "ring shouts" were definitely frowned upon. The result was that in some localities religious

On the plantations the slaves lived in a world without books and schools, or the fine arts they had known in Africa. Folktales, music and dancing became their chief means of self-expression.

11

An unknown artist of the 1790s made this watercolor of "The Old Plantation" somewhere in South Carolina. It is a rare record of the stick dance done to a drum and a stringed instrument.

Negro dancers entertain the crowd in a detail from The Militia Training, an 1841 painting by James G. Clonney.

THE BREAKDOWN

An illustrator for Harper's Weekly *drew this scene in 1861. A "thumping ecstasy," one visitor called such dances.*

Dancing was one of the slaves' favorite pastimes, enjoyed on special holidays and Saturday nights. One observer described the jogs and shuffles as "dancing all over," every part of the body moving at the same time.

Blind Tom, the 20th child of a Georgia slave, made his master a fortune on concert tours. Colonel Bethune falsely billed him as an idiot whose musical genius was due to some strange magic. Tom died at 59, exploited to the end.

A well-known banjoist in Richmond was Sy Gilliat, painted by an unknown artist. The Virginia musician died in the early 1820s.

meetings and revivals were forbidden by the slave owners. Sometimes, in spite of prohibitions, they were held anyhow, and it was said that in order to work off their suppressed jubilation at such times slaves sometimes put their heads under washpots so their shouting could not be heard at the

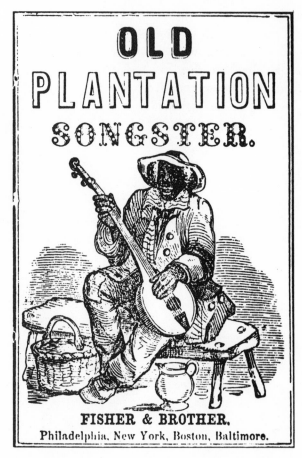

OLD PLANTATION SONGSTER.

FISHER & BROTHER,
Philadelphia, New York, Boston, Baltimore.

A small paperback containing the words to the popular melodies.

Big House. On the other hand—perhaps as much for their own amusement as that of the slaves—many masters encouraged weekend revels rather than revivals where blacks might dance the juba and sing as loud as they wished. But such doings, too, infuriated religious whites (mostly poor whites who did not own slaves) and they set out to suppress the rhythmic enjoyment of the blacks wherever they could. One Florida plantation owner wrote in 1829 concerning "his Negroes" that "A man calling himself a minister got among them. It was now sinful to dance, work their corn or catch a fish on Sunday." And a worried South Carolina planter wondered whether among slaves "The very abolition of singing and dancing as a result of religion . . . was not likely to produce even greater evils than it professed to cure." But some slaves, with few resources to resist Christian white pressures, were afraid to sing their own songs. However, they did, and when whites heard them, they were considered "natural born entertainers" with musical charm.

Perhaps it was the interest of white roustabouts in Negro music which saved from oblivion the secular songs and dances of the slaves. The birth of ragged white minstrels in blackface (with an eye toward making money from these plantation songs) certainly salvaged a part of Negro musical expression from near extinction by the religious zealots of the slave states. Although the white minstrels exaggerated Negro humor, distorted Negro rhythms, and burlesqued the dancing, enough of the basic beat of the blacks went into minstrelsy —along with some of the innocence and charm of their ethnic material—so that something of the Negro's contribution remained to make a definite and continuous imprint on the field of American entertainment.

Cover of a song book.

15

"JUMP JIM CROW"

Wheel about and turn about
An' do jist so—
An' ebery time I wheel about
I jump Jim Crow . . .

A little black slave boy singing this refrain and cutting capers on a street corner, so the story goes, caught the attention of an itinerant actor-singer named "Daddy" Rice. Rice was a New Yorker born in 1808 who wandered into the South as a young man, sometimes entertaining, sometimes acting, sometimes working as a stage carpenter or all-round theatre helper. Some say the city was Louisville, others say Cincinnati, where Rice observed the jigging lad. Anyhow, he picked up from this little black boy both his song and his dance, and with it Rice became famous. "Daddy" Rice blackened his face like the little colored boy and dressed in rags when he sang "Jump Jim Crow," and he pranced on stage with such syncopated hilarity that audiences demanded encore after encore. Another entertainer performing in burnt cork, Dan Emmett, borrowed the song from Rice and, as one of the first full-time minstrel men, carried it with acclaim throughout the country. "Jump Jim Crow" thus became the

16

JIM CROW.

NEW YORK.

Published by E. Riley & Hall, N. / Brooklyn C°.

Thomas Dartmouth Rice in his comic representation of Jim Crow. He added other Negro portraits to his act—a town dandy, a flatboatman, a plantation hand —and enjoyed huge popularity in the 1830s and 1840s. He met the same success in London. The painting on the opposite page shows Rice on stage at the Bowery theatre in New York, almost mobbed by his fans.

cornerstone of what was to be for eighty years America's most popular form of entertainment, the blackface minstrels.

Hundreds of white minstrels performing in burnt cork borrowed not only the Southern Negro's songs but his dance steps, his jokes, and his simple way of speech as well—which they distorted into what became known as "Negro dialect." White entertainers North and South literally made millions of dollars from Negro material. The Negroes themselves, barred from most theatres as spectators and segregated in others, could seldom see a minstrel show, and at that time they were not allowed to perform in them.

Negro dancing and what Negroes did with their bodies when singing fascinated white entertainers. The group amusements of the plantation blacks and their big-city counterparts seemed to possess powers of sure-fire communication in the theatre. Widely imitated were the jigs and jubas of the black field hands and the cakewalks of the house servants. The plantation stick dance became a standard comedy number for the minstrels in which a white made up as a very old blackamoor tottered on stage in rhythm to do the most amazingly grotesque steps and leaps over his cane. The contrast between decrepitness and surprising agility made for hilarious low comedy.

"Patting juba" became an accompaniment to a whole series of intricate dance steps whose rhythms fascinated even the poets of the mid-1800's, and caused writers like Edgar Allan Poe and Sidney Lanier to explore the possibilities of working the varied beats into verse. The Negro custom of creating rhythms for dancing without instruments became a part of the white minstrel routines—"striking the hands on the knees, then striking the right shoulder with one hand, the left with the other—all the while keeping time with the feet and singing." One of Poe's friends observed, "There is no such rhythm as this in Greek poetry —nor in fact in any other nation under the sun."

Of juba patting, Sidney Lanier wrote, "Here music is in its rudest form, consisting of rhythm alone . . . the most curious noise, yet in such perfect order it furnishes music to dance by . . . I have never seen it equalled in my life." The

uniqueness of expression derived from the Negro gave American minstrelsy its *raison d'être* and its character. "They play antics with the high heaven of sound," noted *Recollections of a Southern Matron* in 1838. Certainly so valuable to their master did some slave musicians become that three black music makers in Louisville were described in 1844 as being worth $1500 each. When the three ran away to the North, several thousand dollars was expended trying to trace their whereabouts and get them back.

Many slaves made their own instruments. Isaac Williams of King George County in Virginia related, "When we made a banjo, we would first of all catch what we called a ground hog, known in the North as a woodchuck." And its hide, tanned, would be stretched over "a piece of timber fashioned like a cheese box." Another way of making a banjo, as some slaves remembered from Africa, was to stretch a bladder over a calabash, and secure the strings on a raised bridge over the bladder. Homemade percussions came from boxes covered with sheepskin, called gumbo boxes. Bamboulas were made from casks covered with cowhide and beaten with beef bones. Other forms of percussion were little bells on ankles; bamboo tubes, one struck against another; the jawbones of animals whose dried teeth created a rattling sound; crude triangles forged by hand; and long hollow bones clicked together "like castanets, but five times as large." The professional minstrel men adapted such slave instruments to their own uses on the stage.

In Congo Square, a large dusty space in New Orleans where slaves were wont to gather on Sundays and holidays, drums from Africa were played. Sometimes a dozen, simultaneously played with all the other improvised forms of percussion, created a marvellous complexity of rhythms. Northern tourists and crowds of local whites gathered to listen and watch the wildest of dancing. But when sunset came, so an account of 1808 states, "the city patrols show themselves with their cutlasses, and the crowds immediately disperse." Some musicologists believe that jazz was born before sunset in Congo Square. Certainly the basic beat was there all day long.

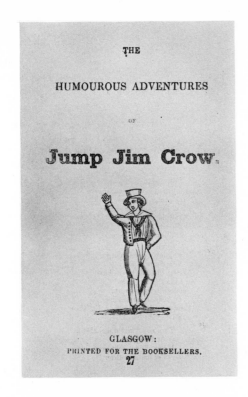

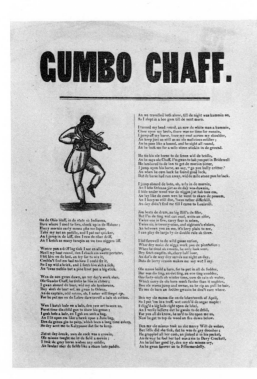

Broadsides came off-press by the thousands, spreading the hit songs of the minstrel shows.

THE MINSTRELS

The singing Lucas who performed throughout the North before the Civil War. Alexander C. Luca (top), Cleveland O. Luca (center left), Alexander C. Luca, Jr. (center right), and John W. Luca (bottom). In 1859 the Lucas teamed up with the celebrated white abolitionists, the Hutchinson Family, meeting the bitter prejudice of some audiences for daring publicly to associate together.

The Virginia Minstrels became the first blackface show to play in New York. Headed by Dan Emmett of "Dixie" and "Jump Jim Crow" fame, it opened on the Bowery in 1843 and was a hit. It was soon followed by the Virginia Serenaders, the Kentucky Minstrels, the Ethiopian Minstrels and similar troupes, all male and all white. It was a quarter of a century after

20

When the Georgia Minstrels changed managers Sam Lucas was still the star.

A sentimental song of 1878, dedicated to the popular Sam Lucas.

"Ethiopian Quadrilles" were featured by Dan Emmett's Virginia Minstrels, the first blackface company. Emmett, a Virginian, was partnered by three Yankees.

CITY HALL, GLASGOW.
FOR ONE NIGHT ONLY.
THE ORIGINAL VIRGINIA MINSTRELS
(from America).
MESSRS. R. W. PELHAM, D. D. EMMIT AND J. W. SWEENY beg to state that at the request of several families of distinction they intend giving
A GRAND ETHIOPIAN CONCERT
in the above hall on
SATURDAY EVENING, FIRST, JUNE 15, 1844, when they will be assisted by the celebrated Irish singer and representative of eccentric characters, MR. W. G. ROSS. The Virginia Minstrels feel assured, from the reception they have met with in America, England and Ireland, their first visit to this town, and the great success which has attended their concerts at the Waterloo Rooms, Edinburgh, they cannot fail to please and enlighten the public of Glasgow as to the slaves and free blacks of the United States. Their songs are all new, and set to the most precious gems of real negro melody. Each person plays on an instrument such as the slaves use on the plantations in the Southern parts of America. R.W. Pelham, tambourine; D. D. Emmit, violin; J. W. Sweeny, banjo; and F. M. Brower on the bone castanets—forming a complete band of negro music, and a true copy of the ups and downs of negro life. NOTE.—Not a trace or shade of vulgarity is mixed up with this original attempt at introducing a new and better school of negroism; and nothing shall be offered, either in word, look or action that can, in the least degree, offend the most fastidious taste. They will portray, through the medium of songs, dances, refrains, lectures, sayings and doings, the oddities, peculiarities, eccentricities, whimsicalities and comicalities of the sable gems of humanity.
PROGRAMME—PART FIRST.
Introductory Air—Merely to get the instruments in tune.
Song, "Old Dan Tucker," showing how Dan got up in the world, and how he got down again..............Mr. F. M. Brower and chorus
Song, "Old Mr. Brown," who was cast away on the James River, and saved himself by sculling the boat to land with the old banjo..................
Mr. R. W. Pelham and chorus
Song, Irish, "Widow Machree."..........Mr. W. G. Ross
Song, "Jenny, Get Your Hoe-Cake Done," with banjo accompaniment......................Mr. Sweeny
Song, "Walk Along, John," a chicken-roost adventure....................Mr. Emmit and chorus
Grapevine Twist, or Match Slave Dance...................Messrs. Brower and Pelham
The music on the banjo by Mr. W. J. Sweeny.
PART SECOND.
"Old Tar River," a song on no particular subject, rather bordering on the sentimental.....................Mr. Sweeny and chorus
Song, "Boatman's Dance," a favorite song, in imitation of the Ohio boatmen......Mr. Pelham and chorus
Song, Irish, "Paddy Carey."................Mr. W. G. Ross
Song, "I'm Gwine ober de Mountains, or Jake Coon's Adventure with his Sweetheart Crossing the Alleghany Mountains".....Mr. F. M. Brower and chorus
Song, "De Old Gray Goose, or the Troubles of a Married Life."..................Mr. Emmit and chorus
Song, "Take Your Time, Miss Lucy Long," a highly popular melody, which has always been received with one universal shout of applause (with heel and toe variations)........Messrs. Pelham and Brower
PART THIRD.
A Locomotive Lecture by..............Mr. F. M. Brower, who will give a correct imitation of a locomotive in operation, with the steam whistle accompaniments, and also relate the full particulars of his first love with Miss Roxiana Snowdrop, and of their visit to a ball, etc.
PART FOURTH.
Song, "Dandy Jim from Caroline," a Negro courtship, marriage, and what becomes of him afterwards.....................Mr. Sweeny and chorus
Song, Comique, "The Stage-struck Hero."..Mr. W. G. Ross
Mr. Emmit will sing his original parody of "The Fine Old Colored Gemman," accompanying himself on the banjo in a manner calculated to make all guitar players turn pale with delight.
Conundrums and trans-Atlantic sayings in any quantity, by the minstrels. The evening's entertainment will conclude with two of the most celebrated slave dances of America, viz.:
Corn Husking Jig.....................Mr. R. W. Pelham.
Marriage Festive Dance................Mr. F. M. Brower.
The music will be played by Mr. J. W. Sweeny and Mr. D. D. Emmit.
Dress circle, 2s.; reserved seats, 1s.; gallery, 6d. Programmes of the entertainments will be distributed through all parts of the hall. Doors open at 7; concert to commence at 8 precisely.

A NOVEL, NATURAL, NATIONAL
Colossal Afro-American Exhibition
"BLACK AMERICA"
Opening Saturday Afternoon, May 25

AMBROSE PARK,

Field Hands from the Cotton Belt.

500 Colored Men and Women,

"OLD FOLKS AT HOME."

Phenomenal Natural Voices.

Buck and Wing Dancing.

A Great Sociological Exhibit

"The Man Who Freed the Slave."

General Price of Admission, 25c.

In 1844 the original Virginia Minstrels took abroad their "true copy of the ups and downs of Negro life," as this Glasgow clipping shows.

"The lovable, bright side" of Negro life in "the sunny South," complete with cabins and cotton fields, was presented in this "colossal" post-Civil War show.

24

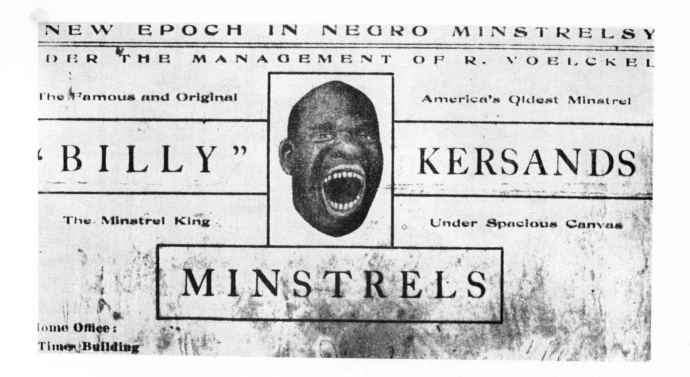

NEW EPOCH IN NEGRO MINSTRELSY

UNDER THE MANAGEMENT OF R. VOELCKEL

The Famous and Original

America's Oldest Minstrel

"BILLY"

KERSANDS

The Minstrel King

Under Spacious Canvas

MINSTRELS

Home Office:
Times Building

This youthful group is "Miss Hattie Delano's Original Alabama Pickaninnies."

the birth of professional minstrelsy before a Negro aggregation came into being. This was Lew Johnson's Plantation Minstrel Company. Although many of this troupe's members were quite dark—being Negro—they nevertheless followed the custom of the white minstrel troupes and blackened their faces and circled their lips with red or white to make their mouths twice normal size. But, as a large group of Negroes performing for the first time on the American stage, they brought with them their indigenous qualities and the genuine basic beat. They revealed new dances, songs and comedy routines that the whites had not yet appropriated. The stop-time taps, the sand and the Virginia essence were introduced. Among the early

Elizabeth Taylor Greenfield, the concert singer, was born a slave in Natchez in 1809, but at the age of one year was taken to Philadelphia by a Quaker woman and educated in freedom. Her voice, one critic said, "ranged 27 notes, from a sonorous baritone to a few notes above even Jenny Lind's highest." She was the first American Negro musician to win more than local recognition, making a success in Europe in the 1850s. She died in 1876.

The cover of James Bland's song book. Born free in 1854, he became a famous composer in his early twenties.

26

The "mostest" of everything was promised in this touring tent show, including Negro comics wearing burnt cork.

Negro stars of minstrelsy in Johnson's and succeeding companies were Wallace King, the falsetto singer billed as "The Man With The Child Voice"; Charles Cruso, droll monologist, and the two famous Bohee Brothers who danced the soft-shoe to the accompaniment of their own banjo playing.

In 1865 a Negro, Charles Hicks, organized the Georgia Minstrels, a colored company that became so successful that it was soon taken over by a white manager, Charles Callender. Callender made the show into a highly lucrative attraction that toured the United States for a number of years. Later, under the name of Haverly's European Minstrels, it went abroad. It was headed by two stars, Billy Kersands who could put a cup and saucer in his mouth, and Sam Lucas who became known as the Grand Old Man of the Negro theatre. Lucas' career spanned almost half a century, for he lived to play the title role in the first motion picture version of *Uncle Tom's Cabin* in 1915. Richards and Pringle, Hicks and Sawyer, and McCabe and Young formed other very successful colored troupes. And in 1893 Primrose and West organized the first racially mixed company in America, The Forty Whites and Thirty Blacks.

Early minstrels consisted of a minimum of fifteen men on stage in Part One, arranged in a semicircle shaking tambourines as the curtain rose. In the center stood an elegantly attired interlocutor, while downstage at each end were the gaudily dressed comedians, Mr. Bones and Mr. Tambo. The quick repartee of these end men traditionally made a fool of Mr. Interlocutor, whose duty it was to absorb their impudent punch lines to the delight of the audience. Between each end man and the interlocutor sat the singing banjo players, tambourine shakers, and vocal soloists—at least one very high tenor and one very deep bass. At the command of the interlocutor, "Gentlemen, be seated," the show began, loud and lively. Rousing choruses, vocal combos, banjo solos, sentimental ballads, comedy songs, dances, rapid-fire gags and jokes came without pause. And Part One usually ended with a vigorous "walk around" in which each individual performer in turn detached himself from the semicircle to prance around the stage.

Central Park Garden

Charles Callender .... Lessee and Manager
R. G. Little .... Stage Manager

CALLENDER'S
Georgia Minstrels
(Organized Twelve Years)

PROGRAMME—PART FIRST.

Tambos....KERSANDS & DEVONEAR
 Interlocutor........WM. MORRIS
 Bones....ANDERSON & GRACE
Overture.............CALLENDER'S GEORGIA MINSTRELS
Linda Love .. .. Jas. Grace
Whispering in the Twilight .... Sam Jones
Hope I may find de Band............. P. Devonear
I hear the old songs yet ... . Wm. W. Morris
Daffney, do you love me yet?.. .... C. Anderson
John's gone down on the Island... .... B Kersands
Sallie Darling .... Dick Little
Concluding with the uproarious Sketch
BRUDDER BONES' BABY.
—TEN MINUTES INTERMISSION.—

PART SECOND
☞ THE ETHIOPIAN NIGHTINGALE
W. E. LYLE........ in his Female Portraitures

THE TROUBADOUR QUARTETTE
In their Camp-Meeting Refrains.
MORRIS, DEVONEA, JONES, LITTLE.

THE HEN CONVENTION!
Barnyard Imitations............BOB MACK.
— TEN MINUTES INTERMISSION —
The ludicrous Burlesque, entitled
When the Cat's away
the Mice will play
G. Washington .P. Devonear | And. Jackson   J Grace
Ben.... Billy Kersands | Susanna W. Elmer Lyle
—FIVE MINUTES INTERMISSION—
BILLY KERSANDS & THE "INFANT"
In their Cotton Field Corousel.
Concluding with a genuine Plantation Walk-around
AMONG DE SUGAR CANE
Sunday Evening, July 22nd
SACRED CONCERT AT 8 O'CLOCK
Cameron & Co. Printers, New York.

Billy Kersands, the comic star, gave dancing lessons to British royalty when the company toured abroad.

He would then jig front and center to dance until breathless, retiring to great applause.

In Part Two or the Olio, recitations, monologues, specialty songs, dances and comedy skits held sway. One of the comedy men usually played a wench in bustle, wig and swishing skirts—a forerunner of the stereotyped Topsy of the *Uncle Tom* shows. A burlesque skit frequently concluded the performance. With the decline of the minstrels, the Olio expanded into an entire evening's entertainment to become known, in the form of separate acts, as vaudeville.

Before the minstrel pattern became set, some individual white entertainers appearing in blackface were already amusing audiences at fairs, in variety halls and with small circuses. Some individual Negro performers, too, such as Andrew Allen, a non-slave, began singing minstrel songs as early as 1815 before white audiences in the North. One such Negro singer, Picayune Butle, is said to have first created "Old Zip Coon," which a young white performer of the period, George Nichols in Purdy Brown's Circus, introduced as "Turkey In The Straw." Under this title, and ascribed to white authorship, it became an American standard.

A New England colored group, the Luca Family —father, mother and four sons—were a singing sensation on tours throughout the North before the Civil War. According to newspaper reports, the Lucas were received with "the wildest enthusiasm" in Boston in 1853. That same year Elizabeth Taylor Greenfield, billed as "The Black Swan," sailed for England where her success was so great that she was called upon to give a command performance for Queen Victoria at Buckingham Palace.

Another Negro singer, James A. Bland, also attracted the attention of British royalty. He had gone to England as a minstrel man in blackface, but he remained there as a star for years without the aid of burnt cork, singing his own songs in concerts. Bland, born of a free Negro family in Long Island, attended Howard University and became a trained musician who not only composed but arranged his own songs. As a youth he had acquired a banjo and began to make up music. One night when he was still in his teens, he had the temerity to go backstage at the Ford Theatre in Washington and play some of his melodies for a famous white minstrel, George Primrose. This veteran performer was so taken by the Negro lad's songs that a week later in Baltimore he sang one of

Amateur concerts and theatricals were popular pleasures. William C. Nell of Boston, pioneer Negro historian and an abolitionist, produced and performed in the Histrionic Club's show in 1858.

them in his show. The song was "Carry Me Back To Old Virginny."

A few years later, young Bland himself became a minstrel man. He joined Haverly's Minstrels just before that show sailed for London, and instantly the handsome young singer caught the public fancy. Shortly Bland's songs were sung in all the British music halls. Years later another young Negro destined to be a great songwriter began his career with a minstrel show. He was W. C. Handy, composer of the "St. Louis Blues," who headed the band for Mahara's Minstrels.

In the nineteenth century, minstrelsy was the first professional training ground for the Negro in American entertainment. But its gradual decline began after the advent of motion pictures. Large groups of performers in blackface ceased to exist. However, individual entertainers, both colored and white, continued to work under cork in vaudeville for many years. Bert Williams, the great Negro comic, performed in blackface until his death in 1922. With white comedians the tradition continued until Eddie Cantor died in 1964. Among the whites other than Cantor who continued to entertain in blackface long after the death of the minstrels were Al Jolson, Frank Tinney, Lou Holtz, George Jessel, Moran and Mack as the Two Black Crows, Tess Gardella as Aunt Jemima, and Amos and Andy in radio and television for some forty years.

A hit from the beginning, Bland's 1878 song is still an American favorite.

30

The white manager of Haverley's, one of the early all-Negro minstrel companies, promptly signed James Bland when he heard his songs. The college-educated performer was soon billed as "The World's Greatest Minstrel Man."

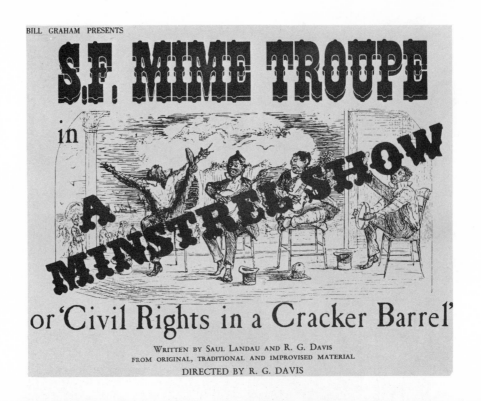

A new kind of minstrel show called Civil Rights in a Cracker Barrel *was born on the West Coast in 1965. With an interracial cast, the San Francisco Mime Troupe converted the old art form into a vehicle for anger and satire.*

"UNCLE TOM'S CABIN"

The Rev. Josiah Henson, the original of Uncle Tom, escaped from slavery, became a preacher, and helped in the Underground Railroad. Meeting Harriet Beecher Stowe by chance, he told her his story, and became the model for her novel's hero.

Next in popularity to the minstrels for many years were the "Tom Shows"—dramatizations of Harriet Beecher Stowe's famous *Uncle Tom's Cabin*, the book which Lincoln implied helped to bring about the Civil War, and which became the world's best seller next to the Bible. As a play, *Uncle Tom's Cabin* became an enormously popular tear-jerker. It was performed throughout the North for many years.

With each of the Tom troupes there was usually "a passel of darkies and a brace of hounds." The Negroes sang plantation songs behind a scrim as Little Eva went to heaven, or the bloodhounds chased Eliza across the ice. In Canada and the Far West, some touring companies advertised "genuine Negroes and real bloodhounds" as a major attraction. But the principal actors were customarily all white, including those who played Uncle

After the Civil War, Henson was still capitalizing on his link with Uncle Tom.

Tom and Topsy. These characters were always made up sooty black. And Topsy was sometimes interpreted as a "wench" in the minstrel manner by a female impersonator. The last white actress to play Topsy in New York was Fay Bainter, with Otis Skinner starred as Uncle Tom, in a Players Club production in 1933. Since that time the old drama has seldom been revived. However maudlin and melodramatic it might have been, *Uncle Tom's Cabin* in its day was a sure-fire show and the kind of attraction which, like the minstrels, drew large repeat audiences on tour season after season.

The famous whipping scene was evidently a popular attraction.

A poster for the first New York production, in 1853. Whites played all the Negro characters.

35

All the major characters and scenes were featured in this billposter for one of the many touring companies.

Uncle Tom's Cabin first opened in 1853 in the small town of Troy, New York, where it played an amazing one hundred performances before moving on to New York City. There it ran for a year at the National Theatre, sometimes giving three performances a day. At one time four companies were playing simultaneously in New York, with the result that a large number of Negro singers were working for the first time in metropolitan theatres. But it was not until 1877, so far as is known, that a Negro played the leading role of Uncle Tom. This happened when Gustave Frohman's white Comedy Company was stranded in Richmond, Kentucky. Charles Frohman records in his biography that suddenly his brother Gustave

"had an inspiration. Then, as always, *Uncle Tom's Cabin* was the great life-saver of the harassed and needy theatrical organization. . . . 'Why not have a *real* Negro play Uncle Tom?' said Gustave. So he wired Charles as follows: GET ME AN EVA AND SEND HER DOWN WITH SAM LUCAS. BE SURE TO TELL SAM TO BRING HIS DIAMONDS. Sam Lucas was a famous Negro minstrel who had been with the Callender company. He sported a collection of diamonds that made him the envy and admiration of his colleagues. Gustave knew that these jewels . . . meant a meal ticket for the company."

So it was that Sam Lucas came to play Uncle Tom. More than thirty years later, in casting the

The New York Herald in 1853 announced that a Jim Crow section was available at the theatre for Negroes who wished to see the story of life under slavery.

initial *Uncle Tom's Cabin* in a three-reel film version, Hollywood remembered that Sam Lucas played the role on stage. But in the second motion picture version in 1913, Tom was played by a white actor, Harry Pollard. However, in the $2,000,000 feature brought to the screen by Carl Laemmle in 1926, the title role of Uncle Tom was again played by a Negro, James Lowe. However, as a stage play during its long years of popularity across America, *Uncle Tom's Cabin* seldom used Negro actors, only singers. And its starring role—like that of Shakespeare's *Othello*—was usually reserved for a white in blackface.

After the Civil War, a New York production boasted of its "200 Genuine Colored People" and advertised the Georgia Jubilee Singers as an added attraction.

UNCLE TOM'S CABIN,
No 2
THE SLAVE MOTHER.

BALLAD
BY
GEORGE LINLEY.

LONDON CHAPPELL 50 NEW BOND STREET

Balladeers rushed in with many songs on almost every aspect of the play, from Eliza's crossing of the ice to little Eva's deathbed scene.

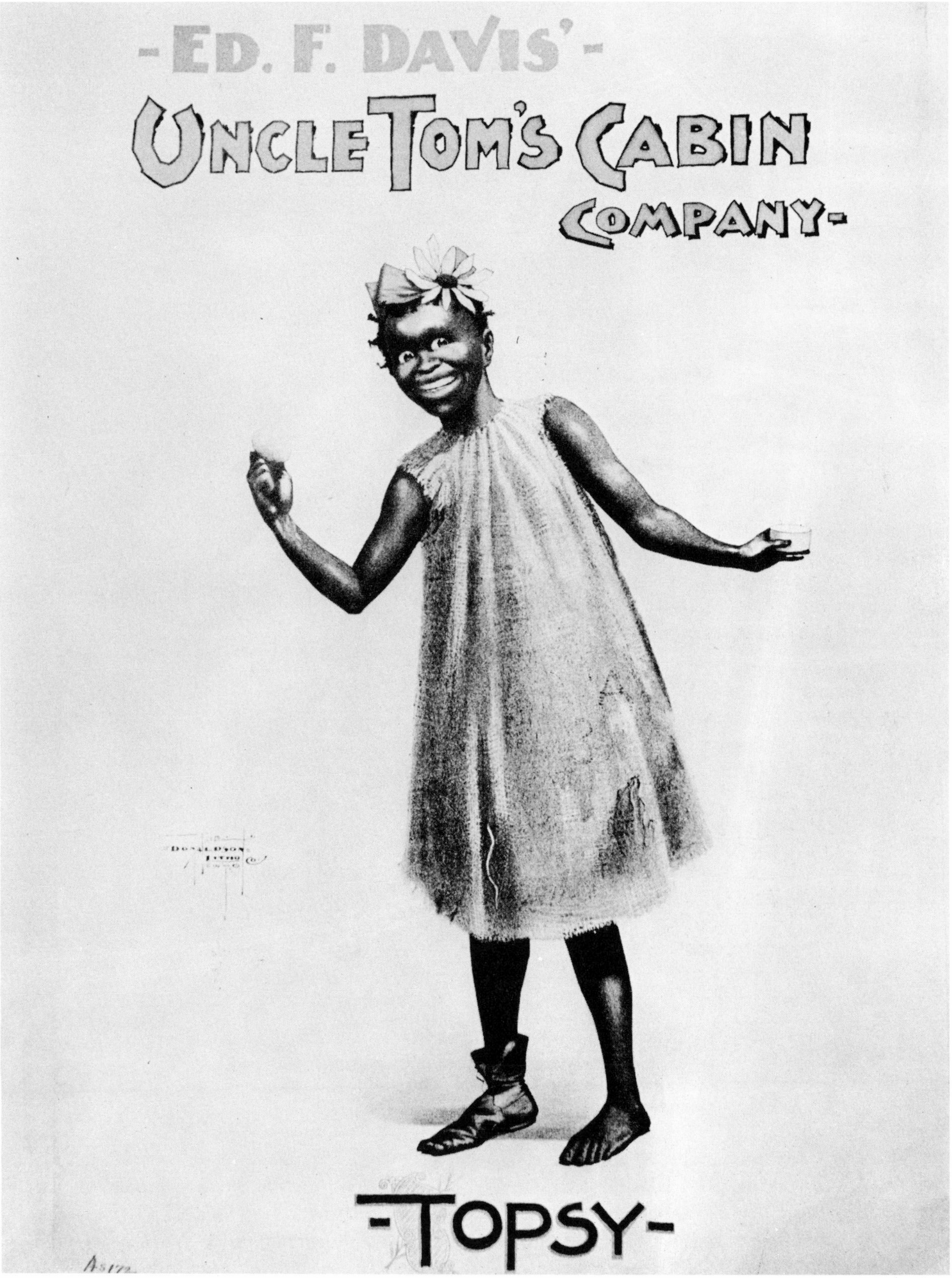
-ED. F. DAVIS'-
UNCLE TOM'S CABIN
COMPANY-
-TOPSY-

IRA ALDRIDGE

Aldridge stars as Zanga in The Revenge.

The first American Negro drama group, the African Company, antedated professional Negro minstrels by some forty years. Although only semiprofessional, the African Company managed to give performances of Shakespeare and other classics in Manhattan with a fair degree of regularity. Their stage was located in a ramshackle structure called the African Grove at the corner of Bleecker and Mercer Streets in lower New York, near the One-Mile Stone which

40

Ira Aldridge as a young actor in Europe.

A playbill for the African Company. Note the slave market scene and the pantomime of Obi, a Negro character. Ira Aldridge's first glimpse of the theatre came through this company.

marked its distance from City Hall. There the first Negro Othello, James Hewlett, performed in 1821. *Richard III* was also a part of the company's repertoire. Although the audiences were largely colored, the *National Advocate* reported that they had "graciously made a partition at the back of the house for the accommodation of whites." But white hoodlums who came to laugh and jeer eventually forced the closing of the Negro playhouse. However, the determined little group of black actors continued to give plays from time to time in other rented localities. It was this company that inspired a colored youth named Ira Aldridge to become an actor, and the first international Negro star.

Aldridge was born in New York about 1807 and had, as a teenager, played the part of Rollo in Sheridan's *Pizarro* in an amateur production. He had also watched James Hewlett perform Shakespeare. But Ira's father, a minister who did not approve of the theatre, sent his son to the University of Glasgow for an education. Young Aldridge left college to become an actor in London, and by 1833 was successfully performing Othello at Covent Garden and touring the provincial theatres of the British Isles. The great Edmund Kean saw Aldridge on stage in Dublin and engaged him to play Othello opposite Kean's Iago. Together they were a great success, touring both England and the Continent for two years. To his role of Othello Aldridge added those of Macbeth, Shylock and King Lear. Playing many parts, Shakespearean and otherwise, throughout Europe, Ira Aldridge settled abroad and never returned to the United States.

Aldridge was not only a great tragedian, but an amazing comedian as well, able to move an audience to tears one night and to laughter another, to turn with ease from the Moor of Venice to a farce like *The Paddock*. Aldridge also had a fine singing voice, and sometimes interpolated into his performances folksongs in the language of whatever country he might be appearing. This, of course, endeared him to the populace. Although his performances were usually in English (while local actors read their lines in their own tongue), foreign audiences loved him. A Russian commentator, M. P. Pogodin, who saw Aldridge in the role

pulled him from the theatre to his hotel. Throughout Europe for thirty years audiences greeted him with acclaim, and the papers showered him with praise. He was loaded with honors—the Order of Chevalier conferred by the King of Prussia, the Cross of Leopold by the Czar of Russia, the Golden Order of Service from the Royal House of Saxony and many others. Aldridge died on tour in Poland in 1867. In the Shakespeare Theatre at Stratford-on-Avon today there is an Ira Aldridge Memorial Chair. In the United States there is an Ira Aldridge Society founded "to advance the cultural cooperation of people of all colors and creeds." A biography has been written about him called *IRA ALDRIDGE, The Negro Tragedian,* by Herbert Marshall and Mildred Stock.

Playing Othello opposite Kean's Iago, Aldridge toured Europe for two years.

James Hewlett played Richard III in the African Company of New York. He was the first Negro to play Othello, probably in 1821.

of a slave, Mungo, declared: ". . . such is the power of his spirit, such is the might of his art, that you surrender to him from the very first minute; you understand what he says, you apprehend all that he feels, you listen to every beat of his heart . . . every stage of human passion . . . expressed by this Negro with incredible power. . . . In my imagination I saw the history of a whole people."

As King Lear, Aldridge's white makeup was so convincing that a French writer who witnessed a performance in St. Petersburg said that Lear's own daughter, Cordelia, "would never have known that her father was a Negro." Aldridge achieved such great popularity in Moscow that the students unhitched the horses of his carriage and themselves

Theatre, Belfast.

BY PERMISSION OF SIR STEPHEN MAY, SOVEREIGN.

EXTRAORDINARY
Combination of Talent.

THE

AFRICAN ROSCIUS

Has the honour of announcing to the Nobility, Gentry, and Public, generally, that his

BENEFIT

AND LAST APPEARANCE

WILL TAKE PLACE

On Thursday Evening, July 9, 1829;

ON WHICH OCCASION THE CELEBRATED

Mr. Kean Jun.

Will make his First Appearance in Belfast, in the character of OROONOKO.

Mr. SWAN,

Of the Theatre Royal Dublin, will make his First and only Appearance, this season, and DANCE
A Celebrated Highland Fling and Sailors' Hornpipe in Character.

The performances will commence with the representation of the Tragedy of

OROONOKO.

Oroonoko,	by	Mr. KEAN, Junior,
Aboan,		by the AFRICAN ROSCIUS.

Governor, Mr James—Blandford, Mr Rae—Hotman, Mr Livingstone—CaptainDriver, Mr W. Alexander—Stanmore, Mr Gibney
Imoinda, Miss Richardson.

END OF THE TRAGEDY,

A Fantasia on the Flute, by Mr. Brocas.

THE CELEBRATED

MATHEWS

Having alluded to a Comic Incident in the career of the AFRICAN ROSCIUS, and founded on it one of
his most Whimsical Hits, in his " TRIP TO AMERICA," the Public are respectfully informed, that (by
Particular Desre of numerous Parties,) THE AFRICAN ROSCIUS will Sing (in Character) the Celebrated
Negro Medley of

"OPPOSSUM UP A GUM TREE."

In the course of the Evening THE AFRICAN ROSCIUS will also Sing an entire New Song, entitled

"The Negro Boy,"

Written Expressly for himself by J. Bissett Esq. of Leamington Spa.

A Turkish PAS SEUL by Miss FAIRBROTHER.

To conclude with the Operatic Play of

THE SLAVE.

Gambia, - - by the AFRICAN ROSCIUS.
Malcolm, (a Scotch Naval Officer,) Mr VERNON, (His First Appearance on any Stage,
in which Character he will sing " SLOWLY WEARS THE DAY," " and MY NATIVE HIGHLAND HOME."
The Governor of Surinam, Mr Seymour,
Capt. Clifton, Mr Rae—Col. Lindenburg, (in the Dutch Service,) Mr W. Johnson—Sam Sharpset Mr James—Somerdyke Mr. Hart.
Mathew Sharpset, (a resident in Surinam,) Mr Macarthy—Fogrum, (a Londoner on his travels,) Mr W. Alexander.
Jailor, Mr Livingstone—Planter, Mr Coyle—Mrs Lindenburg, Miss Richardson—Stella Miss Rae—Miss Von Frump, Miss Macarthy.
Zelinda, Miss McKeever—Ladies of the Colony, Mrs James and Miss C. Fairbrother

An early poster, in which Aldridge is referred to as "the African Roscius," after the famous actor of ancient Rome. Here in Belfast in 1829, he played opposite the great Edmund Kean in Oroonoko, or the Royal Slave, a very popular play in Britain for over 75 years. Aldridge also sang a "celebrated Negro medley."

44

THEATRE ROYAL, PLYMOUTH.

W. 26.]   Lessee and Manager,—Mr. J. R. NEWCOMBE, 5, George Place, Plymouth.   [N. 129.

SECOND NIGHT OF THE ENGAGEMENT OF
MR. IRA ALDRIDGE
THE CELEBRATED
AFRICAN ROSCIUS

After an absence of Three Years from England, during which period he has had the distinguished honour of appearing before Frederick William, King of Prussia; the Queen, Prince, and Princess Royal, of Prussia, and the Court; Francis Joseph the First, Emperor of Austria; the Arch-Duchess of Austria, and the Imperial Family; Frederick Augustus of Saxony, and the Queen Maria; the King and Queen of Holland; the Duke and Duchess of Saxe Cobourg Gotha; the Queen of Sweden; General Jellachich, Ban of Croatia; from whom he has received the most flattering encomiums for each and every Performance honoured by their presence. During the Engagement, Mr. IRA ALDRIDGE will have the honour of appearing in his most celebrated characters of Othello. Shylock, King Lear, Macbeth, Richard the Third, Gambia, Bertram, Mungo, Virginian Mummy, Alambra, Three Fingered Jack, &c.

On TUESDAY, August 14, 1855,
Her Majesty's Servants will enact MORTON's popular Play of

THE SLAVE;
OR, THE BLESSINGS OF LIBERTY!

This Drama pleads the cause of the Slave,—and, as such, is entitled to more than common consideration. It is delightful when our amusements are thus rendered conducive to humanity. A Negro rebellion having taken place at Surinam, the oppressed very naturally turned upon their oppressors and gave them a taste of arbitrary rule. Among the Negroes is Gambia, a favourite Slave, who acts as their mediator with the Governor: for their faults he entreats his mercy; for their helplessness his pity; for their wrongs his protection. He had not joined in the rebellion; since Liberty, when linked with Rapine and Cruelty, might prove a worse state than even Slavery.

Gambia, the Slave - - Mr. IRA ALDRIDGE

Colonel Lindenburgh	Mr LAWRENCE	Somerdyke		Mr LINDON
The Governor of Surinam	Mr WARDE	Officer		Mr LOCKE
Matthew Sharpset	Mr C. HUMPHRYS	Gaoler		Mr KIMBER
Captain Clifton	Mr C. FREDERICKS	Malcolm		Mr NEWTON
Fogrum	Mr FRED. LLOYD	First Planter		Mr CHARLES
Sam Sharpset	Mr HARRY CHESTER	Second Planter		Mr ADAMS
			Mrs C. BOYCE	
Zelinda's Child	Zelinda		Stella Clifton	Mrs LINDON
	Miss LINN		Mrs. Lindenburgh	Mrs WARDE
Miss Von Frump	Miss CROSS			

NEW COMIC SONG,
"THE RATCATCHER'S DAUGHTER," with the popular "DONKEY GALOPE," Mr. FRED. LLOYD.

To conclude with the Musical and Laughable Farce of

THE PADLOCK.

Don Diego....Mr HARRY CHESTER   Leander....Mr C. FREDERICKS   Students....Messrs NEWTON and LOCKE

Mungo, the Slave - - - - Mr. IRA ALDRIDGE

(Which has been universally acknowledged to be one of the most finished and perfectly natural delineations of the true Negro Character on the Stage,) and in which he will sing

"Dear Heart, what a terrible Life I'm led,"   "Opossum up a Gum Tree,"   and "Negro Boy."

Leonora........Mrs LINDON   Ursula........Mrs HARDING

On WEDNESDAY,—"MACBETH." Macbeth....Mr. IRA ALDRIDGE.   Lady Macbeth..Mrs. C. BOYCE. To conclude with the Extravaganza of "QUEEN MAB."
On THURSDAY,—By Desire, "OTHELLO" will be repeated. Othello......Mr. IRA ALDRIDGE.
On FRIDAY,—The Entertainments will be under the Patronage of Sir COLEMAN RASHLEIGH, Bart. and —SPICER, Esq.,
STEWARDS OF THE RACES.

Tickets to be had of Mr. P. E. ROWE, Music Warehouse, Box-Office, George Street, where Places for the Boxes may be secured.

PRICES AS USUAL.]   Doors open at Half-past Six o'Clock. To commence at Seven.   [KEYS, PRINTER, PLYMOUTH.

The playbill lists some of Aldridge's honors and mentions his best roles.

EARLY MUSICALS

Sissieretta Jones, the "Black Patti."

Bon-Bon Buddy,
The chocolate drop—
The chocolate drop,
That's me.

So ran a song made famous by George Walker in the musical *Bandana Land* shortly after the turn of the century. Walker was a dynamic singing comedian who performed without the aid of blackface, dressed well on stage and off, and was good-looking. Gradually more and more Negro entertainers began to appear behind the footlights looking like themselves, rather than burlesques of their race. Slowly the tradition of minstrel exaggerations began to give way to a non-blackface pattern in Negro musicals which incorporated large choruses of pretty girls. At first, however, these shows were not termed musicals. They were called "coon shows" in con-

The idolized team of Bert Williams and George Walker, in a cakewalk number. To distinguish them from white comedians in burnt cork, they were billed for a time as "Two Real Coons."

BLACK PATTI TROUBADOURS

DIRECTION VOELKEL & NOLAN

THE BUCK-DANCING CONTEST

This all-Negro company featured Sissieretta Jones, whose great voice led critics to call her the Black Patti after the opera star, Adelina Patti. The show's climax came with a group of operatic arias instead of the usual cakewalk finale.

trast to the minstrels and Tom shows. But they laid the groundwork for public acceptance of Negro women and of the Negro male on the stage in other than burlesque fashion. A Bon-Bon Buddy behind the footlights, handsome in brown and beige, twirling a cane, doffing a stylish derby hat and strutting in rhythm backed by a chorus of brownskin beauties, brought a sparkling new dimension to American entertainment. The early Negro musicals also brought to the theatre some of the most glorious singing in the world.

Sissieretta Jones was a stunning woman with a gorgeous voice. She began her career as a concert singer, appeared at the White House, and was signed for roles in *Aïda* and *L'Africaine* at the Metropolitan in 1892, but that plan was never

carried through. Instead, she continued her concert tours until a show built around her, *Black Patti's Troubadours*, conceived by Negro writer Bob Cole, was produced. Under white management, this attraction toured the country for several years, with Black Patti (as she was billed) appearing only in the second act in songs and operatic arias.

The first all-Negro musical show produced, conceived, directed and managed entirely by Negroes was Bob Cole's *A Trip To Coontown* in 1898, a show with a story line, credited with being the first colored musical comedy. Sam Lucas, the famous comedian who had played Uncle Tom, starred in this attraction which ran for three seasons. It had been preceded in the Nineties by other less elabo-

48

rate but also successful Negro revue-type productions like *The Creole Show* which began in 1891 and played a full season in Chicago during the World's Fair, *The South Before The War, The Octoroons,* and in 1896 the first all-Negro company to perform on Broadway proper, *Oriental America.* These shows made various innovations in Negro entertainment. One was that all of them presented beautiful women beautifully dressed, both as principals and in the chorus. They also

Saturday Matinee and Night, May 23.

Black Patti Troubadours,

VOELCKEL & NOLAN, Props. and Mgrs.

In a Musical Comedy Entitled

DARKTOWN'S CIRCUS DAY.

C A S T.

Josiah Johnson, the Poo-Bah of Darktown..John Green
Mariah Johnson, his wife "with an eye on Josiah".......................Anthony D. Byrd
Primus...................................... { Their sons, "with a { ....Will Cook
Reuben .... } love for the circus" } ....Chas. Bougia
Little Willie, their youngest, with "lengthy aspirations"....................Jas. Crosby
M'mselle Hoplightly, "the queen of the arena"....................................Ida Forcen
Prof. Slackenback, with a circus on his hands ....J. Ed. Green
Handy Andy, with troubles of his own......................................Bobby Kemp
Policeman 7-11, "a guardian of the peace,"................................Leslie Triplett
Bill Barber, "a circus spieler with the dope"....................................Mac Allen
Henri Tenori, "from the oprea"..James Worles
Percy Hamfat, an actor..J. P. Reed

BELLS OF DARKTOWN.

Bessie Gilliam. Nettie Lewis. Jeanetta Murphy, Olivette Williams, Sarah Green, Emma Thompson, Lizzte Taylor, Mau le Turner, Henrietta Perceaud. Mable Turner, Ella Carr.

Candy Butchers. Peanut Vendors, Animal Attendants, Actors, Actresses, Freaks, Monkeys, Bears, Elephants and others.

SYNOPSIS.

SCENE I.—Exterior of Darktown Circus.   SCENE II.—Interior of Darktown Circus.
SCENE III.—Interior of Theatre.   TIME—Present.

During the action of this sketch the following musical numbers will be introduced:
"When the Circus Comes to Town,"Chorus, "Strolling around the Circus Tent," Entire Company, "Castle on the Nile." Jas Crosby and Company, "What Became of the Monk," Messrs. Kemp, Byrd, Crosby and Triplett, "Mandy," Ida Forcen and Chorus. "Aint Going to Stay Here Any Longer," John Green and Chorus, "Under the Bamboo Tree." Nettie Lewis and Bobby Kemp Finale--Buck Dancing Contest.   Intermission

PART II.

EMMA THOMPSON, Comedienne.
AROUND THE CAMP FIRES IN THE PHILIPPINES.
JAMES CROSBY. Bon Mots of 1903.
M. SI-SIERETTA JONES, the Black Patti.
BOBBY KEMP'S Wang Doodle Four.
MAC ALLEN. Slack Wire Equilibris.
WILLIAM NICHOLS, Mimic.

Messrs. Voelckel and Nolan present selections from Graud and Comic Opero in costume including BLACK PATTI (Mme. SISSIERETTA JONES), Sarah Green, Contralto; James E Worles, Tenor; J Ed. Green, Baritone. James P. Reed, Bass; and a chorus selected from the best negro voices in the country.

Conspirator's Chorus, (Mme. Angot)..Company
"Miserere" (Travatore) ....BLACK PATTI, J. E. Worles and Chorus
"In Lovers Lane"...James P. Reed
"Behold the Queen" (Ensemble) ....Chorus
"Waltz Song" (Belle of New York) ....BLACK PATTI and Company
"Quintette" (Martha)....BLACK PATTI, Sarah Green, James Worles, J. Ed. Green and A. D. Byrd

ORCHESTRA SELECTIONS.

ANTON GLOECKNER, Musical Director.

March—In Dahomey..Johns
Overture—"Celtic...St. Clair
Reverie—Falling Star ....Richmond
Waltzes—Hearts Courageous..Blanke
Characteristic—Nasturtium..Jones
March—Ching a Ling a Loo..Hoffman

employed trained musicians like the young song writer, J. Rosamond Johnson, and they incorporated into their scores newly composed songs as well as operatic arias.

When commercial managers discovered that money might be made from using the talents of trained Negro musicians like Johnson—who had studied at the New England Conservatory of Music, and who was the brother of the poet James Weldon Johnson with whom he wrote songs—white impresarios were quick to take advantage of such abilities. A new era opened for the Negro in American entertainment. At the turn of the century the Johnson brothers together wrote such show tunes as "Under the Bamboo Tree," "My Castle On The Nile," "Since You Went Away," and the Lillian Held hit, "The Maiden With The Dreamy Eyes," and wrote with Bob Cole, "Lazy Moon" and "Congo Love Song." J. Rosamond Johnson became the composer of several musical shows including *Shoo-Fly Regiment*, and *Red Moon* in which he sang and acted.

With the most famous Negro poet, Paul Laurence Dunbar, the composer Will Marion Cook in 1898 wrote *Clorindy—The Origin of the Cake Walk*. Based on ragtime using the syncopated beat

Contestants for the cakewalk crown.

New York Syncopated Orchestra
50—Players and Singers—50

Will Marion Cook, Conductor
Orchestra Hall---Chicago, Illinois
Michigan Boulevard, bet. Jackson Boulevard and Adams Street
Wednesday Evening, Feb. 12, 1919

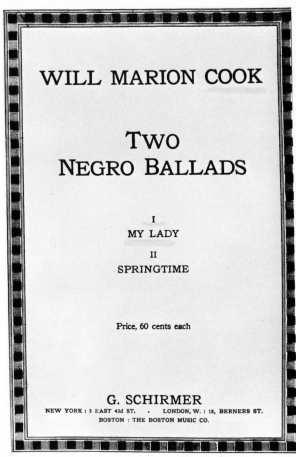

WILL MARION COOK

TWO
NEGRO BALLADS

I
MY LADY

II
SPRINGTIME

Price, 60 cents each

G. SCHIRMER
NEW YORK : 3 EAST 43d ST.   •   LONDON, W. : 18, BERNERS ST.
BOSTON : THE BOSTON MUSIC CO.

Will Marion Cook was one of the most notable musical comedy composers of the early 20th century. Later he took his jazz band on tours of the U.S. and Europe, helping to establish the popularity of Negro music.

Will Marion Cook.

that the slaves brought with them from Africa, this musical was an instantaneous hit at the Casino Roof in New York, with Cook as its musical director and Ernest Hogan and Belle Davis as the cakewalking couple. Will Marion Cook was a graduate of Oberlin College. He later pursued his musical studies with Joachim in Europe and under Anton Dvořák at the National Conservatory in New York. It was Cook who wrote "Bon Bon Buddy," the famous "Rain Song," the Bert Williams hit, "I May Be Crazy But I Ain't No Fool," and "Exhortation." Will Marion Cook composed and orchestrated the scores for the famous Williams and Walker shows that established the Negro on Broadway.

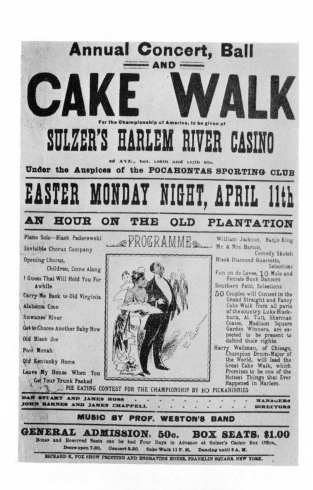

Bob Cole, made up as "Willie Wayside." He wrote hit musicals with the Johnson Brothers.

Actor, producer, singer, composer—Ernest Hogan of Kentucky could do it all. He modernized the end man's style and wrote some of the earliest ragtime tunes. He died in 1909.

52

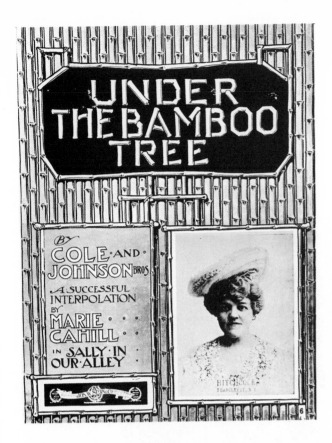

One of the big song hits of the turn of the century, written by Bob Cole and the two Johnsons.

The composer, J. Rosamond Johnson, at the piano, with Taylor Gordon, the singer. They toured theatres abroad, singing spirituals and popular songs.

BERT WILLIAMS

Keith's During Week of Jan 5. 1914.

When *In Dahomey* opened in 1902 at the New York Theatre in Times Square, it established the team of Bert Williams and George Walker as the top Negro stars in both America and England. The show had a London run of seven months. As part of the Prince of Wales' ninth birthday celebration, the company received a command to perform at Buckingham Palace. There Williams and Walker introduced the cakewalk to royalty, and it became the social fad of Europe. Other highly successful Williams and Walker musicals followed—*Abyssinia* in 1906, *Bandana Land* in 1907. For most of their musicals, the entire book, music and lyrics were by the Negro writers, Cook, Vodery and Rogers. But

shortly after *Bandana Land* closed, George Walker died and the great starring combination of Williams and Walker came to an end.

In 1910 Bert Williams joined the famous *Follies* as a star. Performing in blackface, he was the only Negro in this otherwise all-white company, appearing in various editions of the show on Broadway for a decade, and touring all America. Of him another great comedian, W. C. Fields, once said, "Bert Williams is the funniest man I ever saw." He was once described by Heywood Broun, who wrote that Williams "stood still in the center of the stage and used no gesture which travelled more than six inches" yet, with his droll pantomime, his laughter-through-tears comedy and wry songs—like

A scene from Bandana Land, *at the Majestic Theatre in New York. George Walker stands by while Bert Williams confides in Ada Overton Walker. This was their last show together, for Walker died soon after.*

Bert Williams in one of his Ziegfeld Follies sketches. Born Egbert Austin Williams in 1875, Bert's first years were spent in Antigua, British West Indies. He grew up in San Francisco, where he learned to sing and play several instruments.

THE NEW YORK THEATRE

Occupying the entire block on Broadway, between 44th and 45th Sts.

KLAW & ERLANGER, ... Proprietors and Managers

Evenings at 8.15.   Matinees Wednesday and Saturday at 2.15

PRICES, 25c., 50c , 75c., and $1.00.

WEEK COMMENCING MONDAY EVENING, MARCH 30, 1903.

HURTIG & SEAMON present

WILLIAMS and WALKER

IN THEIR NEWEST SUCCESS

IN DAHOMEY

A Musical Farce, in Three Acts.

Music by Will Marion Cook.   Lyrics by Paul Lawrence Dunbar.   Book by J. A. Shipp

GEO. H. HARRIS, Manager,   CHAS. F. WIEGAND, Business Manager.

Cast of Characters

Shylock Homestead, called "Shy" by his friends..........BERT A. WILLIAMS
Rareback Pinkerton, "Shy's" personal friend and adviser.. GEO. W. WALKER
Cicero Lightfoot, president of a colonization society,...., ...Pete Hampton
Dr. Straight (in name only), street fakir,................Fred Douglas
Mose Lightfoot, brother of Cicero, thinks Dahomey a land of great promise.Wm. Barker
George Reeder, keeps an intelligence office... .... lex Rogers
Henry Stampfield, letter carrier, with an argument against immigration.
                                                          Walter Richardson
Me Sing, keeps a chop suey factory.....................Geo. Catlin
Hustling Charley, promoter of Get-the-Coin syndicate ....J. Shipp
Leather, a bootblack...........................Richard Connors
Officer Still...........................Geo. Pickett
Messenger Rush, but not often.......................Theodore Pankey
Bill Primrose..James Hill
Cecilia Lightfoot, Cicero's wife....................Mrs. Hattie McIntosh
Mrs. Stringer, dealer in forsaken patterns, also editor of fashion notes in
   "Beanville Agitator"   ....Mrs. Lottie Williams
Rosetta Lightfoot, a troublesome young thing...............Aida Overton Walker

Colonists, Natives, etc.

"I'm In The Right Church But The Wrong Pew" —he always sent audiences into gales of laughter. "Oh Death Where Is Thy Sting," "Woodman, Spare That Tree" and "Come After Breakfast, Bring Along Your Lunch, and Leave Before Suppertime," were among the songs he made memorable, and his musical pantomime of a poker player was widely acclaimed.

In the *Follies* Williams usually had only one spot, entering late in the show to a lugubrious chord from the orchestra. First a lone white-gloved hand with slowly moving fingers would protrude from the wings, followed by a long black-suited arm. Then a second hand and arm followed. Before his body appeared just the movement of his two hands could make an audience howl. His solo act was usually limited to less than half an hour, and he would always exit to a roar of applause. Williams' recordings sold in the hundreds of thousands, and at one time his salary was equal to that of the President of the United States. Yet on tour this money-making star often had to sleep in third-rate, segregated hotels; or if he stayed in white hotels with the rest of the *Follies* company, he usually had to ride the freight elevator and take his meals in his room. He once said, "It is no disgrace to be a Negro, but it is very inconvenient." At the age of 47, in 1922, Bert Williams died.

It was in San Francisco that Williams teamed up with young Walker, who had strayed west from his native Kansas. Early in their twenties they made a hit at Koster and Bial's Theatre in New York, doing the cakewalk for a record six-month's run.

Playing Rufus the Redcap, Bert Williams did a comic sketch with Leon Errol in one of the Ziegfeld Follies.

"Bob" Cole   Lester A. Walton   "Sam" Corker   Bert A. Williams   James Reese Europe   Alec Rogers

"Tom" Brown   J. Rosamond Johnson   Geo. W. Walker   Jesse A. Shipp   R.C. McPherson (Cecil Mack)

"The Frogs," a theatrical association of the early 1900s. Most of the best talent seems to have been on hand for this photo.

JUST ABOUT EVERYTHING

Among Barnum's early exhibits were the 14-year-old Carolina twins, Millie and Christina, born linked together in North Carolina.

The essence of show business is nerve. "A sucker is born every minute," P. T. Barnum, the great circus man, once declared. Barnum had begun his career in 1835 by exhibiting what was at that time his one and only attraction, Joice Heth, a withered Negro crone said to be over one hundred years old. She was a slave whom Barnum purchased and boldly presented to the public as having been George Washington's nurse. From the gawking crowds that paid their money to look, his take averaged $1500 a week.

When Barnum established his combined circus and menagerie in 1871, he called it "The Greatest Show On Earth." Later the Barnum and Bailey sideshows exhibited Jo-Jo the Dogface Boy and Zip the Pin-Headed Man. Both of these oddities of nature were gentlemen of color. Also colored was one of the first sets of Siamese Twins exhibited by the same circus. Numerous Fat Ladies of enormous proportions have been Negroes—and not always connected with circuses: Big Maybelle became a popular blues singer, as did Beulah

LITH.&PUB. BY CURRIER&IVES.   162 NASSAU ST. NEW YORK.

"WHAT IS IT"?

Is it a lower order of **MAN**! *Or is it a higher order of* **MONKEY**! *None can tell! Perhaps it is a combination of both. It is beyond dispute* **THE MOST MARVELLOUS CREATURE LIVING.** *It was captured in a savage state in Central Africa, is probably about 20 years old, 4 feet high, intelligent, docile, active, sportive, and* **PLAYFUL AS A KITTEN.** *It has the skull, limbs and general anatomy of an* **ORANG OUTANG** *and the* **COUNTENANCE** *of a* **HUMAN BEING.**

TO BE SEEN AT ALL HOURS AT BARNUM'S MUSEUM.

Currier & Ives lithographed Barnum's popular "Gallery of Wonders," playing in No. 12 on the public's curiosity about little-known Central Africa, and reflecting the racist view of the Negro as semi-human.

Bryant who appeared at the Newport Jazz Festival and toured abroad. Tree-top tall Negro giants included a handsome mountain of a man exhibited before the Civil War, Admiral Dot, who stood 7 feet 11 inches tall and weighed 600 pounds; years later Big George featured in the Hippodrome musical, *Chu Chin Chow*, in New York and London. At the opposite poles in size, Pee Wee Marquett was a professional midget. And yard-high Princess Wee Wee, performing with six-foot-tall Willie Bryant, was the tiniest singing comedienne on the Negro vaudeville circuit and a long-time feature of the Whitman Sisters Company.

Negroes in show business, at one time or another, have been just about everything anybody else has been, from performers to impresarios. J. Lawrence Freeman was a pioneer composer and producer of operas in Harlem in the Twenties. Mary Caldwell Dawson presented both operas and concerts along the Eastern seaboard, as did Azalia Hackley in the Midwest. Both women often acted as narrators or mistresses of ceremonies—their aim being to popularize among Negroes the best in the musical arts. In less serious media, Negro jazzers played on Mississippi River boats in the old days, and in black jug bands on New Orleans parade floats. Today folk singers like Odetta, Leon Bibb,

From the "What Is It?" approach, the circus moved, many years later, to the exhibition of African tribesmen.

JOICE HETH IN PHILADELPHIA.

This venerable colored lady was on exhibition at Masonic Hall, Philadelphia, in the Summer of 1835, as per the subjoined advertisement, clipped from *The Pennsylvania Inquirer* of July 15 of that year. Her owner was then R. W. Lindsay of Jefferson County, Ky., and he it was who was exhibiting her, and also a bill of her sale, dated Feb. 5, 1727, and conveying her from Augustine Washington, county of Westmoreland, Va., to Elizabeth Atwood, it being represented in that document that she was then fifty-four years old, and had been the nurse of George Washington. Selling out his grocery business, and buying Joice Heth for $1,000, P. T. Barnum began life as a showman, exhibiting her in New York, Philadelphia, Boston, Albany, and other cities. She died in February, 1836, and at her post-mortem examination the physicians questioned that her age was quite so great.

CURIOSITY.—The citizens of Philadelphia and its vicinity have an opportunity of witnessing at the Masonic Hall one of the greatest natural curiosities ever witnessed, viz., JOICE HETH, a negress, aged 161 years, who formerly belonged to the father of General Washington. She has been a member of the Baptist Church one hundred and sixteen years, and can rehearse many hymns, and sing them according to former custom. She was born near the old Potomac River, in Virginia, and has for ninety or one hundred years lived in Paris, Kentucky, with the Bowling family.

All who have seen this extraordinary woman are satisfied of the truth of the account of her age. The evidence of the Bowling family, which is respectable, is strong; but the original bill of sale of Augustine Washington, in his own handwriting, and other evidences which the proprietor has in his possession, will satisfy even the most incredulous.

A lady will attend at the hall during the afternoon and evening, for the accommodation of those ladies who may call.

An ancient Negro slave offered Barnum his entry into show business in 1835. Note her bill of sale from the Washington family was allegedly dated 1727.

Len Chandler, and Brownie and Sonny perform everywhere from Carnegie Hall to Cairo, while colored performers like Babs Gonzales and Adelaide Hall are engaged for ship's concerts on the big trans-Atlantic liners.

In vaudeville Wee Georgia Woods was an amazing ventriloquist; Allie Brown a daring slack-wire walker; Wilton Crawley danced, juggled and balanced a lighted lamp on his head while playing the clarinet. Peg Leg Bates of the wooden limb was for years a featured performer. And Ernest Hogan, "The Unbleached American" who composed "Pasmala," played the longest single vaudeville run in history—44 weeks on the New York

Admiral Dot, the Negro giant of pre-Civil War days, as he appeared in carnivals and sideshows.

blues singer. During that period there was a daring lady lion tamer, Bessie Coleman, performing under canvas; and fifty years later at Miami Beach's Jungleland as an attraction for the winter tourists, Emanuel Ruffin daily put the snarling kings of the veldt through their paces in a circular outdoor cage. Other Negroes wrestle alligators for a living in Florida.

Over the years there have been numerous black bronco busters with the rodeo shows playing the big state fairs and yearly at Madison Square Garden. A top star for a decade with the Miller Brothers travelling *101 Ranch* was the husky Negro cowboy Bill Picket, who single-handed could throw a bull by the nose. Another top bull-dogger and lasso artist was Thryl Latting. "Being a Negro in rodeos can be an asset," Latting declared, "because people pay extra attention to you."

Most circuses and carnivals at one time or another have had Negro acrobats, contortionists, magicians like the Great Gowongo and, of course, belly dancers sometimes passing as dark-skinned Orientals. And the heavyweight boxing champion of the world, Jack Johnson, gave nightly exhibition bouts at Broadway's Flea Circus. The Turtle Woman of the Coney Island freak shows was colored.

The Harlem Globe Trotters, performers as well as athletes, have been hailed as the world's most wonderful basketball clowns. In the professional Roller Derby skating contests that tour the arenas from fall to spring, Darlene Anderson was given the Rookie-of-the-Year Award in 1958. Mabel Fairbanks, Holquina Peterson, Sterling Bough and Elsie Robinson have been figure skaters with the big ice carnivals. Today the Playboy Clubs employ pert brownskin "bunnies," and lovely colored models parade down runways in the Ebony Fashion Fair and other touring-style shows. Among the glamorously gowned stars of the *Jewel Box Revue* are the brownskin female impersonators, Mr. Billie Day and Mr. Mel Michaels. From the "jive" art of professional wrestling to go-go dancing *au-discothèque*, from carnivals to Carnegie Hall, from minstrels to musicals, medicine shows to the Met, Negroes have taken part in every phase of American show business.

Roof in the early 1900's. With carnivals and medicine shows around the turn of the century, pretty brownskin Toy Brown was a snake charmer, as was Madam Cow Cow Davenport, the wife of the

Esther Sutherland, billed as "The Biggest Thing in Jazz."

Mr. Billie Day (left) of Pittsburgh, famous for his impersonations of Billie Holli-
day and Lena Horne. Also with the Jewel Box Revue was Mr. Mel Michaels,
(right) whose specialties are impersonations of Eartha Kitt and Pearl Bailey.

T·O·B·A·

That So-Different Southern Four.

The T.O.B.A. was a busy Negro vaudeville circuit extending after the first World War from New York to Florida, Chicago to New Orleans. Performers nicknamed it Toby, or Tough On Black Actors, because it paid so little money, except to headliners. For those with top billing, however, the Theatre Owners Booking Association might mean work for 52 weeks a year at good salaries. Bessie Smith was a headliner, as were Butterbeans and Susie, Kid and Coot, Wilbur Sweatland and his clarinet, Brown and Brown, S. H. Dudley and his Mule, Hamtree Harrington, Tom Fletcher, the operatic soprano Fannie Wise, and the Whitman Sisters. Sweet Mama Stringbean (whose real name was Ethel Waters) sometimes played the Toby circuit. Among its most

Bill "Bojangles" Robinson, the great dancing star.

Starting Monday Night!

Coming Here in All Its Splendor

The SUPREME COLORED SHOW of the World

THE RECOGNIZED REPRESENTATIVES OF THE SHOW WORLD PRESENT THE GREATEST ARRAY OF PERFORMERS EVER GATHERED TOGETHER.

SMART SET

AND THE ORIGINAL

MA RANIEY, The "Great "BLUES" SINGER

The GREATEST COLORED SHOW ON EARTH

50 CELEBRATED THEATRICAL CIRCUS **50**
AND OPERATIC STARS

A RIOT OF FESTIVITIES SET IN A CANVAS OF GORGEOUS BEAUTY UNLIKE ANY OTHER PREVIOUS ATTEMPT IN MODERN TENT SHOWS.

THIS SHOW ONLY PLAYS LARGE CITIES AND IS THE BIGGEST ATTEMPT IN THE COLORED SHOW WORLD.

Come and See==You Will Be Surprised

America's Greatest Singing and Dancing Chorus
WITH THE MOST WONDERFUL COSTUMES EVER SEEN IN THIS CITY

FUNNY COMEDIANS		THE BIGGEST BEVY OF SINGING AND DANCING GIRLS YOU HAVE EVER SEEN
ACROBATS		
GRAND OPERA STARS		
IMPERIAL Troupe of Tossing Turning, Tumbling CLOWNS in Feats of Daring		

In all the world no show like this—It is the only Big Show Coming This Season and you can't afford to miss it.

Admission Adults,	27c War Tax, 3c	**30c**
Children,	18c War Tax, 2c	**20c**
Reserved Seats,	18c War Tax, 2c	**20c**

Doors Open at 7:00 p. m.
Performance at 8:15 p. m.

Everything Clean, Moral and Refined

FOLLOW THE CROWD TO THE BIG TENT

prosperous theatres were the Regal in Baltimore, the Howard in Washington, the 81 in Atlanta, the Booker T. in St. Louis, and the Monogram in Chicago. The Grand on Chicago's South Side, a rival theatre to the Monogram, had a sort of semi-permanent musical stock company, headed for a long time by an excellent comedian, Billy King. In Atlanta S. H. Dudley also had a partially permanent company, in which as a youth Nipsey Russell acquired his sense of comedy. There were many theatres in the country then catering almost exclusively to colored audiences—places where young Negroes could work on stage and so become audience-wise. The decline and slow death of the T.O.B.A. during the Depression was a real loss to colored performers.

Some of the more solid aggregations like Moss and Frye, the acrobatic Crackerjacks, the Golden Gate Quartet, the Southernaires, and the Four Harmony Kings became favorites on the white vaudeville circuits—Pantages, Loew's, the Keith Orpheum combine—while others worked the independent Negro theatres that remained, like the Lincoln and the Alhambra in Harlem, and much later the Apollo. Negro quartets have long found favor with the public—from the Four Prophets, the Black Diamonds, and the Hamtown Students before 1900 to the Deep River Boys and the Mills Brothers, whose foursome lasted as headliners from the Twenties to the Sixties and who were so popular from the beginning that they never played the T.O.B.A.

On the white vaudeville circuits which Bert Williams sometimes played between *Follies* engagements, Bill "Bojangles" Robinson of the tapping feet became the highest salaried colored star. Buck and Bubbles, Sissle and Blake, U.S. Thompson, singer George Dewey Washington, Stump and Stumpy, the dancing Nicholas Brothers and the Berry Brothers were featured performers. Popular comics were Dusty Fletcher of *Open The Door, Richard* fame, Mantan Moreland, Pigmeat Markham and Tim Moore—who played a blackface

Ma Rainey (misspelled in the poster) was featured in Smart Set, *the world's "supreme" colored tent show.*

69

Robinson lampooned Jewish comedians. Johnson and Dean were famous cakewalk artists in vaudeville and, as a tribute to the beauteous female half of the team, a special song was written, "Miss Dora Dean." Singers Cole and Johnson were early two-a-day favorites. Sand dancer Eddie Rector, the pantomimist Johnny Hudgins and Ethel Waters were spotlighted as singles, and in his old age the composer and blues trumpeter, W. C. Handy, was a featured part of Joe Laurie's *Memory Lane* act.

Many colored performers, particularly in the early stages of their careers, alternated between the Negro variety houses and the white ones. But,

Bill "Bojangles" Robinson

Born in an Ohio river town in 1873, Tom Fletcher got his start when a travelling Uncle Tom show asked the boy to fill in as a plantation hand. At 15 he joined a minstrel company for $5 a week "and cakes" (board and lodging). He died at 81, the day his recollections of a long life in show business went to press.

Scotsman in kilts before he became the first colored Kingfish in the changing Amos and Andy series.

In 1911 Billy Kersands, the comedian of the minstrels, played the Loew Circuit, dancing with two billiard balls in his mouth—which was larger than Joe E. Brown's. "If God ever wanted to make my mouth any bigger," said Kersands, "He would have to move my ears." Also dating from minstrel days, the dancing comedian Ernest Hogan lived to become a vaudeville favorite. Around 1900 Mr. and Mrs. Tom McIntosh toured with a variety skit called *The King of Bivarid.* Later, Hume and Botrell, and Al and Mamie Anderson, were actors of color who did straight dramatic sketches on the vaudeville stage. In Yiddish dialect Cooper and

70

Sissle and Blake wrote Shuffle Along *and played white vaudeville, too.*

of course, the goal of every vaudeville artist of whatever race or color was the Palace on Broadway. Some performers from the Negro T.O.B.A. circuit eventually made it there and saw their names blown up into top billing—Bill Robinson most notably. His funeral cortege in 1949 made a point of wending its way through Times Square, past the Palace Theatre where the playbills outside once advertised in enormous type: BOJANGLES WORLD'S GREATEST TAP DANCER. As the flower-covered funeral car passed the Palace, a band played "Give My Regards to Broadway."

Bob Cole (left) and the Johnson brothers, James Weldon (center) and J. Rosamond. Their musicals pioneered Negro entertainment on Broadway.

Craine's Smiling Sunbeams, an oldtime vaudeville act.

BIRTH OF JAZZ

Sidney Bechet

Louis Armstrong was born July 4, 1900, just about the time that jazz was crystallizing into band and orchestral form. Thus his life spanned the growth into maturity of America's most indigenous music—music on which he himself became so great an influence. Jazz, with its basic beat, has had from its beginnings a close relationship with the theatre, and the elements of jazz have been woven into the scores of many American musicals and popular songs. Without the blues, what would Tin Pan Alley have done? Where would rock and roll have been? What

would have happened to the nightclub business, the recording industry, and the jukebox combines?

When Buddy Bolden's horn sounded in old New Orleans, it sounded so loud it could be heard all the way from Canal Street downtown to Lake Pontchartrain. Louis was a child then, but he determined to learn to blow a horn like Bolden, and he did. His trumpet has since been heard around the world. In the early days of his professional career, Louis played in dance bands such as those at the Royal Gardens in Chicago and Roseland in New York. Then he played in nightclubs, both

for dancing and to accompany shows. He played in pit bands in Broadway revues such as *Hot Chocolates,* and in one was featured on stage. As a "scat singing" actor, Armstrong played Bottom in *Swingin' The Dream* adapted from Shakespeare's *A Midsummer Night's Dream* at the Center Theatre in 1939. As a concert and jazz festival headliner for years, Louis Armstrong and his combos toured the world from Africa to Australia. He might well be called "Mister Jazz Himself."

From old New Orleans, the city of the Mardi Gras and the marching bands, came many great jazz players and composers—Jelly Roll Morton, the pianist who wrote "Tiger Rag," trumpeter King Oliver, trombonist Kid Ory, clarinetists Bunk Johnson, Barney Bigard and Sidney Bechet, and banjo-playing Johnny St. Cyr. Farther up the Mississippi in Sedalia, Missouri, Scott Joplin was beating out his "Maple Leaf Rag" in 1899. In Memphis and St. Louis W. C. Handy was dreaming the blues. On riverboats, in carnivals and circuses, with minstrels, on the vaudeville stage and in nightclubs many of the early jazz musicians became popular solo entertainers or featured performers in show bands; Joe Oliver's musical clowns, for instance, took San Francisco by storm in 1921, but later became the more elegant Creole Band performing in tuxedos and diamonds.

At Proctor's Theatre in New York in 1905, the Memphis Students opened. They are thought to be the first jazz band ever to play a theatre engagement. They were singing musicians (not students, and *not* from Memphis) who put on such a good show that they were soon booked for the Olympia in Paris, the Palace in London and the Schumann Circus in Berlin. With the band was dancer Ida Forsyne, soloist Abbie Mitchell, and comedian Ernest Hogan, as well as dancing conductor Will Dixon and the famous stick-juggling drummer, Buddy Gilmore.

In 1912 the Clef Club's Syncopated Orchestra of 125 men featuring mandolins, banjoes, guitars, cellos and basses against a background of ten pianos,

Miles Davis

introduced symphonic jazz to Carnegie Hall. With the instrumentation augmented by human voices, the concert was a sensation. Its conductor was James Reese Europe. As director during World War I of the Fifteenth Regiment Band of the 367th Infantry, he first introduced brass-band jazz to major European cities under the Allies. Ford Dabney's jazz orchestra was for a number of years a show feature at Ziegfeld's Roof. In 1919 Will

Louis Armstrong

75

Nina Simone

Lionel Hampton

Sonny Rollins

Duke Ellington

Marion Cook's Syncopated Orchestra performed for a long period at the 44th Street Theatre. Many Negro show bands in ensuing years filled theatre and nightclub bookings everywhere, sometimes featuring comedy musicians like Stuff Smith or Ray Nance, or singing-dancing-jiving conductors like Louis Jordan, Lucky Millinder or Cab Calloway, or highly entertaining musical showmen like Lionel Hampton with his vibraphones.

The Newport Jazz Festival and other such mammoth fetes from Boston to Monterey, Chicago to Cannes headline Negro jazz artists. At these

Count Basie

77

James Reese Europe

outdoor programs at least three aggregations—those of Duke Ellington, Louis Armstrong and Count Basie—became almost yearly fixtures. Dizzy Gillespie, Horace Silver, Charlie Mingus, Miles Davis and other musical showmen were in great demand at the festivals and elsewhere, as well as jazz and blues singers such as Billie Holiday, Dinah Washington, Sarah Vaughan, Dakota Staton and the inimitable Nina Simone. The Norman Granz combination, *Jazz At The Philharmonic,* with the great Ella Fitzgerald as soloist, toured most of the world.

Pianists like Mary Lou Williams, Hazel Scott, Dorothy Donnegan, Art Tatum, Teddy Wilson, Oscar Peterson, Erroll Garner, Don Shirley, Thelonius Monk and Billy Taylor gained fame in the concert and record fields. The folk singers and guitarists since the days of Blind Lemon Jefferson and Leadbelly have also shared the spotlight with jazz men, among them Lonnie Johnson, Leroy Carr, Big Bill Broonzy, Josh White, Memphis Slim, Brownie McGhee, Sonny Terry with his harmonica and Odetta. Since 1900 there have been many great Negro folk and jazz performers: Bud Powell, Cozy Cole, Eric Dolphi, Cecil Taylor, Ornette Coleman, John Lewis, Max Roach. The musical personalities of some, like that of Charlie Parker, have greatly influenced the changing styles of jazz in both performance and composition. But perhaps the two greatest single influences on jazz, and certainly the possessors of the hardiest careers of all, were Louis Armstrong and Duke Ellington, makers of happy music for a full half century.

Ornette Coleman

THE BLUES

W. C. Handy

Behind jazz is always the blues. And the greatest of blues singers, Bessie Smith, became a top-drawer attraction—but *only* among Negroes in Negro theatres. She never quite made it elsewhere, but she was a star in Harlem, on Chicago's State Street, and on the T.O.B.A. circuit throughout the South. Her "race records" sold in the millions. Perhaps in her day she was too basic for the general public—even in the Twenties when primitivism in Negro art was a fad. Bessie did not attempt to entertain. She simply stood still and shouted the blues without trick arrangements or orchestral refinements—and she rocked the joint. Before the days of microphones, Bessie could be heard for a mile. When she sang in tent shows in the South, nobody needed to pay admission to *hear* her. But, of course, if they wanted to *see* her, people bought tickets.

Her Negro following was enormous, but the one time that she was featured in a Broadway nightclub she did not draw. Her engagement lasted only three days. And it was not until after her death in 1937 that the record industry chose to really acknowledge her artistry. Then John Hammond of Columbia Records declared, "To my way

Bessie Smith

Jelly Roll Morton

Joe Williams

of thinking, Bessie Smith was the greatest artist American jazz ever produced. In fact, I am not sure that her art did not reach beyond the limits of the term *jazz*." And Mezz Mezzrow wrote, "She didn't have any mannerisms . . . to send those golden notes of hers on their sunshiny way. She just stood there and sang, letting the love and laughter run out of her, and the heaving sadness, too . . . and swayed just a little with the glory of being alive and feeling."

There were in the same era three other blues-singing Smiths, Mamie, Trixie and Clara, all unrelated. Mamie was the first blues singer to record,

and her "Crazy Blues" was a best seller on the Negro market. In the light of her large sales, legend has it that she asked for more than $50 a recording session and was therefore frozen out of the record industry and died in obscurity. But in her heyday with her Jazz Hounds, of which Coleman Hawkins was a teenage member, Mamie Smith made some exciting discs. All of the Smiths were top-notch blues shouters.

Other fine performers not quite as famous as the Smiths in the Twenties were Alberta Hunter, Lizzie Miles, Sara Martin and Bertha "Chippie" Hill whose recording of "Trouble In Mind" is a classic. Preceding these was Ma Rainey, who put the blues on the map in Southern tent shows long before Bessie Smith was born.

Among the great male blues singers and instrumentalists were Tampa Red and Georgia Tom, Pine Top Smith, Cow Cow Davenport, Jimmy Yancey and T-Bone Walker. Later came Champion Jack Dupree, Jimmy Rushing and Joe Williams (once of the Count Basie band) who later recreated the style of the old blues in Harry Belafonte's television production, *The Strollin' Twenties*. Many composers, including George Gershwin, borrowed heavily from the blues. But the greatest transcribers, arrangers or composers in the blues idiom have been Negroes—Jelly Roll Morton, Mule Bradford, Spencer Williams, Clarence Williams and, of course, W. C. Handy. Certainly the blues might be said to have been the cornerstone of jazz.

Alberta Hunter, one of the few Negro women hit song writers of the blues era.

SONG WRITERS

One of the most popular song writers of the 1890s was the Ohioan, Gussie L. Davis. He wrote both words and music of many hits.

Feelin' tomorrow like I feel today,
I'll pack my trunk and make my get-a-way. . . .

So says the "St. Louis Blues." And an old Shelton Brooks song affirms the same theme:

Some of these days you'll miss me, Honey . . .

These lines became a sort of identifying trademark for the famous white singer, Sophie Tucker, over a period of fifty years. "Some of These Days" was written in 1910 by Brooks, who also was the composer of "Darktown Strutters Ball" in 1915. Many all-time hits were conceived by Negro lyricists and composers, from James Bland's "Carry Me Back To Old Virginny" (which is the official song of that state) to various rock-and-roll numbers Elvis Presley made into best sellers.

Among the American songs of Negro authorship that have become standards are not only the great "St. Louis Blues" and "Memphis Blues" by Handy, but Duke Ellington's "Sophisticated Lady," "Mood Indigo" and "I'm Beginning to See The Light"; J. Rosamond Johnson's "Li'l Gal," Will Marion Cook's "Rain Song," Bert William's "Nobody,"

Shelton Brooks is best known now for his "Some of These Days," but he wrote many other popular songs.

Fats Waller's clowning at the piano entertained millions when he appeared in such movies as Stormy Weather.

Sy Oliver, songwriter and arranger, leading a recording session.

Fats Waller and Andy Razaf combined to write such hits as "Ain't Misbehavin'" and "Honeysuckle Rose." For this tune they were joined by J. C. Johnson, composer of "The Charleston" and "Old Fashioned Love."

Maceo Pinkard's "Mammy" introduced by Al Jolson, Fats Waller's "Honeysuckle Rose" with Andy Razaf's lyrics, Benton Overstreet's "There'll Be Some Changes Made," Clarence Muse's "When It's Sleepy Time Down South," Sissle and Blake's "I'm Just Wild About Harry," J. P. Johnson's "Old-Fashioned Love," Alberta Hunter's "Downhearted Blues," Ella Fitzgerald and Chick Webb's "A Tisket, A Tasket," "I Don't Want To Set The World On Fire" by Bennie Benjamin, "Lover Man" by Jimmy Davis and Roger Ramirez, Ledbetter's "Goodnight, Irene" and Erroll Garner's "Misty."

The earliest Negro writer to produce a long series of hits was Gussie L. Davis who for over two decades, beginning in 1866, published a great many popular ballads including "The Lighthouse By The Sea," "The Fatal Wedding," "If I Could Only Blot Out The Past" and "The Baggage Coach Ahead," a Nineties favorite still sung today. Among the more prolific of colored songwriters since 1900 (besides some of those already mentioned) are Alex Rogers, Cris Smith, R. C. McPherson, Clarence Williams, Spencer Williams, Perry Bradford, J. C. Johnson, Louis Jordan, Leon and Otis Renee, Don Redmond, Sy Oliver, Billy Strayhorn, Walter Bishop, Irving Burgie, Oscar Brown, Jr., Ray Charles of the Big Beat and, in the rock-and-roll field, Otis Blackwell, Joe Tex, Charlie Singleton and Titus Turner.

Phil Moore's "Shoo-Shoo, Baby," Nat King Cole's "Straighten Up And Fly Right," Louis Jordan's "Is You Is Or Is You Ain't My Baby" and Zilner Randolph's "Ol' Man Mose Is Dead" are outstanding novelty songs, as are "I Want Some Seafood, Mama" by Fats Waller, "Flat Foot Floogie With The Floy Floy" by Slam Stewart, Bud Green and Slim Gaillard, and Slam Stewart's "Hit That Jive Jack." Dizzy Gillespie's "Oops Papa Da" and "Salt' Peanuts" are brilliant nonsense numbers; likewise the swinging folk-game chant, "Hambone, Hambone," with its hand clapping, leg patting juba style percussion. The manner in which these songs are sung and improvised upon is as much a part of a performance as are the words or music—Fats Waller's crazy syllables, Ella and Louis' scat singing or that of Babs Gonzales can turn almost any basic beat number into a lunatic romp. And Cab Calloway's *hi-de-hi-de-ho* vocalizations seemed to originate "out of this world" like the "speaking in tongues" of the slaves during their ring shouts a long time ago. Cab's *hi-de-ho* chorus made a hit of "Minnie The Moocher"

Many Negro songwriters have remained anonymous in relation to the major part of their output, particularly in the first quarter of the century when, because of poverty, it was often customary for composers to sell their compositions outright or to permit white publishers or arrangers to put their names on the songs. One of the most famous

American songs is a case in point. A Negro barber in Philadelphia, Richard Milburn, who was a fine guitar player and a melodious whistler, made up a song one day which he himself sang and played for some time before a publisher learned of it and sought him out. Milburn's song was called "Listen To The Mocking Bird" and the title page on the first published copies in 1855 read: "A Sentimental Ethiopian Ballad—LISTEN TO THE MOCKING BIRD—Melody by Richard Milburn—Written and Arranged by Alice Hawthorne." Mrs. Hawthorne was a local white woman, the mother of a young composer, Septimus Winner—who sometimes published under his mother's name rather than his own. "Listen To The Mocking Bird" sold so well that in 1856 a second edition was published—but only *one* name appeared on the title page as writer —that of Alice Hawthorne. Milburn's name disappeared from the credits and has never been associated with the song since. Old-time Negro composers shrug, "'Twere often thus."

Oscar Brown, Jr., composer, singer, actor, one-man show.

"Lover Man," one of the song standards, was written by Jimmy Davis (below) with Roger Ramirez.

David Martin, jazz pianist and composer of the score for Simply Heavenly.

89

Fletcher Henderson, pianist and arranger, was leading a band at Roseland on Broadway in the 1920s. A college-trained Southerner, he became the arranger for the Benny Goodman band at its peak in the 1930s.

HAPPY FEET

Avon Long.

In the Twenties it seemed as if all Harlem was dancing—and Harlemites set the rest of the world to dancing, too. The leg-flinging Charleston, which some say had nothing at all to do with South Carolina but originated with the kids of Harlem, swept the world. J. P. Johnson wrote a song to go with the dance and introduced it on Broadway in *Runnin' Wild*. Then Bricktop, followed by Josephine Baker, took it to Paris, and Frisco (the black Frisco, not the white one) did the Charleston in London. In quick succession for a decade new Negro dances followed, and some caught on with a wide public—the droll Black Bottom, the shim-sham-shimmy with its freeze-in-place break, the pixie-like truckin' raising a pointed finger, and above all the long popular Lindy hop originating at the Savoy Ballroom in 1927, perhaps on the very night that the happy ending of Lindbergh's flight across the Atlantic was announced.

The Savoy in Harlem, an institution for many years, was a dance emporium known as the Home of Happy Feet, where downtown whites and uptown Negroes came to "trip the light fantastic,"

Ida Forsyne, American dancer who became the cakewalking toast of Russia shortly after the turn of the century when she came to perform and stayed for almost a decade. Living to a ripe old age, she aided Jerome Robbins in choreographing his "Cakewalk" for the New York City Ballet.

to clap hands to the Charleston, to truck around the floor with arms akimbo, and to swing out in the Lindy hop, the dance that started the ballroom custom of couples no longer remaining close together as they dance. It was the Lindy that later turned into the rocking rhythms of the jitterbug. Nightly at the Savoy, Leroy (his only known name) danced for fun, but often with such clusters of downtown people around him that he decided to open a dancing school for those who wanted to learn his steps. Whitey also, and a group of the Lindy hoppers at the Savoy became professionals and travelled around the world swinging from Harlem to Hong Kong. Al and Leon swung out of the Savoy up to the Newport Jazz Festival. But the most amusing swinger of all was Snakehips Earl Tucker whose hips were a swivel. Attired in a wide-sleeved satin blouse, everything shaking, sleeves fluttering as if in a gale, rhinestone belt glittering in the spotlight, Snakehips in prohibition

Explosion on a Harlem street corner.

THE LINDY HOP

"Oh, *swing it, Mister Charlie—swing it!*" Whirling thru the Lindy Hop at the Savoy Ballroom, where, for from forty cents to a dollar, one can dance to the hot strains of two bands until dawn, with scarcely any lull in noise or music.

To the left, Earl *"Snakehips"* Tucker, originator of that weird dance, the "Snakehips." Gliding sensuously back and forth, tapping a continual one-two-three — one-two-three, he peers out at the audience. Satin blouse, diamond belt, a contemptuous, quivering, black pearl, bathed in a sea of light. More than contortion, it is perfect muscle control, climaxed in his crying near the wings, with his blouse and belt fluttering like a gale-whipped flag.

tap tap tap

clap clap clap

"Shim—sham—shimshamshimmy—aw, shim—sham—shimshamshimmy. Now it's to the left—tap—now it's to the right—*Mr. Eddie, Mr. Eddie* ain't treatin' me right—aw, shim—sham—shimshamshimmy!"

SNAKEHIPS

THE BREAK

Everyone poised momentarily before continuing the mad pace. Another break—and that's the "Sham."

TRUCKIN'

"Truck on down!" Small's Paradise revue getting into the swing of things. In all of Harlem the waiters are usually the finest exponents of any new dance step. They see them all—revues and entertainers come and go—and, too, they have usually waited in every club and cabaret in Harlem. Lithe, trim men, ambidextrous with trays, they bask in reflected glamour.

DOWN TO THE VERY BRICKS

To be specific and technical, the very finest dancers, the *"deepest"* truckers, the *"solid senders"* of the art are the street urchins. There is no step, no movement, which they cannot execute; no words to any song written they do not know.

Bill Robinson and Cab Calloway entertaining at the Cotton Club.

days never failed to make even the most drunken of nightclub patrons sit up and take notice, using his feet merely for propulsion since his body did all the rest.

Besides Bill Robinson, other audience-pleasers of the Twenties who Charlestoned, trucked or tapped their way to fame were Avon Long and Cora LaRedd at the Cotton Club; Pete Nugent; Eddie Rector, smoothest sand dancer of all; Ida Forsyne back from long years in Europe; the ballroom dancers, Meares and Meares; exotic Louise Cook; handsome Jimmy Atkins and also Tommy Atkins; little Pops Whitman; the high stepping Berry Brothers; U. S. Thompson; Peaches and Duke; Arthur Bryson; Dewey Weinglass; and the

best of the female tap dancers, Baby Alice Whitman. A bit later came Bunny Briggs, Bill Bailey, Marie Bryant, the Four Step Brothers and the Hillman Brothers. In nightclubs the Harlem chorus girls were said to form the hottest and fastest chorus lines in New York. Harlem's happy feet influenced many of the dancers and choreographers of Broadway shows. Blond Gilda Gray became famous with her expert version of the Harlem Shimmy which she claimed she invented and which gained her a featured spot in the Ziegfeld Follies. Harlem in the Twenties went truckin' on down to Broadway, and Bea Palmer, Anne Pennington and even Texas Guinan learned to do the Charleston and the Black Bottom.

96

"SHUFFLE ALONG"

The team responsible for Shuffle Along. From the left, Eubie Blake, Flournoy Miller, Al Mayer (producer), Noble Sissle and Aubrey Lyles. Miller and Lyles had begun as a playwriting team while students at Fisk University.

Sissle and Blake wrote the songs for *Shuffle Along*. Miller and Lyles wrote the book, and the four of them produced, directed and starred in it. After various vicissitudes the show finally arrived in New York in 1921. It was a smash hit. *Shuffle Along* began the vogue for Negro singing and dancing that lasted throughout the Twenties. Thereafter for a decade colored musicals on Broadway were top box-office attractions. From them there came to fame three scintillating stars, Ethel Waters, Florence Mills and Josephine Baker. The writers for most of these shows (until Dorothy Fields, Jimmy McHugh and Harold

Arlen came along) were Negroes. Besides Noble Sissle and Eubie Blake, there were Fats Waller and Andy Razaf, J. P. Johnson, J. C. Johnson, Tom Lemonier, Donald Heyward, Porter Grainger and Maceo Pinkard.

Top arrangers in the Twenties were Will Vodery, Jimmy Mundy, Tom Whaley, Charles L. Cooke and Don Redmond. There were also blues shouters like Mattie Hite, Lucille Hegamin and Mary Stafford who could sing louder than any nightclub band. At the Paradise in Atlantic City before the days of microphones, any one of these singers could be heard for blocks away on a quiet

Josephine Baker, daughter of a St. Louis washerwoman, went from waitress to dancer in the chorus of Shuffle Along *and then to stardom in the Folies Bèrgeres.*

The chorus and the comics in Chocolate Dandies, *the Sissle and Blake success of 1924-25.*

night. If you were a pedestrian approaching the club from the boardwalk, *first* you would hear the singer, then, as you got nearer, you might hear the band. This style of vocal projection old-timers termed, "throwing it from the velvet." Featured singing artists in the Twenties included Valaida Snow, Edith Wilson, Josephine Hall, Lottie Gee, Ada Ward, Walter Richardson, Adelaide Hall, Gertrude Saunders, Alberta Pryme, Daniel Haynes and Maude Russell. Comedians besides Flournoy Millery and Aubrey Lyles, were Billy Higgins, Eddie Green, Glen and Jenkins, Doe Doe Green, Mantan Moreland, Sandy Burns, Tim Moore, Gallie de Gaston, Blues McAllister, Frank Radcliff and Johnny Hudgins.

Shuffle Along was conceived primarily for Negro audiences. It was produced on a shoestring, rehearsed in New York, and scheduled to open at the Howard Theatre in Washington. But when the cast from Harlem got down to Pennsylvania Station by subway, they found the producers did not have enough money for rail tickets to the Capital. Some threatened to back out. But the show did open in Washington that night, played two successful weeks there, and earned enough to go on to Philadelphia for a week. There Sissle and Blake tried to persuade the owner of the Dunbar to invest the extra thousand dollars they needed

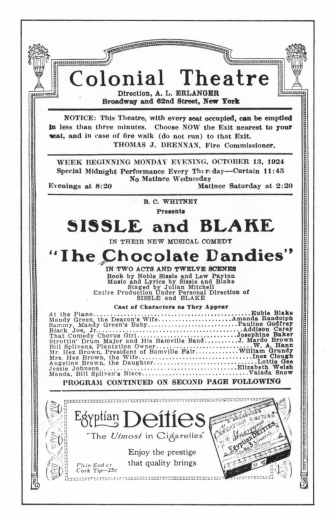

99

The chorus of Shuffle Along poses with one of the show's composers, Noble Sissle. The 1921 hit played at the 63rd Street Music Hall.

Costume sketches for Josephine Baker.

to brighten up the second-hand costumes. No luck. He refused to put in a penny. Nevertheless, the show came to New York. But no Broadway theatre was available, so they opened in 1921 at the Sixty-Third Street Theatre—a considerable distance from the Great White Way.

But Providence smiled. Overnight *Shuffle Along* became such a hit that double lines formed on the sidewalk for tickets, a motor car and taxi jam developed in the block, and the Traffic Department had to make Sixty-third a one-way street. *Shuffle Along* became the most successful Negro musical in New York since the days of Williams and Walker. And Florence Mills (who replaced Gertrude Saunders) was the toast of Broadway.

Shuffle Along was loaded with talent. The diva-to-be, Caterina Jarboro, and the future star, Josephine Baker, were among the chorus girls.

Flournoy Miller, the author of musicals, also starred as a comedian.

William Grant Still played oboe in the orchestra, and the composer-conductor-to-be, Hall Johnson, was also in the pit. One of the famous blues-singing Smiths, Trixie, sang "He May Be Your Man But He Comes To See Me Sometimes." The score was crammed with song hits—"Bandana Days," "The Gypsy Blues," "Love Will Find A Way" and "I'm Just Wild About Harry." It ran for over a year in Manhattan and two years on the road. It started a trend in Negro entertainment that did not abate until the Great Depression arrived.

For a decade following *Shuffle Along* a succession of Negro musicals came to Broadway, most of them successful. *Put And Take*, conceived by Irving Miller, immediately followed *Shuffle Along*. In 1922 came *Strut Miss Lizzie* by Creamer and Layton; then *Seven-Eleven*. The charming *Liza* with a score by Maceo Pinkard was a 1923 hit. That same year Leonard Harper's *Plantation Days* went to London. In 1924 Lew Leslie built *Dixie To Broadway* around Florence Mills, and Miller and Lyles' *Runnin' Wild* opened. The latter created a sensation with the Charleston. In 1925 Sissle and Blake's *Chocolate Dandies* began its long run. In 1926 Florence Mills starred in Lew Leslie's *Blackbirds,* and in 1927 there was Miller and Lyles' *Rang Tang* which began rehearsing the day Lindbergh flew the Atlantic. Ethel Waters starred in *Africana,* and Irving Miller's *Dinah* introduced a dance called the Black Bottom. Meanwhile at the Cotton Club and Connie's Inn in Harlem, as well as at the Plantation downtown, there were excellent revues. On Broadway for 518 performances Bojangles starred in Lew Leslie's *Blackbirds of 1928,* and that same year Miller and Lyles produced *Keep Shuffling*. In 1929 *Hot Chocolates* made a hit of Fats Waller's song, "Ain't Misbehavin'," just about the time America headed for the Depression and the bottom fell out of show business for Negroes and whites alike.

For only five short years following *Shuffle Along*

The star of New York, London and Paris began as "Baby Florence Mills," a cakewalk champion at six. This is Edward Steichen's portrait of her as she played in Dixie to Broadway, *in 1924.*

What The World's Notables Say

"My evening at The Plantation restaurant was a most delightful one. Apparently you have done everything to provide a place of entertainment that is charming and unique in all of its many features."
DAVID BELASCO.

"The Plantation is a heart-gladdening revelation. Yours to the last curtain."
LEON ERROL.

"Smart, snappy, unique, delightful; deserves its immense popularity."
NORMA TALMADGE.

"A revelation to me and an agreeable one. The speediest, snappiest show and smartest atmosphere in delightful combination."
RAYMOND HITCHCOCK.

"For novelty, entertainment, service and fun, it is unexcelled."
Sincerely,
LOUISE GROODY.

"I found the Plantation one of the most original and unique Supper Rooms in the World."
MORRIS GEST.

"Am glad to sincerely say how much I have enjoyed the Plantation."
IRVING BERLIN.

"The most up-to-date idea that has been offered the 'Milky Way' in many a Moon."
FRANCES WHITE.

"I found the Plantation very artistic and enjoyed the novel entertainment."
ARTHUR HAMMERSTEIN.

"The Plantation is CLASS personified, in entertainment, atmosphere and the fashion parade of smart people. It's delightfully different and the Best Ever."
NORA BAYES.

"Society has a new toy, and this latest fad of the town is The Plantation. This charming American Room is quite quaint and seems certain to become the vogue."
S. JAY KAUFMAN.

"The Plantation is the most novel and attractive place of its kind to be found in America or Europe."
ANTONIO SCOTTI.

"It is wonderful, bewildering and beautiful. I've never seen anything excel the novelty of the entertainment."
FLORA ZABELLE.

"The Plantation? There is no place in the World like it"
Says
WALTER CATLETT.

"I know of no more delightful After Theatre playground than the Plantation."
VINCENT SERRANO.

"The Plantation does not grow cotton but Silk. Food, orchestra, show—everything is fine as silk."
SAMUEL SHIPMAN.

"The Plantation is a new note and a most welcome one: it gives us the spirit of America instead of Europe."
EDGAR SELWYN.

The Plantation was a restaurant at 50th and Broadway. Its musical shows featuring Florence Mills had a great vogue.

Florence Mills reigned as an international star—New York, London and Paris. Then she died, still young, and at the height of her fame. She had worked hard in show business all her life. She was eight years old in 1900 when she sang in Williams and Walker's *Sons of Ham.* She was with the Panama Trio on the Barbary Coast and in the Plantation Ten in vaudeville. Her life had not been an easy one. For a time during her childhood, the Gary Society for the protection of impoverished children took her under its wing. When Lew Leslie carried her from Broadway to Europe, she had already been working and travelling almost continuously for 25 years and was no stranger to the rigors of the one-night stand. Nevertheless, she remained so dainty, simple and charming—willow-frail and pixieishly pretty—that people everywhere wanted to reach out their arms to protect and love

Eddie Green was another comedian who could write his own sketches. Here he is in Hot Chocolates, *a Broadway show of 1929. Later he was featured in* Duffy's Tavern, *a popular radio series.*

Adelaide Hall in Blackbirds of 1928. *Later she entertained in Europe for years.*

her—without knowing why. Perhaps it was because, beneath the sparkle of her theatre personality in the spotlight, something seemed to sigh:

> *Never had no happiness,*
> *Never felt no one's caress.*
> *I'm just a lonesome bit of humanity*
> *Born on a Friday, I guess . . .*

That is the verse which introduced the song she made famous, "I'm A Little Blackbird Looking For A Bluebird, Too." On her return from London, Florence Mills died suddenly in New York in 1927. As her funeral cortege wound slowly through Harlem, an airplane overhead released a flock of bluebirds.

BROADWAY DRAMA

James Weldon Johnson in his *Black Manhattan* calls April 17, 1917, "the date of the most important single event in the entire history of the Negro in the American theatre. . . . It was the first time anywhere in the United States for Negro actors in the dramatic theatre to command the serious attention of the critics and of the *general* press and public." The occasion was the presentation at the Garden Theatre by poet Ridgely Torrence of three plays, *The Rider of Dreams, Granny Maumee* and *Simon the Cyrenian*, with a cast of Negro actors, a number of whom had been with the Lafayette Players. George Jean Nathan, leading critic of the day, gave the evening high praise and placed two of the actors, Opal Cooper and Inez Clough, among the top-ten performers of the year. This was an excellent beginning for colored artists in

Paul Robeson in the 1925 revival of The Emperor Jones.

The Pulitzer Prize play of 1926, In Abraham's Bosom, *by Paul Green, featured*
Rose McClendon and Frank Wilson.

A scene in the Theatre Guild's great success, Porgy, with Rose McClendon
(left), Frank Wilson and Evelyn Ellis.

109

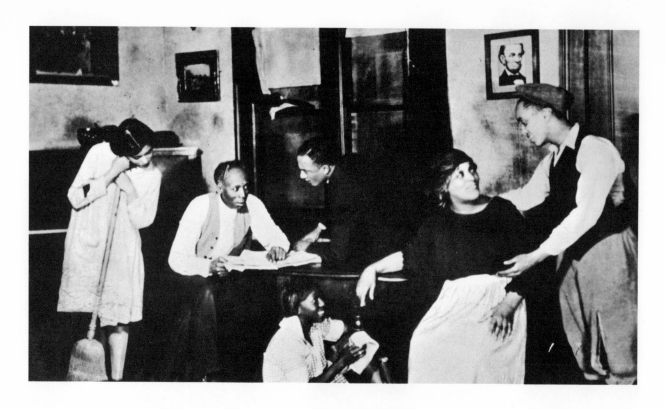

A scene from the 1929 Harlem, *one of the earliest Broadway plays authored by a Negro, Wallace Thurman, in collaboration with William Jordan Rapp.*

serious drama on Broadway. But the Torrence plays did not run very long. The day after the opening, the United States declared war on Germany.

Three years later in Greenwich Village, Eugene O'Neill's *The Emperor Jones* became the next production involving Negroes to excite New York playgoers. As a result its star, Charles Gilpin, received the Spingarn Medal in 1920 for the highest achievement by any American Negro during the year, and the Drama League voted him one of the ten people that season who had done most for the theatre. Eugene O'Neill's next play also caused excitement—although for racial reasons rather than theatrical. It was *All God's Chillun Got Wings,* featuring Paul Robeson and Mary Blair. The plot

Paul Robeson with Mary Blair in All God's Chillun Got Wings. *The O'Neill play about an interracial marriage was presented at the Provincetown Playhouse in New York in 1924.*

Oscar Polk and Ruth Attaway in the original 1936 production of the Kaufman & Hart hit comedy, You Can't Take It With You.

In Lillian Hellman's portrait of post-Civil War Southerners, The Little Foxes, *which began its long Broadway run in 1939, Abbie Mitchell played Addie and John Marriott played Cal.*

concerned an interracial marriage. When the press learned that Robeson was to kiss blond Miss Blair's hand on stage, a mighty protest arose from public and press, with editorial demands for the banning of the production lest it cause riots. Nevertheless, the play opened, and nothing untoward happened. But due to this internationally publicized controversy, young Paul Robeson and the young O'Neill both became widely known.

Other plays in succeeding years involved with the problems of miscegenation included *Mulatto, Brass Ankle, Blood Stream, Strange Fruit, Mamba's Daughters, Deep Are the Roots, Mandingo, Octoroon* and, of course, *Othello*. But none caused such a furor as did O'Neill's early drama. Following O'Neill, the Paul Green plays, *In Abraham's Bosom* (which received the Pulitzer Prize in 1926) and *House of Connelley,* gave opportunities to excellent Negro actors like Rose McClendon, Abbie Mitchell, Frank Wilson and Jules Bledsoe. *Lulu Belle* cast white Leonore Ulric and Henry Hull as its mulatto leads, but the rest of the company was almost entirely Negro, and DuBose and Dorothy Heyward's *Porgy* (which later became *Porgy and Bess*) had a cast composed of the finest Negro actors ever assembled in one production up to that time: Rose McClendon and Frank Wilson, plus Georgette Harvey, Evelyn Ellis, Richard Huey, Leigh Whipper and Jack Carter. Staged by the Theatre Guild and directed by Reuben Mamoulian, *Porgy* was the great dramatic hit of the Twenties and had a very long run in both New York and London.

Then came the socially slanted plays of the Thirties like *Never No More* by James K. Millen, John Wexley's *They Shall Not Die* (about the infamous Scottsboro Case), and the Paul Peters and George Sklar play, *Stevedore,* with Rex Ingram and Edna Thomas among others. Serious plays of Negro life by liberal white playwrights attracted Broadway audiences but received no consideration at all on radio or in Hollywood. The mechanical media gave Negro actors a chance only as comics, and then mostly in very stereotyped presentations. The silver screen was for many years black America's daily betrayal before millions of people.

NO GREEN PASTURES

Richard B. Harrison, who played De Lawd in The Green Pastures. *Born in Canada of parents who were fugitive slaves, he moved to Detroit where he worked as porter and waiter. He began his theatrical career as a dramatic reader for Negro clubs, schools and churches. He was over 65 years of age before getting his first chance in the legitimate theatre in the Marc Connelly play.*

Depression days were indeed hard days for Negro actors. But fortunately *The Green Pastures* came along to hire a considerable number of them. This was a Negro folk fable dramatized, directed and produced by whites to be performed by Negroes. It had a certain charm, and such good actors that they gave the play an almost authentic folk feeling. Also its adaptor and

director, Marc Connelly, secured the wonderful Hall Johnson Choir as a singing orchestra in the pit. And Connelly achieved perfect casting in Richard B. Harrison, the man who played De Lawd. Tall, fatherly, dignified, white-haired Mr. Harrison had been for forty years an elocutionist reciting Shakespeare in Negro schools, churches and clubs across the country. He had also taught

The building of the ark, a scene from The Green Pastures. *Noah was played by Tutt Whitney, Gabriel by Wesley Hill, Adam by Daniel L. Haynes, and Abraham by J. A. Shipp.*

correct speech in colored colleges. Mr. Harrison was a complete stranger to Negro dialect so, for his role in *The Green Pastures,* he had to be coached in colored dialect by a white actor who once had played darkey parts. Being a mulatto, he also had to use dark makeup. "Gangway for de Lawd Gawd Jehovah!" was Harrison's entrance line as he stepped on stage. From that first moment on, audiences for years were captivated by his humorously reverent and beautiful portrayal of De Lawd and his portrayal of Gawd's problems with his "chillun" in heaven as well as on earth. *The Green Pastures* was what Broadway calls a "smash hit."

Richard B. Harrison was well over sixty before he set foot on the Broadway stage. He gave 1,568 straight performances of De Lawd without missing a single one. On tour after the New York run, the company of almost a hundred actors and singers travelled 40,000 miles performing from coast-to-coast. Because of Jim Crow the colored cast usually had to stay in third-rate rooming houses and sometimes eat at hamburger stands. After five years of *The Green Pastures,* when Harrison returned from his last long tour, he said, lapsing into the dialect of his play, "I'm plumb tuckered out." Shortly afterwards he died in Manhattan.

Harrison had been plagued in many cities by the irony of a black man playing God in white theatres where Negroes were barred or were segregated in the top gallery. Negro organizations picketed the playhouses in a number of these cities. When *The Green Pastures* was scheduled to play the National Theatre in Washington where no Negroes at all were admitted, a committee of prominent colored citizens in the Capital asked its star some weeks in advance to cancel the engagement. Although in anguish concerning the situation, Harrison refused. Then the cast itself threatened to go on strike on the eve of the opening. Some of the actors were arrested in Washington, and others discharged from the company, but the show went on. Richard B. Harrison, its star, famous though he had become, thereafter lost considerable prestige in the eyes of the Negro people. Certainly, for those who could not even see the play, *The Green Pastures* was no green pasture at all.

THE FEDERAL THEATRE

THE
FEDERAL **·USA· WORK PROGRAM WPA** **THEATRE**

HALLIE FLANAGAN
National Director

PHILIP W. BARBER
Director of Production for N. Y. C.

Presents

THE NEGRO THEATRE

PRODUCTION OF

THE CASE OF PHILIP LAWRENCE

Based on the drama "Eleven P. M."

By GEORGE MacENTEE

Production Supervised and Directed by J. A. (Gus) SMITH

A Negro Theatre program. The sets for this play were the work of Perry Watkins, the first Negro scenic designer on Broadway. The Federal Theatre gave him his first chance to work on several plays and then Guthrie McClintic commissioned him to design Mamba's Daughters.

During the Depression Negroes in entertainment fell upon evil days. Except for the long-running *Green Pastures* that opened in 1930, there were no green pastures for colored performers, singers or dancers for a long time. Had it not been for the Federal Theatre in those lean years, many Negro actors would have found it impossible to exercise their craft. Mantan More-land once told a tale about a barnstorming troupe which was touring the South in those days and had not been paid for weeks. But one day the manager announced excitedly that he had a wire that the house was sold out at their next stop, a city in Arkansas. Mantan was delighted. He would be paid. When he arrived in town by bus, the landlady where he had rented a room said, "I'll

Orson Welles gave his Federal Theatre production of Macbeth *a Haitian setting and an all-Negro cast. Standing at the center right are Edna Thomas as Lady Macbeth and Jack Carter as Macbeth. In the center is Service Bell as the king. At left center is Canada Lee as Banquo. The overture was James P. Johnson's "Yamekraw," the voodoo chants and dances were by Asadata Dafora Horton, and the chorus was conducted by Leonard de Paur.*

cook a wonderful dinner for you, so just take a nice hot bath and get ready to eat before show time."

While Mantan was in the bathroom, he heard a bit of rain and wind outside, but paid no attention. When he came to the dinner table, he asked the landlady, "Where is the theatre, ma'am?"

The landlady answered, "Well, I hate to tell you, but a cyclone just blowed it away."

The Federal Theatre Project established by the government's Works Progress Administration in 1935 proved a godsend to colored actors during the Depression. In the big cities Negro units were set

A scene from Haiti *at the Lafayette Theatre in Harlem, with Rex Ingram and Elena Karam.*

up, and in some white groups token integration took place. The Project gave Negroes a chance for the first time to learn something about stage management, lighting and other technical matters relating to backstage activities—an opportunity the commercial theatre never allowed due to the objection of the white stagehands union and other craft syndicates. Even Negro-owned theatres formerly had to have white stagehands. And in colored movie or vaudeville houses, according to union rules, only *white* operators could run motion picture projectors or operate spotlights. Negroes could do all these things in the Federal Theatre. In New York there was not only an excellent unit directed by John Houseman at the Lafayette in Harlem, but colored actors were to some extent integrated in the Broadway units in the *Living Newspaper* productions and other shows. Negro

Turpentine *was a social play by J. A. Smith and Ben Morell exposing the evils of the Southern labor-camp system.*

playwrights, too, were given a chance to see their scripts come alive, and actors thirsty for juicy parts had an opportunity to play them in Harlem, Chicago and Los Angeles.

Edna Thomas was a fascinating Lady Macbeth at the Lafayette in the Orson Welles' production of a tropical *Macbeth* laid in Haiti; Jack Carter played the lead, Canada Lee was Banquo and Service Bell the King. Chicago presented an all-Negro *Swing Mikado* in 1939 with Gilbert and Sullivan music played in jazz tempo. On the West Coast the Clarence Muse production of Hall Johnson's *Run Little Chillun* ran for months. The Seattle theatre group produced a new play by a Negro playwright, Theodore Browne's *Natural Man*. It also did classics ranging from *Lysistrata* and Shakespeare to *Androcles and the Lion* with colored casts. When by an act of Congress in 1939 the Federal Theatre was abolished, it was a great loss to Negro actors and to young technicians anxious to continue the backstage training they could not get elsewhere.

DRAMA IN HARLEM

Clarence Muse was educated as a lawyer but was diverted into the theatre. He was a writer-director-producer for years with Negro theatres in New York and Chicago before he became one of Hollywood's best-known Negro actors in the 1940s.

Twenty years or so before the Federal Theatre came to Harlem, there were excellent stock companies flourishing in the Negro community, presenting musicals and plays which usually had a week's run. The Anita Bush Players performed at the Lincoln Theatre at 135th and Lenox. And in 1914 the amusement critic, Lester Walton of the *New York Age*, leased the Lafayette to establish a stock company. The Lafayette Players presented varied fare including grand opera, and for the Shakespeare Tercentenary produced *Othello* with Edward Sterling Wright of Boston in the leading role. Other cities also had all-colored stock companies—Dallas, Kansas City, the Howard Players in Washington, the Pekin Theatre Company in Chicago. But the Lafayette in Harlem was the most famous.

The Lafayette acquired great popularity with its uptown presentations of downtown hits—*Madame X, On Trial, Dr. Jekyll and Mr. Hyde, The Count of Monte Cristo,* and even the Jewish comedy *Potash and Perlmutter* performed by Negroes. It

was in *Within The Law* that ebony-dark Clarence Muse made a great hit—performing the role of the lawyer in whiteface. Muse, who had enormous popularity with Harlem audiences and whose rich deep voice was well known, used a gimmick in this play which never failed to bring the house down. At his initial entrance, Muse first began to speak off stage, carrying on a brief conversation while still out of sight. The audience would think, "There comes Clarence," but they were unprepared for what was to happen—the very dark Muse stepped on stage *completely white*. Astonished pandemonium always broke out. Applause shook the theatre. *Within the Law* in Harlem became an S.R.O. hit. Later in *Dr. Jekyll and Mr. Hyde* Clarence Muse again appeared in white face.

Another story concerning caucasian makeup is that of a beautiful brownskin actress in a Midwestern stock company who always played *Camille* in white makeup and a blond wig. To cover her arms throughout the play, the dark star wore long white gloves. One night during the death scene at the end of the play when she reached up to hug her beloved Armand, the sleeves of her lovely lace nightgown fell so far down toward her shoulders that the upper portion of each dusky arm was exposed—uncovered by gloves. At what was usually a very moving moment in the play, a male voice from the audience boomed out, "Lady, you're getting ready to die—and ain't took off your gloves yet!" The spectators could not stop laughing until the final curtain.

But in spite of occasional absurdities of this nature, colored stock companies produced good plays and developed some excellent actors, a number of whom later performed on Broadway. Charles Gilpin came from the Pekin Theatre Company in Chicago to join Anita Bush in Harlem and then the Lafayette Players. That large company already included names like Abbie Mitchell, Laura Bowman, Evelyn Ellis, Frank Wilson, Edna Thomas, Andrew Bishop, Inez Clough and Jack Carter.

A scene from Anna Lucasta, *with Hilda Simms and Canada Lee.*

1923 was the year Willis Richardson's play, The Chip Woman's Fortune, *was presented at the Lafayette Theatre.*

From the Lafayette, Gilpin went directly to Broadway to play a featured part in John Drinkwater's *Abraham Lincoln*, and a few years later he created the title role in *The Emperor Jones*. This part, performed at the Provincetown Theatre, made Gilpin the first Negro actor to be widely acclaimed in a straight dramatic role. Previously, colored stars had all come to fame as singers or dancers.

Following the Lincoln and the Lafayette, the Alhambra Theatre in Harlem formed a semipermanent company of performers including the comics, Amanda Randolph and Teddy Blackmon. A short-lived group called the Negro Folk Theatre presented a double bill at the Lafayette: Oscar

Charles Gilpin was the son of a Southern day laborer and a trained nurse. Born in 1878, he entertained wherever he could, in county fairs, restaurants, minstrel shows, until he got a foothold in the drama in the early 1900s. By 1916 he was directing the Lafayette Theatre company. Above left he is shown as himself, in center as the Negro clergyman in Drinkwater's Abraham Lincoln, *his first Broadway part in 1919, and right as Brutus Jones in* The Emperor Jones, *his greatest success.*

Wilde's *Salome* with Evelyn Preer, and *The Chip Woman's Fortune* by Negro playwright Willis Richardson. In 1940 Theodore Ward attempted to form at the Lincoln a repertory theatre called The Negro Playwrights Company, but during its first production—Ward's own play, *Big White Fog* —the struggling company's difficulties with white theatrical unions forced it to close. Previously the Suitcase Theatre, a small group performing weekends in 1936–1937 in a fraternal hall in Harlem, had chalked up the longest run to date for a single play in that community—135 performances of *Don't You Want to Be Free?* by Langston Hughes.

Earl Jones in the leading role of Harlem's longest running play, Don't You Want To Be Free?

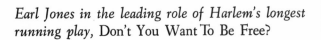

124

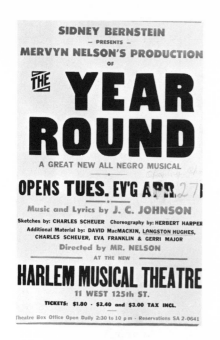

Posters for theatrical productions in Harlem.

But not until the Rose McClendon Players formed their Theatre Workshop, offering a Subscription Series of three plays a year by Negro playwrights, did a Harlem community group achieve any sort of permanency. The McClendons, as they were known, were founded in 1937 by Dick Campbell and endured until 1942, giving such young men and women as Fred O'Neal, Ossie Davis, Helen Martin, Maxwell Glanville, Claire Leyba and Freddie Carter their first opportunities to perform, rehearsing and playing in the evenings after they had finished their daily jobs elsewhere in factories or kitchens. Among the playwrights whose work was presented for the first time were George Norford, Loften Mitchell, Warren Coleman and Abram Hill whose comedy, *On Striver's Row*, became a Harlem hit and was often revived thereafter.

A few years later in the basement of a public library, the American Negro Theatre directed by Abram Hill came into being, and its acting group included Sidney Poitier and Harry Belafonte, who there developed their burgeoning talents in plays by or about Negroes. However, the theatre's only production that went from Harlem to Broadway was not a play of Negro life at all, but a comedy by Philip Yordan about a Polish family, adapted for performance by colored actors. The American Negro Theatre's presentation of *Anna Lucasta*, with Hilda Simms as Anna, opened uptown. It was such a hit in Harlem that it was taken to Broadway in 1944 where it ran for almost three years, chalking up 957 performances. Another company played for forty weeks in Chicago, and a third toured New England. *Anna Lucasta* years later was made into a motion picture—in fact, two pictures—one with a white cast including Paulette Goddard, and subsequently a second film with a Negro cast starring Eartha Kitt. Unfortunately, commercial success in the long run did not do the American Negro Theatre any lasting good. The group consciously began to aim its uptown productions at downtown consumption, thereby losing its ethnic touch as well as its community audience. It soon fell apart. Since that group there has been nothing like it in Harlem for the development of either actors or playwrights.

125

THE SPIRITUALS

The original Fisk Jubilee Singers, painted in England in 1873 by Edmund Havel, court painter to Queen Victoria.

Sometimes I'm up,
Sometimes I'm down
Sometimes I'm almost
To the ground . . .
Oh, yes, Lord!

The spirituals—the sorrow songs of bondage —have long been musical staples. Ever since 1871 when nine Fisk Jubilee Singers, all students dressed in hand-me-downs from Northern missionary barrels, left their poor campus in Nashville to sing themselves into the hearts of America and Europe, the spirituals have been a beloved part of our cultural heritage. Aside from continual use in religious services, the spirituals have been sung over the years by minstrel performers, folk artists, folk choruses and trained choruses, by Paul Robeson and Harry Belafonte, and by almost all colored concertizers appearing in Carnegie Hall. Formal arrangements of the spirituals have been made by such outstanding musicians as Nathaniel Dett, Harry T. Burleigh, Hall

THE
SHEPPARD
JUBILEE SINGERS!

GENUINE COLORED PEOPLE!

UNDER THE LEADERSHIP OF ANDREW SHEPPARD.

Thirty years a Slave, formerly the property of Gen. Robert E. Lee, at Arlington, Va., emancipated by Abraham Lincoln's Great Proclamation of Freedom. All having been Slaves, they give the truest and best representation of Slave Life on the Old Plantation, which for Harmony and Melody is unsurpassed.

Organized by Rev. Father Hawley,

City Missionary in Hartford, Ct., for over Thirty Years.

DOORS OPEN AT 7 P. M.   CONCERT AT 8 P. M.

Admission 25 and 35c. Children Half Price.

S. S. BASSEY, Manager.

Robert E. Lee's former slave led this band of singers. The concert was arranged by Father Hawley, a Catholic priest of Hartford who was dedicated to helping the poor, often with the aid of benefit lectures by Mark Twain.

127

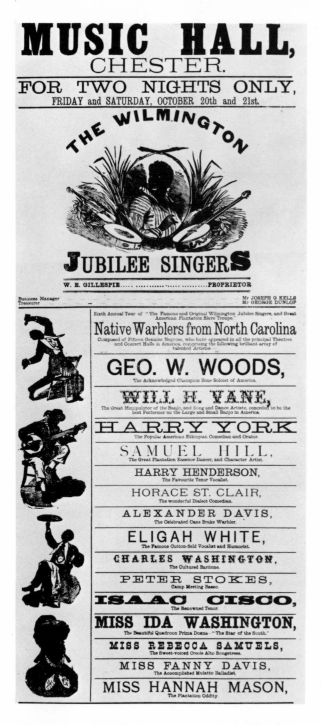

MUSIC HALL,
CHESTER.
FOR TWO NIGHTS ONLY,
FRIDAY and SATURDAY, OCTOBER 20th and 21st.

THE WILMINGTON
JUBILEE SINGERS

W. E. GILLESPIE.............................PROPRIETOR

Business Manager ——— Mr JOSEPH G KELLS
Treasurer ——— Mr GEORGE DUNLOP

Sixth Annual Tour of "The Famous and Original Wilmington Jubilee Singers, and Great American Plantation Slave Troupe."

Native Warblers from North Carolina
Composed of Fifteen Genuine Negroes, who have appeared in all the principal Theatres and Concert Halls in America, comprising the following brilliant array of talented Artistes.

GEO. W. WOODS,
The Acknowledged Champion Bone Soloist of America.

WILL H. VANE,
The Great Manipulator of the Banjo, and Song and Dance Artiste, conceded to be the best Performer on the Large and Small Banjo in America.

HARRY YORK
The Popular American Ethiopian Comedian and Orator.

SAMUEL HILL,
The Great Plantation Essence Dancer, and Character Artist.

HARRY HENDERSON,
The Favourite Tenor Vocalist.

HORACE ST. CLAIR,
The wonderful Dialect Comedian.

ALEXANDER DAVIS,
The Celebrated Cane Brake Warbler.

ELIGAH WHITE,
The Famous Cotton-field Vocalist and Humorist.

CHARLES WASHINGTON,
The Cultured Baritone.

PETER STOKES,
Camp Meeting Basso.

ISAAC CISCO,
The Renowned Tenor.

MISS IDA WASHINGTON,
The Beautiful Quadroon Prima Donna—"The Star of the South."

MISS REBECCA SAMUELS,
The Sweet-voiced Creole Alto Songstress.

MISS FANNY DAVIS,
The Accomplished Mulatto Balladist.

MISS HANNAH MASON,
The Plantation Oddity.

Another band of jubilee singers of the 1870s who specialized in portrayals of slave life before Emancipation. When they showed what revivals and camp meetings were like, the press reported "the audience laughed, applauded, almost shouted with joy, and did everything except get up to join in an impromptu jubilee."

Johnson, John Work, William Boatner and Margaret Bonds; and by Morton Gould, Fred Waring and Robert Shaw. Many composers have utilized the spiritual themes—from Dvorak's *New World Symphony* to Duke Ellington's "Dear Old Southland," and Jan Meyerowitz in the musical interlude of his opera, *The Barrier*. Roland Hayes and Marian Anderson became as celebrated for their singing of spirituals as for their lieder. And "Dry Bones" has saved the life of many a vaudeville quartet.

Beginning their first tour, the Fisk Jubilee Singers gave their first program of spirituals on a wintry night in Cincinnati. The next day they stopped at Wilberforce in Ohio, the oldest of Negro colleges. "Then they went, fighting cold and starvation, shut out of hotels and cheerfully sneered at, ever Northward," wrote W. E. B. DuBois, "and ever the magic of their song kept thrilling hearts, until a burst of applause in the Congregational Council at Oberlin revealed them to the world. They came to New York and Henry Ward Beecher dared to welcome them, even though the metropolitan dailies sneered at his 'nigger minstrels.' So their songs conquered till they sang across the land and across the sea, before Queen and Kaiser, in Scotland and Ireland, Holland and Switzerland. Seven years they sang, and brought back a hundred and fifty thousand dollars to found Fisk University." This money also built the first brick structure on their campus, Jubilee Hall.

Pioneer Negro singing groups a half century ago basing entire programs largely on the spirituals were Slater's Jubilee Singers and the popular Sheppard Jubilee Singers. Hall Johnson formed his famous choir in the Twenties with spirituals as their basic fare. His singers performed in concert halls, in Radio City Music Hall and in motion pictures. Wings Over Jordan later became a very popular choir; on Sunday mornings at one time this group had a weekly radio show on a national hook-up. Eva Jessye's Choir, Leonard DePaur's Infantry Chorus, and the Utterbach Concert Ensemble, as well as Evelyn Freeman's Exciting Voices and the Jester Hairston groups on the West Coast made effective use of spirituals. Rosamond Johnson and Taylor Gordon in the Twenties carried

Slayton's was obviously a dignified, conservative group of concert artists.

Wednesday Evening, Feb. 28th, 1872.

TO COMMENCE AT 8 O'CLOCK P. M.

OPERA HOUSE!

Grand Luca Concert.

OLMSTEAD LUCA

—THE—

Celebrated Black Pianist,

(Just returned from Europe after an absence of ten years,) has the
pleasure of announcing a

CONCERT!

—ASSISTED BY—

Madame A. A. Luca,
Contralto.

Mr. A. A. Luca,
Tenor and Violinist.

PROGRAMME.

PART I.

1. OVERTURE—"Tancredi,"...................................ROSSINI
   VIOLIN AND PIANOFORTE.
2. SONG—Good bye Sweetheart,...........................HATTON
   MR. A. A. LUCA.
3. PIANOFORTE SOLO—"Le Reveil Du Lion." (Op. 115)....KONTSKI
   OLMSTEAD LUCA.
4. TWO PART SONG—"The Wish,"......................MENDELSSOHN
   MADAME LUCA & A. A. LUCA.
5. PIANOFORTE SOLO—Polka de Concert......................O. LUCA
   OLMSTEAD LUCA.
6. DUETT—Bridge of Sighs.................................WHITE
   MESSRS. A. A. & O. LUCA.

PART II.

7. AMILEE WALTZES....................................LANNER
   VIOLIN AND PIANOFORTE.
8. ROMANZA—"O can it be,".............................MATTEI
   MR. A. A. LUCA.
9. PIANOFORTE SOLO—Sonata Pathetieque, (Op. 13)......BEETHOVEN
   OLMSTEAD LUCA.
10. DUETTINO—"I live and love thee,"..................CAMPANA
    MADAME LUCA & MR. A. A. LUCA.
11. PIANOFORTE SOLO—"Andante & Rondo Capriccioso," (Op. 14) MENDELSSOHN
    OLMSTEAD LUCA.
12. DUETT—"What I live for."..............................
    MESSRS. A. A. & O. LUCA.

☞ The Grand Pianoforte used on the occasion is from WM. KNABE & CO.,
kindly furnished by Mr. JOHN SELTZER & CO.

PRICES OF ADMISSION:

Reserved Seats, 75 Cts.   Unreserved Seats, 50 Cts.

Tickets to be obtained at the Music Store of JOHN SELTZER & Co.

Nevins & Myers, Printers, 71 North High Street, Columbus, Ohio.

Leon Bibb came up from Louisville to sing in the chorus of Broadway musicals and then to take featured roles. He has sung folk songs, ballads and show tunes for audiences throughout America and Europe.

Like many other singers, Josh White began as a child in a church choir. He became noted for his songs of militant protest, especially "Strange Fruit."

These Lucas of the 1870s may have been the generation that followed the pre-Civil War Luca Family of vocalists and instrumentalists.

Odetta, born in Alabama, has spent most of her time in California. Trained in opera, she turned to folk music.

the jubilee songs to Europe in vaudeville-concert form, as later did many singing foursomes such as the Deep River Boys and the Golden Gate Quartet. Paul Robeson's debut concert in Greenwich Village was a concert of spirituals. And Josh White, Leon Bibb, Odetta and many others have made use of spirituals in nightclub appearances.

Voices, Inc., the Afro-American Folkloric Group, and Abdul, Dismond, and Pryor, perform them on the college circuit. Morton Gould's *Spirituals for Strings* is a recent recording hit. With new words, old spirituals have become part and parcel of the "freedom movement," and of the repertoires of most young folk singers.

COLORED COMPOSERS

Ulysses Kay

Serious colored composers, many of whom have used ethnic themes in the larger musical forms, include Edmund Jenkins, Florence Price, William Dawson, Howard Swanson, Clarence Cameron White, Ulysses Kay, Gordon Parks, Coleridge Taylor Perkinson, Hale Smith, William Grant Still and Margaret Bonds, whose *Spiritual Suite For Piano* and *The Ballad of the Brown King* have had widespread performances. Edmund Jenkins, who grew up as a member of his father's famous Jenkins Orphan Home Band in South Carolina, wrote *Charlestonia: A Negro Rhapsody For Full Orchestra*, which was performed in 1924 in Paris and Brussels. Florence

Price played her *Piano Concerto* with the Chicago Symphony Orchestra under Frederick Stock, who in 1932 also programmed her *Symphony In E Minor* for several performances. And in 1935 Leopold Stokowski conducted the Philadelphia Orchestra in William Dawson's *Negro Folk Symphony*.

Howard Swanson's *Short Symphony* was performed in 1950 by the New York Philharmonic Symphony Society and the following year at the Edinburgh Festival. In 1954 the New Orleans Philharmonic Symphony presented Clarence Cameron White's *Elegy*. Ulysses Kay's works have been played by the Tucson Orchestra and the Rochester Eastman Orchestra. In Venice under

Nathaniel Dett

Hall Johnson

Howard Swanson

the baton of Negro conductor Dean Dixon, *Symphonic Set For Piano and Orchestra* by Gordon Parks received its first performance. And Hale Smith's orchestral piece commissioned by the Louisville Orchestra in 1962 and performed by the Cleveland Orchestra has commanded attention. Coleridge Taylor Perkinson's *Concerto No. 1 For Viola and Orchestra* had its world premiere by the Orchestra of America at Philharmonic Hall in New York in 1965.

However, the most frequently performed Negro composer of symphonic music has been William Grant Still. His *Africa: A Symphonic Poem* was first presented in New York in 1929 and later at Rochester's Eastman School of Music. In 1935 came the premiere at Carnegie Hall of his *Afro-American Symphony* played by the New York Philharmonic. A year later, when Still directed the Los Angeles Philharmonic in a selection of his own works at the Hollywood Bowl, he became the first Negro in America to conduct a major symphony orchestra.

Dean Dixon was the first Negro to achieve an entire career solely as a symphonic conductor, at first in the United States and then in Europe where he directed major orchestras for many years. As guest conductor at age 28 at Lewisohn Stadium in the summer of 1943, he became the first Negro to baton the one-hundred-year-old New York Philharmonic. In 1949 Dixon conducted the *Radiodifusion Française* in Paris. Soon thereafter he became one of the three resident conductors of the Gothenberg Symphony, and subsequently directed major orchestras all over Europe. In 1960 he accepted a post in Frankfurt, Germany, to take charge of the Hessian Radio Orchestra. Rome's *Il Momento* termed Dean Dixon "a conductor with an enormous talent."

Everett Lee is another colored conductor whose career was largely based in Europe, as was that of West Indian Rudolph Dunbar, who lived for a time in the United States but went to Europe while still a young man. In California Henry Lewis became one of several conductors of the Los Angeles Symphony.

There have been many distinguished Negro choral conductors—Nathaniel Dett of the Hampton Institute Choir; Hall Johnson who eventually retired to devote his talents to arranging; Eva Jessye who directed every *Porgy and Bess* ensemble and also conducted her own choral groups between productions of the Gershwin show; Leonard DePaur whose Infantry Chorus achieved fame after World War II, and who continued to conduct other male ensembles that toured on four continents; and Clinton Utterbach of the Utterbach Ensemble, a vociferous singing group projecting spirituals in the gospel manner.

Distinguished concert pianists of color include Hazel Harrison, Armenta Adams, Philippa Duke Schuyler, Natalie Hinderas, Eugene Haynes and Andre Watts, who in 1965 at age 18 appeared in New York's Philharmonic Hall as soloist in Chopin's *F Minor Concerto,* and was described by one metropolitan critic as performing "with an eloquence and poetry that has the freshness of youth and the inborn maturity of the greatest talents."

Most Negro concert artists, certainly in the early days of their careers, did many performances in colored churches, community centers and the auditoriums of Southern Negro colleges. Roland Hayes and Marian Anderson gave concerts before predominantly Negro audiences before they became famous. The Harlem churches, often under the sponsorship of their women's clubs and encouraged by the National Association of Negro Musicians, have presented many young artists uptown long before downtown New York became aware of their talents.

The Countee Cullen Branch of the New York Public Library and both the Harlem Y.M.C.A. and Y.W.C.A. branches give their facilities without charge to young singers and instrumentalists. For several seasons in The Little Theatre of Saint Martin's Episcopal Church on Lenox Avenue, Coffee Concerts under the direction of Raoul Abdul (himself an excellent baritone) presented a fine series of programs where many Harlemites heard for reasonable prices such outstanding artists as Carol Brice of City Center Opera, Muriel Rahn, Betty Allen and Edward Lee Tyler; Marion Cumbo and Kermit Moore, cellists; pianists Armenta Adams, Margaret Bonds and Natalie Hinderas.

Margaret Bonds

William Grant Still

CARNEGIE HALL

The young contralto, Marian Anderson, in 1928. She was educated in the Philadelphia public schools and first sang at the age of six at the Union Baptist Church there. When she was 12 she was singing professionally in church concerts. She won a competition in 1926 that brought her a debut at Lewisohn Stadium in New York.

An historic evening for black singers of concert music occurred at Carnegie Hall on the night in 1923 when Roland Hayes made his debut there. White concert managers previously would not book any Negroes other than singers of spirituals. Only after sensational newspaper reports in 1922 of the Roland Hayes concert at Buckingham Palace before King George V, did American impresarios become interested in the young tenor. Programming as Hayes did not only the spirituals but also Schubert and Brahms, Monteverdi, Wolf and Glinka, his artistry is credited

Roland Hayes, born in a Georgia cabin in 1887, was the first Negro singer to give a concert at Carnegie Hall. His career continued into his seventies.

In Vienna in 1934, the year before Miss Anderson returned to America for the Town Hall recital that made her internationally famous.

with breaking the color bar for Negro singers in the field of serious music. Hailed even in Germany as one of the great interpreters of lieder, for well over a quarter of a century Roland Hayes filled concert halls in America and Europe and paved the way for all other colored singers of classical music. "From the hour of his emergence on the local stage," wrote critic W. J. Henderson, "his color was forgotten. He succeeded . . . in leaving only a conviction of beauty and persuasive eloquence." Ralph McGill, white editor of the Atlanta *Constitution,* wrote of his fellow citizen, "Roland Hayes is a great Georgian."

Three years after Roland Hayes broke the ice for trained Negro singers at Carnegie Hall, the budding Marian Anderson, as winner of the New York Philharmonic Competitions, sang with that orchestra in Lewisohn Stadium, and a few weeks later with the Philadelphia Orchestra of her home town. But it was not until 1936 that an overflow crowd jammed Carnegie Hall to hear the unassuming young contralto who, by that time, had been acclaimed all over Europe. When Toscanini listened to her in Salzburg, he exclaimed to the surprised Miss Anderson, "A voice like yours is heard only once in a hundred years." In the decade that followed she sang all over Europe, Africa and South America, and in one season alone gave seventy concerts in the United States.

In 1939, when denied the use of Constitution Hall in Washington because of color, Marian Anderson sang at the government invitation on the steps of Lincoln Memorial on Easter Sunday before a crowd of 75,000 people. She sang at the inaugurations of both President Eisenhower and President Kennedy, and more than once appeared at the White House. It is estimated that at least 8 million persons around the world have heard Marian Anderson in concert during the forty years of her long career. Millions more heard her on radio, records or television. She gave her farewell Carnegie Hall concert on Easter 1965, and then embarked on her last world tour.

At a recording session. She also appeared many times on radio and television.

138

Miss Anderson singing with the Bombay City Orchestra. She sang before some seven million people during her many concert tours.

William Warfield, Arkansas-born and a graduate of the Eastman School of Music, began as a nightclub entertainer and became one of the leading concert baritones.

Other Negro singers who have graced with distinction the stage of Carnegie Hall include Paul Robeson, Dorothy Maynor, Kenneth Spencer, Camilla Williams, Lawrence Winters, Adele Addison, Berry Allen, William Warfield and Leontyne Price. Todd Duncan, Anne Brown, Inez Matthews, Robert McFerrin, Carol Brice, Lawrence Watson, Grace Bumbry and Shirley Verrett have also had successful concert careers. One of the most popular Negro baritones, Harry T. Burleigh—who was a composer and arranger of distinction as well —seldom gave concerts. But for more than a quarter of a century he was a leading soloist on Fridays at the Hebrew Temple Emanuel and on Sundays at St. George Episcopal Church, both wealthy and fashionable houses of worship in New York City, and his performance of synagogue music was as movingly beautiful as his singing of spirituals, anthems and hymns.

Harry T. Burleigh, composer, arranger, and for over 50 years soloist at one of New York's leading churches.

Paul Robeson, the son of a New Jersey pastor who had been a fugitive slave, won all-American honors on the Rutgers football team and was elected to Phi Beta Kappa. He took a law degree at Columbia, but turned to the stage. He sang his first concert at the Greenwich Village Theatre in 1925.

CELESTE "AÏDA"

A scene from Ouanga, *an opera on a Haitian theme by Clarence Cameron White, composer and violinist. It was premiered in 1956 by the National Negro Opera Company at the Metropolitan Opera House.*

In the days before integration on the American stage, the only operatic role most impresarios thought a Negro woman might sing with plausibility was *Aïda*. Several artists essayed it, usually with second-rate casts, without making any impression on the public. It was not until 1933 when there slithered across the stage of the Hippodrome in New York a tall voluptuous soprano named Katerina Jarboro, that anybody dreamed a Negro singer might make the musty old classic exciting. The dusky diva who did this had been a chorus girl in *Shuffle Along*. By pinching pennies, she managed to study voice. Marrying a man who sympathized with her ambitions, she persuaded him to send her to Europe. She stayed four years in France and Italy, taking vocal lessons, coaching for leading roles, studying languages and haunting opera houses. Then somehow she persuaded somebody to present her in *Aïda* in Milan.

The Italian public liked Jarboro immediately because, in theatrical parlance, she "projected." Provincial houses engaged her for both *Aïda* and *L'Africaine*. Her fame spread, even abroad—"abroad" from the vantage point of Europe, meaning America. She returned to America after seven years—behaving, looking and singing like a star—to

Adele Addison has sung La Boheme with the New York City Opera.

Shirley Verrett, one of the several Negro singers to appear at Spoleto in Italy during the Festival of Two Worlds.

become the first Negro performer to appear with an American opera company. Alfredo Salmaggi signed her for special performances in New York with his company. She triumphed.

When the curtain went down on Jarboro's first *Aïda* in Manhattan, dancer Bill Robinson and singer Paul Robeson were among the hundreds who cheered enthusiastically. Harlem in top hats and tails, pearls and décolleté, had turned out in large numbers for her debut, filling almost half the enormous Hippodrome. Expert publicity filled the remainder of the house with whites. Everybody

Charlotte Holloman, soprano, made her opera debut in The Barrier. *In 1966 she sang with the Saarbrucken Opera.*

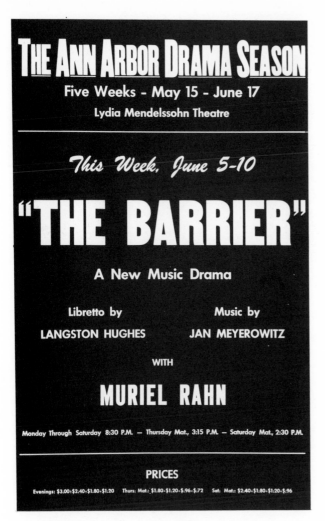

helped open doors for others of her race on the Continent. By the middle of the twentieth century, however, almost every major opera house had Negro singers on their rosters, including Lawrence Winters in Hamburg, Charles Holland in Paris, Olive Morefield with the Vienna Volksoper, Rhea Jackson in Oslo, Therman Bailey in Cologne; Charlotte Holloman, Ella Lee, Annabell Bernard and William Ray in Saarbrücken; and with the Berlin Opera, Gloria Davey, Vera Little and Berryl McDaniel. Other Negro singers often did guest appearances throughout Europe—Margaret Tynes at the Vienna State Opera, Lenora Lafayette at Covent Garden, Shirley Verrett at Spoleto during the Festival of Two Worlds, Kathleen Crawford in various German houses, and Mattiwilda Dobbs at Stockholm's Royal Opera. In Mexico City in 1946 Ellabelle Davis sang *Aïda* with the Opera Nacionale.

The New York City Opera was a pioneer in the

Elabelle Davis sang Aïda *with the Opera Nacional of Mexico City.*

gave Jarboro an ovation as, arms filled with flowers, she knelt center stage at the final curtain and bowed almost to the floor. She was a diva in the grand manner. Her voice and her gestures were large.

Another early diva of temperament with a great flair for showmanship was Madame Lillian Evanti, who combined the first part of her maiden name, Evans, with a part of her husband's name, Tibbs, to become Evanti. Her appearances in Europe preceded Jarboro, and Evanti is thought to be the first Afro-American woman to sing successfully the coloratura roles in *Rigoletto* and *Traviata* in European opera houses. When Madame Evanti left Washington to go to Europe, there were few colored singers in opera. Evanti was a pioneer who

Dorothy Maynor with Serge Koussevitzky, conductor of the Boston Symphony, whose praise at the Berkshire Music Festival in 1939 launched her career as one of the nation's leading sopranos. She was trained under Nathaniel Dett at Hampton Institute.

146

integration of Negro singers, both as principals and in the chorus. In 1946 Todd Duncan sang the roles of Tonio in *Pagliacci* and Escamillo in *Carmen*; Camilla Williams sang *Madam Butterfly*; Lawrence Winters interpreted Amonasro, Tonio and roles in *The Dybbuk, Love of Three Oranges* and *Die Meistersinger*; Adele Addison sang *La Boheme*; Reri Grist sang *Carmina Burana*; Shirley Verrett sang *Carmen*, and William Dupree and Margaret Tynes various roles. Celebrating the company's fifth anniversary in 1949, the William Grant Still opera, *Troubled Island*, laid in Haiti and with a libretto by Langston Hughes, was presented at City Center. It marked the first major production in the United States of an opera of Negro composition. The characters were all Negro. Robert McFerrin was among the singers, but the leading roles were performed by white artists, Robert Weede, Helena Bliss and Marie Powers in blackface. They looked odd, but sang beautifully.

THE METROPOLITAN

Marian Anderson taking a curtain call at her Metropolitan debut on January 7, 1955, when she sang Ulrica in Verdi's Masked Ball.

Just as the great velvet curtains at the Metropolitan Opera House were about to open on the second act of Verdi's *The Masked Ball* on the historic evening of January 7, 1955, when Marian Anderson was making her debut as the first Negro principal to appear with the company, something went wrong. The conductor's light in the orchestra pit signalled for the prelude to the act to begin, and it did. It was played up to the bars at which the curtains were supposed to open, but they did not open. There was a pause; then another tiny light signal and the orchestral prelude began all over. But at the bars for the curtain cue, once more nothing happened. The stage remained dark, and again the music stopped. By this time everyone in the audience was apprehensive. The hearts of Negroes particularly were in their throats. For them the integration of the first colored star into the Metropolitan was a momentous occasion, and all who could gain admission were present in full-force, from the lower floor and the boxes to the top gallery. When the music stopped for the second time they—and many others in the vast audience—held their breath.

The goal of every singer—the stage of the Metropolitan Opera. Marian Anderson with Rudolf Bing, director of the company.

What could have happened backstage? Had Miss Anderson perhaps fallen coming down the dressing room stairs? Or was she (most frightening thought of all) late in arriving? A whispered murmur ran through the audience, "What could be the matter?" Then the orchestra commenced again its brief prelude—and *this* time the curtains parted to reveal Marian Anderson in the role of Ulrica, a soothsayer stirring a smoking cauldron. The delays had been due to a faulty cue light on the conductor's stand. But at last, after thirty years of concert fame, Miss Anderson was now a star of the Metropolitan, being the first Negro diva to break the color bar at America's mansion of music, the Big House of opera. A new day in American integration had begun. *Variety,* "the Bible of show business," said, "Miss Anderson—like Joshua, but more quietly—had fought the battle of Jericho and at last the walls had come tumbling down."

Twenty days after Miss Anderson's debut in *A Masked Ball,* Robert McFerrin as Amonasro in *Aïda* became the second Negro to be featured at the Met. The third was soprano Mattiwilda Dobbs of Atlanta who in 1954 had been the first singer

George Shirley as Narraboth in Strauss's Salome.

Martina Arroyo, soprano of the Metropolitan Opera.

of color to perform at La Scala. On the Met stage in succeeding seasons other Negro voices shared curtain calls with the great stars of the company. By 1965, ten years after Miss Anderson's debut, it was no longer a novelty to find colored artists on the roster. Those who subsequently appeared at the Met in a variety of prominent roles included Gloria Davey, Leontyne Price, George Shirley,

Grace Bumbry as Eboli in Verdi's Don Carlo.

150

Grace Bumbry, Martina Arroya, Reri Grist and Felicia Weathers. But the bright particular star of all the artists, white or Negro, was to be Leontyne Price.

Miss Price was born in Laurel, Mississippi, and attended the Negro college, Central State, in Ohio. There Paul Robeson once heard her sing and helped raise a scholarship fund for further study. She enrolled at Juilliard in New York where she made her opera debut as Mistress Ford in *Falstaff*. Playing opposite William Warfield, whom she later married, Miss Price first came to widespread attention as Bess in *Porgy and Bess*. In 1955 she sang *Tosca* on NBC-TV's Television Opera Theatre and with "Vissi d'arte" created a sensation. She made her formal stage debut in grand opera in San Francisco in *Dialogues of The Carmelites*, followed by *Aïda* in 1960 with the Vienna State Opera and then at La Scala. In 1961 as Leonora in *Il Trovatore* she made her debut at the Met. "It was an exciting night," said *The New York Times*. "Her voice, warm and luscious, has enough volume

Mattiwilda Dobbs as Olympia in Tales of Hoffman.

Gloria Davy as Nedda in Pagliacci.

Felicia Weathers as Lisa in Queen of Spades.

Within a few weeks after Marian Anderson's debut, Robert McFerrin became the second Negro to sing at the Met. He made his debut as Amonasro in Aïda.

154

Leontyne Price, born in Mississippi, attended Central State College (formerly Wilberforce) and the Juilliard School. She made her debut at the Met. in 1961.

In 1966, the Metropolitan for the first time cast two Negro singers in leading roles. Here George Shirley sings Count Almaviva and Reri Grist sings Rosina in the Barber of Seville.

to fill the house with ease, and . . . she took some fine spun phrases in a ravishing pianissimo."

As the reigning "prima donna absoluta" at the Metropolitan, Leontyne Price sang numerous big roles. Her Verdi repertoire included Amelia in *Un Ballo In Maschera*, the title role in *Aïda* and Leonora in *Il Trovatore;* her Mozart roles encompassed Fiordiligi in *Cosi Fan Tutte*, Donna Anna in *Don Giovanni* and Pamina in *The Magic Flute;* and her Puccini specialties were Liu in *Turandot*, the title role in *Tosca*, Cio Cio San in *Butterfly* and Minnie in *The Girl Of The Golden West*, where Miss Price rides a white steed on stage. When the Metropolitan moved from its 76-year-old citadel on Broadway to its present home in the Lincoln Center complex, Leontyne Price had the honor of opening the new house with *Antony and Cleopatra*, an American opera by Samuel Barber which was commissioned especially for the occasion.

Leontyne Price in the title role of Verdi's Aïda.

In the 1955 NBC-TV production of Tosca.

Miss Price in Forza del Destino.

OPERA
ON BROADWAY

The 1942 revival of Porgy and Bess, *as seen by the artist Hirschfeld.*

A number of attempts have been made to create a kind of Broadway opera for popular consumption. In these efforts Negroes have figured prominently as performers and in two cases as librettist or lyricist. One of the earliest serious musical productions on Broadway was Gertrude Stein's *Four Saints in Three Acts* (1934) with a score by Virgil Thomson, which ran for sixty performances, and was revived in 1952 under the auspices of ANTA. Its original all-Negro cast included Beatrice Robinson-Wayne, Edward Matthews, Ruby Greene, Inez Matthews, Charles Holland and Altonell Hines. The 1952 revival included Rawn Spearman, Martha Flowers, Leontyne Price and Betty Allen. Among the dancers were Arthur Mitchell and Louis Johnson.

A year after *Four Saints* was produced, "the first native American folk opera," *Porgy and Bess,* had its world premiere in 1935 under the auspices of the Theatre Guild. With music by George Gershwin, a libretto by DuBose Heyward and an all-Negro cast (except for the police), it ran 124 performances in 1935. Subsequently, it was revived on Broadway by Cheryl Crawford in 1942

A scene from Four Saints in Three Acts, *the Virgil Thomson opera produced twice on Broadway with an all-Negro cast.*

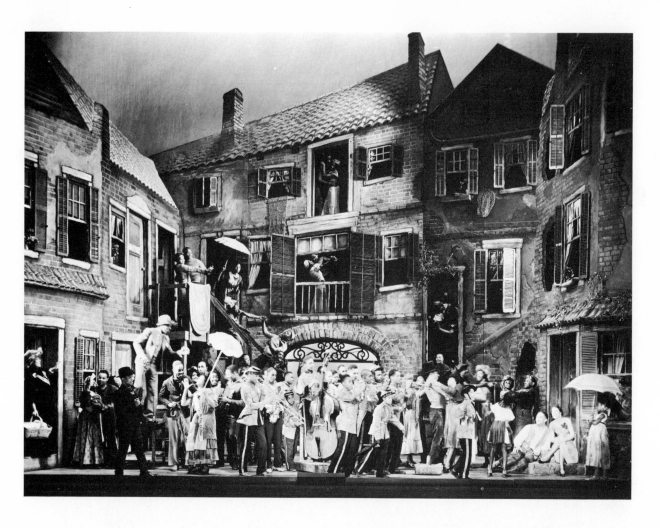

The first production of Gershwin's Porgy and Bess, *with Todd Duncan singing* Porgy.

and ran 286 performances. Again in 1953, after an extensive European tour under the auspices of the State Department, it played at the Ziegfeld Theatre for a long run. The original cast included Todd Duncan, Anne Brown, Ruby Elzy, Warren Coleman, Edward Matthews, John Bubbles and Abbie Mitchell. In the later cast at the Ziegfeld were Leontyne Price as Bess, William Warfield as Porgy, Cab Calloway as Sportin' Life and John McCurry as Crown. Often the New York City Light Opera Company has revived *Porgy and Bess.* Over the years the casts of this perennial attraction have included at various times Etta Moten, Margaret Tynes, Leesa Foster, Irving Barnes, Mar-

tha Flowers, Ruby Elzy, Joyce Bryant, Carol Brice, Georgia Burke, Urylee Leonardos, Avon Long, Veronica Tyler, Andrew Frierson and Gwendolyn Walters.

Shortly before Christmas in 1943, Billy Rose brought to the Broadway Theatre an all-Negro version of Bizet's *Carmen* transplanted to the contemporary South under the title *Carmen Jones.* Its score was arranged by Robert Russell Bennett, and Oscar Hammerstein wrote new lyrics. A run of 231 performances rewarded an excellent cast headed by Muriel Smith and Muriel Rahn as alternate Carmens, Napoleon Reed and Luther Saxon as Joe, Carlotta Franzell and Elton Warren

160

In the 1953 revival of Porgy and Bess, *William Warfield and Leontyne Price, shown here in rehearsal, sang the title roles.*

as Cindy Lou, Glenn Bryant as Husky Miller and Cozy Cole featured on the drums.

Another successful Broadway opera was *Street Scene* with music by Kurt Weill, book by Elmer Rice and lyrics by Langston Hughes, produced in 1947 at the Alvin where it ran for several months. Its cast was integrated with Creighton Thompson, Juanita Hall, Wilson Woodbeck and Helen Ferguson participating. *Street Scene* has frequently been revived by the New York City Opera.

The tremendous success of a revival of Gian Carlo Menotti's *The Medium* at Cleveland's Karamu Theatre featuring Zelma George prompted the producers at the Arena Theatre in the Edison

Muriel Smith (left) and Muriel Rahn alternated as Carmen in the 1943-44 all-Negro version of the Bizet opera, reset in the South and retitled Carmen Jones.

161

A scene from the New York City Opera's revival of Street Scene.

Zelma George singing The Medium *in the 1950 production on Broadway of the Gian Carlo Menotti opera.*

Hotel to bring this highly gifted performer to New York where she played 102 performances in midsummer, 1950. Mrs. George portrayed the Medium as a paralytic in a wheelchair. Leo Coleman (of the debut company) played the gypsy mute for a part of the run.

In November 1950 *The Barrier* opened at the Broadhurst Theatre with a score by Jan Meyerowitz and a libretto by Langston Hughes derived from his play, *Mulatto.* Its principals were Lawrence Tibbett, Muriel Rahn and Wilton Clary, and its supporting cast included as a young girl, Reri Grist, who later became a leading soprano at the Met. The girl's role on tour was sung at one time by Charlotte Holloman, and later by Mattiwilda Dobbs, both of whom later starred at leading opera houses in America and Europe.

In 1952 *My Darlin' Aïda,* based on Verdi's opera, opened on Broadway with Dorothy Sarnoff and other non-Negro leads, but featured such excellent performers of color as Olive Moorefield, William Dillard and Alonzo Bosan, plus a large singing chorus.

William Dupree sang a leading role in the Kurt Weill-Langston Hughes adaptation of Street Scene.

163

CROSSES AND CADILLACS

The Daniels Singers, a gospel youth group.

A form of folk music that developed in the gospel churches of the Negro ghettos and eventually spread to Broadway, Piccadilly Circus and the Grand Boulevards of Paris—to the delight of many and the consternation of others—is gospel singing. "Let us make a joyful noise unto the Lord," the Bible says. Gospel singers do just that. Although originating in a deeply felt religious impulse, the "joyful noise" in the mouths of many professional gospel singers today is certainly aimed at times at ears other than the Lord's. In Las Vegas it conflicts with the clink of gambling coins. But Clara Ward justifies gospel's invasion of the casinos, theatres and nightclubs by saying, "Jesus went into the highways and byways. Why should not we go with our songs?"

Certainly gospel music introduced new elements not only into the theatre, but into the recording industry, radio and television. On discs Mahalia Jackson became a best seller. But although she gave a whole evening's concert at the Newport Jazz Festival, Miss Jackson will not sing in theatres or nightclubs—only in stadiums, churches and con-

Mahalia Jackson, the New Orleans singer, whose record, "Move On Up a Little Higher," was the first gospel hit to sell more than a million copies.

Anna English, in Tambourines to Glory, *the Langston Hughes play with gospel music, presented on Broadway.*

cert halls. Annually for several seasons she packed Carnegie Hall, and has toured abroad.

Gospel singing is the last refuge of Negro folk music and, at its religious source, is largely uncontaminated by influences outside the church. Although it borrows heavily from worldly music, it converts that music to its own use, so gospel's basic beat remains uniquely its own. Black congregations, by frequent spontaneous improvisation, constantly give their songs new and varied nuances. Utilizing many of the old spirituals and hymns and injecting them with a new swing, gospel revitalized contemporary church music. In the pentecostal churches, many congregations have created brand-new songs for themselves. Frequently published in small folio form and sold for as little as fifty cents, this music reaches a mass audience. Even though few gospel churchgoers read music, they read the words and pick up the tunes from the church organist or song leader and sing along lustily with their congregations, embroidering on the vocalizations at will. The same gospel song may be sung in twenty different ways in twenty different churches—which is one reason gospel, even professional gospel, has such variety.

Once when Mahalia Jackson was rehearsing a song, singing it over and over, her pianist Mildred Falls asked, "Mahalia, why don't you sing it like you did the last time?" Miss Jackson's answer was simply, "Because I don't want to."

Gospel singers enjoy changing as and when they wish, improvising, and carrying on in individual fashion, even in groups. To each his own part in the scale, as the singer wishes. Sometimes sopranos choose to sing the bass line. Real gospel singing as it may be heard is next to impossible to score on paper. Published versions are only approximations. Like the primitive blues, the gospel rhythms, harmonies, vocal leaps, glides and glissandos defy notation. Mahalia Jackson said of gospel singing, "I try to give it the way *I feel,* and most of the time I feel good. Amen!"

Robert Shelton, folk music critic of *The New York Times,* wrote of the gospel style, "This inventive and often mesmerizing genre of religious musical expression has the power to transport the listener wherever he may be, in the crowded con-

166

The Clara Ward Singers.

Hilda Simms in Tambourines to Glory.

fines of a storefront church or in the elegance of Philharmonic Hall." The gospel song-play *Black Nativity* by Langston Hughes, featuring Marion Williams, Alex Bradford, Princess Stewart, Kitty Parham and the Stars of Faith, was the only attraction to play ten consecutive performances at the New York Philharmonic. This was at Christmas, 1962—during a newspaper strike and so without benefit of advertising. Previously, *Black Nativity* had, after its New York run, been invited by Gian Carlo Menotti to The Festival of Two Worlds at Spoleto. There it was a summer success, followed by a year-long tour of Europe, filling such large theatres as the Champs Elysées in Paris and the Criterion in London, and eventually sending a company to New Zealand and Australia. Later a second gospel show by Hughes, *The Prodigal Son*, went from the Greenwich Mews in New York to England, Belgium, Holland and France. Both these attractions were staged by Negro director Vinnette Carroll. Her *Trumpets of The Lord*, also

in the gospel idiom, was an off-Broadway hit and was later produced in Rome.

Alvin Ailey and his dancers on their tour of Europe and Asia employed gospel singer Brother John Sellers to accompany their ballet, *Revelations*. One of the first gospel exponents to invade Europe was Sister Thorpe and her guitar. Mahalia Jackson followed, then the Clara Ward Singers, Prof. Hugh Porter with Sammy Price, Dorothy Norwood and her aggregation, James Cleveland and others. Among America's exciting gospel groups have been the Pilgrim Travellers, the Caravans, the Four Blind Boys, the Swan Silvertones, the Staples Singers, the Roberta Martin Singers, the Nightingales and the Utterbach Concert Ensemble. Star soloists include Norsalus Mackizick, Christine Clark, Dorothy Drake, Charles Taylor, Frances Stedman, Bessie Griffin, Dorothy Love and Edna Gallmon Cooke. Among the many excellent organists are Maceo Woods, Herman Stevans, Marion Franklin and Hampton Carlton. *Gospel TV Time* initiated a popular television series; and Joe Bostic's *Gospel Train* on radio captured a wide audience in the New York area. All major cities now have gospel programs on the airwaves.

Leading songwriters in the gospel field include the onetime blues accompanist for Ma Rainey, Thomas A. Dorsey, whose "Precious Lord Take My Hand" is a standard, and Lucie E. Campbell, composer of "Touch Me, Lord Jesus," "In The Upper Room" and "He'll Understand." The "soul music" of some of the contemporary jazz singers such as Ray Charles, Aretha Franklin, and exponents of the big beat like James Brown, took on the imprint of gospel songs, incorporating their flavor into the "worldly music" and "big rock" of commercial show business. Gospel's excursion into the highways and byways produced some strange fruit, entirely detached from religion. At the height of the vogue, there was even a gospel cabaret in the Broadway area where pretty brownskin waitresses wore angel's wings while serving drinks. And for a time some professional gospel singers became so affluent, even travelling in chauffeur-driven cars, that the old hymn that once moaned, "I cannot bear my burden alone," was replaced by, "Lord, help me get my cross to my Cadillac."

168

Marion Williams and Alex Bradford in the song-play, Black Nativity.

THE APOLLO

Just as Harlem's Savoy Ballroom became an institution, so later did the Apollo Theatre, where over the years most of the leading variety stars have appeared. Josephine Baker, after a triumphant return from two decades in Paris, broke all Harlem box-office records for a ten-day period at the Apollo over Christmas week. Lena Horne, Pearl Bailey, Eartha Kitt, Duke, Count, Louis Jordan, have proven big favorites. Jackie "Moms" Mabley and Pigmeat Markham always panic Apollo audiences. Dusty Fletcher, Eddie Green and Mantan Moreland have also been favorite comedians. As singers, Ella Fitzgerald, Sarah

Vaughan and Maxine Sullivan among others have been great draws, and in recent times all the popular rock and roll singles—Jackie Wilson, James Brown, LaVern Baker, have caused lines down to the corner. Gospel shows, often presented by Doc Wheeler and Fred Barr, send people shouting up the aisles. And among the most popular masters of ceremonies have been Leonard Reed, the late Willie Bryant, Jack Walker and Nipsey Russell.

Very rarely has the Apollo essayed dramatic shows, but one season it presented a few, including the famous *Tobacco Road* with an all-Negro cast in which Powell Lindsay played Jeeter Lester and

Comedians *Tim Moore and Johnny Lee entertain at the Apollo in the late Thirties.*

Estelle Hemsley portrayed the grandmother. Dude was Jimmy Wright. That year Nina Mae Mc-Kinney played the Jeanne Eagels' role in *Rain*. And in Sidney Kingsley's *Detective Story*, Sidney Poitier starred, backed by an excellent cast that included Hilda Haynes, Kenneth Manigault, Jay Riley, William Branch and novelist-playwright-actor Julian Mayfield.

One great contribution to Harlem show business has been the Apollo's weekly Amateur Night. Aspirants in the past who survived the pistol-totin' comic Puerto Rico (who shot performers off the stage) might go on to fame and fortune. Some winners of the Amateur Hour like Ella Fitzgerald and Sarah Vaughan went on to achieve international acclaim. The Apollo is a joyous fun house whose package shows sometimes tour a chain including the Howard in Washington and the Regal in Chicago, and it is the only theatre in Harlem where live entertainment may be seen.

Jimmy Basket with Pigmeat Markham (right), in the blackface days at the Apollo.

From left, Spider Prince, John "Ashcan" LaRue, and John Vigal in a doctor sketch.

A chorus at the Apollo.

Fats Domino takes over.

"The Drifters," one of the many vocal groups popular at the Apollo.

174

Billy Eckstine at the mike, with dancers Charlie Atkins and Honi Coles.

COVER CHARGE

Jackie "Moms" Mabley

During their heyday nightclubs were a major source of experience and income for Negro performers. Ada "Bricktop" Smith Du-Conge, better known as just Bricktop, who once performed on the T.O.B.A. and in Harlem, eventually became the world's most beloved nightclub hostess. Cole Porter, Nancy Cunard, the Prince of Wales, Gloria Swanson, the Aga Khan, Tennessee Williams and thousands of other regular patrons of her clubs in Paris or Rome or Mexico City called her simply Brick. She began her career about the time of the San Francisco earthquake, was a member of the Panama Trio and the Tennessee Ten that included Florence Mills, graduated to Connie's Inn in Harlem as a singing

soubrette, and landed in Paris in 1924 without a penny, having lost her purse on the docks at Havre. Jean Bullard, manager of a little *boîte* on Rue Pigalle in Montmartre, had cabled New York for a quick replacement for the Grand Duc's temperamental star, Florence Embry, a brownskin beauty who one day departed in a huff to open her own cabaret.

Quite unknown in Europe, the freckle-faced young Bricktop at first drew no clientele, but gradually the youthful French novelist Louis Aragon, the American writer Anita Loos, and the key-club queen of New York's prohibition era Belle Livingston, discovered the charm of Brick's big smile and tiny voice, her jolly welcome at each table,

From chorus girl at the Cotton Club, Lena Horne rose to the top ranks in almost every branch of entertainment—cabaret, musical comedy, the movies, television, recordings.

her few little rapid dance steps when she sang, and patrons began to like her—not because she was a great *artiste* but because she was just Bricktop. In a few years she had earned enough to open her own club in Montmartre, and Chez Bricktop's quickly became the most fashionable of Parisian nightspots. It remained so until the outbreak of World War II when she returned to America.

For more than a decade after the war, her new club, relocated on the Via Veneto in Rome, drew the international smart set until Bricktop retired in her seventies to Chicago to write her memoirs concerning the great and near-great she had known.

Since the turn of the century, Negro entertainers thrived as solo performers at private parties for the rich from Fifth Avenue to Newport to

When very young, Ada "Bricktop" Smith was part of a trio called The Panama Girls which played the Pantages vaudeville circuit for three years. The other girls, also to become famous, were Cora Greene (left) and Florence Mills (center).

Bricktop in Paris.

Miriam Makeba

Abbey Lincoln

Della Reese

Erroll Garner

Mary Lou Williams   The Modern Jazz Quartet

Hazel Scott   Red Allen and Buster Bailey

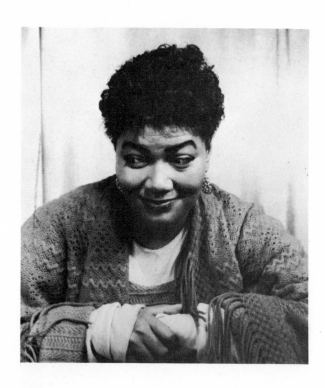

Pearl Bailey

Sam Cooke

Palm Beach. The pianist, Lucky Roberts, was a long-time favorite, as was Nora Holt. And when New York's small East Side nightclubs became fashionable, some colored entertainers became almost permanent fixtures there, among them the "singers' singer," Mabel Mercer (a graduate of Bricktop's in Paris) and Bobby Short, singing pianist, who were often exported to Florida or Montego Bay for guest appearances at rich parties. At the Bon Soir in Greenwich Village, Jimmy Daniels was for years its musical host. There also comic songstress Mae Barnes and guitarist Tiger Haynes were fixtures. Other performers became closely identified with certain clubs—Nina Simone with the Village Gate, Dorothy Donegan with the Embers, Nipsey Russell at Harlem's Baby Grand, Henry Red Allen and combo at Broadway's blaring Metropole, and Dizzy Gillespie in the jazz emporium, Birdland. For a brief period the twist brought Negro dancers into popularity in the clubs, particularly at Smalls Paradise in Harlem. And the discothèque craze gave employment not only to exponents of the Monkey and the Frug, but to singing groups like the Supremes and the Shirelles. Eventually some went swinging into the Copacabana.

After playing for years only in Negro clubs, the stand-up comics of color, with their unique brand of ethnic humor and racial satire in the integration era, suddenly found themselves in demand at the best downtown cover-charge establishments. Booking agencies began to offer them contracts for expensive rooms from New York to Las Vegas. The veteran Jackie "Moms" Mabley, toothless and far past the half-century mark, found herself convulsing the Playboy Clubs with her monologues. And Harlem's Nipsey Russell, Godfrey Cambridge and Dick Gregory appeared in great demand at gilded microphones.

"Isn't this the most fascinating country in the world?" then asked an affluent Dick Gregory with the spotlight in his eyes. "Where else would I have to ride on the back of the bus, have a choice of going to the worst schools, eating in the worst restaurants, living in the worst neighborhoods—and yet average $5,000 a week now just talking about it?"

The Supremes

Ethel Ennis

Cab Calloway

Sammy Davis, Jr.

Sepia singers entered the high-class nightclubs years before the comics did. After the Second World War most big hotels housing supper clubs gradually began to welcome colored musicians and singers. Lena Horne drew the carriage trade from the Fairmont in San Francisco to the Empire Room

Harry Belafonte

at the Waldorf Astoria, as did Pearl Bailey and Katherine Dunham. Both Billy Daniels and Billy Eckstine, as well as Nat King Cole and Johnny Mathis, filled plush cabarets around the country. Ella Fitzgerald, Sarah Vaughan, Dorothy Donegan, Barbara McNair, Leslie Uggams, Diahann Carroll and Nancy Wilson proved top attractions. In the Las Vegas casinos Sammy Davis, Harry Belafonte and Clara Ward and her Singers were show-stoppers. The perennial Mills Brothers continued to remain headliners. And Eartha Kitt's yearly engagement at the Plaza in New York became an event.

The recordings of many of these nightclub performers sold over a million copies—particularly those of Harry Belafonte, Johnny Mathis, Lena Horne and Nat King Cole. As far back as 1938–1939, Ella Fitzgerald's "A Tisket, A Tasket" and Cab Calloway's "Jumpin' Jive" reached the million mark. Later, LaVern Baker was a big seller. The Ink Spots and the Charioteers topped the lists in their day; and Fats Domino's total record sales for his many releases are said to be over 27 million platters. Ray Charles and Sam Cooke had a great jukebox rating, as did Eartha Kitt's seasonal "Santa Baby." Such groups as the Platters, and individual singers in the rock-and-roll manner like Little Richard, Jackie Wilson, Chubby Checker, Mary Wells and James Brown, achieved enormous popularity with teenage buyers, as did various trios and quartets with the basic beat—the Drifters, the Coasters, the Shirelles and above all, the Supremes, a trio of girls brought to fame by Motown Records, the Detroit Negro-owned firm made rich by rock and roll. With them the big beat came to the fore in places where guests wear evening clothes and belong to the "in crowd." Motown originated the "Detroit sound."

Billy Eckstine

Godfrey Cambridge

186

Dick Gregory

Bill Cosby

KARAMU THEATRE

*Nolan Bell, a Karamu actor for over 25 years and its
leading comedian. His roles have ranged from* The
Taming of the Shrew *to* Waiting for Godot *and
Moliere's* The Doctor in Spite of Himself.

Cleveland's Karamu Theatre stands out as
one of the most important tributary theatres in the United States. It was founded
by two young Oberlin College graduates, Russell
and Rowena Jelliffe, in a ramshackle pool hall in
1916, and it was known then as the Gilpin Players, composed entirely of Negroes. Over the years
Karamu has produced almost every play concerned
with Negro life by a white or Negro author, and
is today an interracial community theatre. Housed
in a million-dollar compound, it now contains a
proscenium theatre, an arena theatre, an amphi-
theatre, a concert hall and facilities for a children's
theatre.

Most successful of the playwrights to develop
their craft at Karamu is Langston Hughes, whose
plays have figured in the repertoire from its early
days to the present. Among them are *Little Ham,
Joy To My Soul, Froni Porch, Drums of Haiti*
(which later became the opera *Troubled Island*),

The Karamu Theatre's production of Mozart's opera, Cosi Fan Tutti.

Mulatto, Simply Heavenly with music by David Martin, and *Shakespeare in Harlem,* adapted by Robert Glenn. For more than a quarter of a century, Rowena Jelliffe directed all the plays at Karamu before the project was enlarged to include other directors—Gerald Marans, Junius Edwards and later Ruben Silver.

Aside from the dramas, another important part of the Karamu repertoire has been its musicals and operas performed by an ensemble developed by Dr. Benno D. Frank, whose first efforts there included the American premiere of Carl Orf's *The Wise Woman* and Gian Carlo Menotti's *The Medium* during the opening week of the present

190

building in 1949. Among the most successful productions have been Kurt Weil's *Lost in the Stars*, *Amahl and the Night Visitors*, *Simply Heavenly* and *The King and I*. With the musical assistance of Helmuth Wolfes and J. Harold Brown, Karamu has developed one of the finest lyric theatres in the Midwest.

Karamu players or dancers who have reached Broadway include Frances Williams, Frank Marriott, Isabel Cooley, Clayton Corbin, Leesa Foster, Sherman Sneed, Charles Moore, Walter Nicks, Howard Roberts, Mildred Smith, Leonard Parker, Ivan Dixon, Royce Wallace, Robert Guillaume, Melvin Stewart and Gwendolyn Walters. On its resident roster it has a master comedian in Nolan Bell, who grew up from childhood at Karamu and has performed in many of its productions, as well as taking part in professional summer theatre performances elsewhere. He is especially remembered for his performances in *Androcles and the Lion*, *Noah*, *Waiting for Godot*, and *Simply Heavenly*. Actor Burgess Meredith has said, "The Karamu project is one of the most civilized endeavors existent in the United States today."

A scene from the Karamu production of Harold Pinter's The Birthday Party, *presented also at the Boston Winter Arts Festival in 1966.*

TIMIDITY AND BRAVERY

The Theatre Workshop of the Communications Center

Presents

HEDDA GABLER

By HENDRIK IBSEN

Friday, August 14th, 8:00 P.M.

Ogden Hall

Hampton Institute Summer School

General Admission 25c   Children 10c
Men in Uniform Admitted Free

Negro colleges in the South (and most colored colleges are there) were for many years dominated by orthodox religious denominations who helped to support them with missionary money. Many usually had no theatre groups—play acting in former years was considered an invention of the Devil. However, in more liberal times, campuses like Dillard and Xavier in New Orleans, Fisk in Nashville, Talledega in Alabama, and Howard University in Washington have initiated excellent student productions. They have had such competent directors as James O. Hopson at Talledega, Thomas A. Poag at Tennessee State, Baldwin Burroughs at Atlanta University, Randolph Edmunds at Florida State, and playwright Owen Dodson and staff at Howard. But because of religious pressures and the racial attitudes of many white Southern trustees, colored colleges in general have been most timid in their selection of plays, leaning heavily toward the Greek classics, Shakespeare, and *Lady Windemere's Fan*—often incongruous fare indeed for black students who never see a play about their problems or their own lives.

An exception to this timidity in his directorial leanings was Melvin B. Tolson, for many years at Wiley College in Texas and later at Langston University in Oklahoma. His Log Cabin Theatre at

A scene from In White America, *Martin Duberman's 1963 documentary play in which three Negro and three white actors convert history into drama.*

of course, they could not even buy tickets to local productions. But in a few cities, particularly on the West Coast, race prejudice did not prevent some liberal directors from using colored actors on occasion or, as Margot Jones did in Dallas, from aiding Negroes to set up acting groups of their own. The Pasadena Playhouse in the Forties did an excellent integrated production of Father Dunn's play *Trial By Fire* about restrictive covenants in housing. The Goodman Theatre in Chicago often used colored thespians and dancers, and the Cleveland Playhouse sometimes borrowed actors from the Karamu Theatre as did the Jewish Community Center's Halle Theatre there.

Near the start of World War I, Negroes themselves established the Skyloft Players on the South Side of Chicago. In Los Angeles the early Negro Arts Theatre was directed by Clarence Muse un-

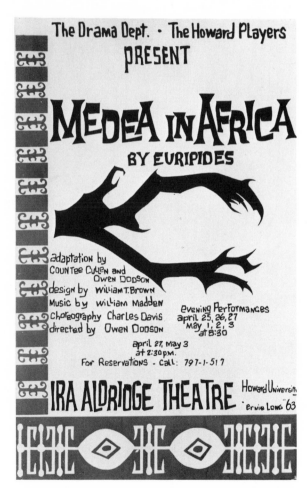

Wiley and his Dust Bowl Theatre at Langston presented plays by Negro playwrights (when Tolson could find them) that faced squarely the problems of the color line in the South. He himself made a dramatization of novelist Walter White's story of a lynching, *The Fire In The Flint*. After its Broadway run he presented *Mulatto,* a drama of miscegenation, and toured it at several colleges in the Southwest. Tolson's productions drew large Negro audiences, and he himself became so popular that he was elected mayor of Langston, Oklahoma, where the college is situated.

White college and regional theatre directors were almost always extremely puzzled as to how to cast Negroes unless in servant roles. Most white regional theatres in the South dared not use Negro actors, whereas Northern theatres seldom desired to do so. Therefore, until very recently, there were scant opportunities in the hinterlands of the United States for colored persons to participate in dramatic activities. And in Southern communities,

From a college student production.

der the sponsorship of the Allied Arts League. And in Hollywood, Nick Stewart's Ebony Showcase involved a number of sepia motion picture artists. Much later in Los Angeles, Frank Greenwood set up the Touring Artists Group presenting topical sketches and plays indoors and out, and achieving in 1966 a controversial success with Greenwood's drama of the Watts riots, *Burn, Baby, Burn.* Following the days of the sit-ins and freedom rides, the Free Southern Theatre with headquarters at Tougaloo, Mississippi, came into being presenting *Waiting for Godot* to cotton farmers and sharecroppers, alternating with *In White America.* They also produced Sean O'Casey's *Shadow Of A Gunman* and Brecht's *The Rifles Of Señora Carrar.* This brave group of actors performed without charge in fields, barns, churches and schools for spectators who could not pay a penny.

PROBLEM PLAYS

Seated at center stage is Ethel Waters, the star of Mamba's Daughters. Scenery was the work of Perry Watkins, the first Negro scenic designer on Broadway.

For a decade after the closing of Broadway's folk fable, *The Green Pastures*, race-problem plays predominated on the Broadway scene and, of course, all of them employed some Negro actors—even *Scarlet Sister Mary* in which Ethel Barrymore played Mary in blackface, a much discussed tour de force at the time. Paul Green's *House of Connelly* and *Roll Sweet Chariot,* DuBose Heyward's *Brass Ankle,* James Knox Millen's *Never No More,* Frederick Schlick's *Bloodstream, Black Souls* by Annie Nathan Meyer, *Stevedore* by Paul Peters and George Sklar, and a stirring drama by John Wexley based on the infamous Scottsboro case were among those illuminating one phase or another of the Negro problem in the early Thirties. *Mulatto* followed with Rose McClendon and, after her death, with Mercedes Gilbert. Then came Martin Flavin's *Achilles Had a Heel,* and in 1939 *Mamba's Daughters* by DuBose and Dorothy Heyward. This play, with Ethel Waters as Mamba, was the most successful of those featuring Negro actors during the Depression decade.

Stevedore, *a militant labor play of the 1930s by Paul Peters and George Sklar,
was produced by the Theatre Union. Jack Carter is seated at far right, with Leigh
Whipper next to him, and Rex Ingram leaning forward in the center.*

They Shall Not Die *told the story of the Scottsboro boys, almost railroaded to the electric chair in Alabama.*

From the nightclubs, vaudeville and the musical theatre, Ethel Waters brought a surprising new power to the dramatic stage. She gave an additional human dimension to the conventional "Mammy" of old—one of both dignity and gentleness—that endeared her to theatregoers without the use on stage of the handkerchief-head dialect and broad humor of former days. In her portrayals of illiterate Negro mothers of the South, Ethel Waters was a mistress of the "laughter through tears" technique which she brought to perfection in her highly hailed performance of Berenice in Carson McCullers' *The Member of the Wedding.* Presented at

the Empire Theatre in 1949, the play received the Drama Critics Circle Award as the best American play of the season.

In the spring just preceding America's entry into World War II, the dramatization of Richard Wright's best-selling novel, *Native Son,* with Canada Lee as Bigger, opened for a modest run. But during the first war year nothing of dramatic consequence involving Negroes occurred on Broadway. Other than *Othello,* with its single Negro actor, the same might be said for 1943. The war years were not fruitful for the Negro in drama until 1944 when *Anna Lucasta* came downtown from

Harlem to become the longest running all-Negro play in Broadway history. It survived 957 performances, a Chicago and an Eastern Seaboard company, a long cross-country tour, a London season, and two subsequent motion picture versions, one white and one colored—not *in* color, but with Negro actors. *Anna Lucasta's* amazingly talented cast of not-yet-famous actors included Hilda Simms, Canada Lee, Georgia Burke, Earle Hyman, Frederick O'Neal, Hilda Haynes and Alice Childress.

Lillian Smith's 1945 drama of miscegenation, *Strange Fruit*, introduced to the theatre the talented Jane White. And *Deep Are the Roots* found the young Gordon Heath playing opposite Barbara Bel Geddes. He was a soldier back from the wars. The following season Earle Hyman had a prominent role in *The Duchess of Malfi*. That year also Maxine Wood's drama, *On Whitman Avenue*, concerning Negro housing with Canada Lee in the lead, chalked up 148 performances. But *Jeb*, which introduced Ossie Davis in his first important part, that of a wounded veteran returning to the race-baiting South, lasted only a week. Theodore Ward's *Our Lan'* had fourteen performances in 1947, but Sartre's *The Respectable Prostitute*, about a young Negro framed on a Southern murder charge, ran at various times and in different theatres off and on Broadway for months. ANTA's Experimental Theatre presented an all-Negro production of Gorky's *The Lower Depths* adapted to the American South, with Gorky's vagrants all colored. It failed, but produced for a short time excellent performances on the part of Ruby Dee, Maurice Ellis, Fredi Washington and Henry Scott. Off Broadway the Blackfriars' Guild presented Father Dunn's *Trial by Fire* which, like *On Whitman Avenue*, dealt with the problem of Negroes seeking occupancy of a decent home. In this Pauline Myers was excellent.

"OTHELLO"

Paul Robeson as Othello and Uta Hagen as Desdemona in the Theatre Guild-Margaret Webster production of 1943.

With Jose Ferrer as Iago and Uta Hagen as Desdemona, the Theatre Guild in October 1943 presented Paul Robeson in *Othello, The Moor of Venice*. It became an immediate box office success and established a record run for any Shakespearean production on Broadway. It also made Robeson a star in his own country after ten years of European triumphs. In 1930 Robeson had performed the role in London, following by a hundred years the first Negro, Ira Aldridge, to play Othello in England. Both, but a century apart, were enormously successful. Of Ira Aldridge's opening performance at Covent Garden, the London *Standard* reported that he was "called upon by the unanimous acclamation of the whole house who, upon his appearance, rose *en masse* to receive him with burst of applause, waving of hats, handkerchiefs, etc. . . . ," and after a curtain speech he retired "amidst enthusiastic cheering."

Playing 296 performances of Othello, *Robeson established a record for Shakespeare on Broadway.*

200

Robeson's Othello also received enthusiastic English acclaim. He created the effect "of a soul bombarded by thunder and torn by lightning," one commentator said. Another declared, "From the moment that he appears in the beginning to his last sigh at the end, the man is gigantic in power . . . Robeson calls for our pity, wrings our hearts, thrills us with his agony because we see him as the plaything of fate, a man great enough for the gods to take an interest in." After his Manhattan opening thirteen years later, *Life* recorded that "Robeson received one of the most prolonged and wildest ovations in the history of the New York theatre."

Terming the Broadway production as staged by Margaret Webster "magnificent," John Chapman wrote, "It is an *Othello* of depth and body and rich sound, and in its title role Paul Robeson has majesty . . . a voice whose resonance and deepness almost pass belief . . . This new *Othello* with a Negro in the title role making love to a white Desdemona, is worlds apart from being a cheap theatrical trick. There is nothing cheap or titillating about it. It presents a black man of dignity and intelligence in the role of a black man of dignity and intelligence." The *New York Post* termed the six-foot-three actor "the most imposing personality on Broadway today." Among the honors Robeson received was that of being named the best male performer of the season, and the granting of the annual Award for Good Diction from the American Academy of Arts and Letters. In 1945

he received the Spingarn Award for artistry in song and theatre. When the play closed in New York after 296 performances, it took to the road on a cross-country tour that lasted two seasons.

In 1959, to open the celebration in England of the hundredth anniversary of the Stratford-on-Avon Shakespeare Memorial Theatre, Robeson again played Othello, with Sam Wanamaker as Iago and Mary Ure as Desdemona. Robeson was then 61 years old and had undergone ten years of political difficulties in the United States due to his acknowledged left-wing leanings. At Peekskill in 1949 a stone-throwing mob disrupted his concert and the Ku Klux Klan burned crosses as far away as Florida. Robeson was boycotted by producers and concert managers, so he could not perform. For a decade he was denied a passport by the government, so he could not travel. But when he was permitted to go abroad again, the Associated Press cabled to the American papers this report of his English welcome in April at Stratford-on-Avon: "Paul Robeson made theatrical history last night in William Shakespeare's hometown. He opened the Shakespeare Memorial Theatre's 100th season as Othello. He kissed blond Mary Ure six long times. He became the first Negro to play the part of the Moor in this celebrated theatre's history. He answered 15 curtain calls, was applauded and then cheered . . . Robeson turned in an amazing performance." *The New York Times* correspondent wrote, "His *Othello* ranks among the best that I have ever seen."

SHAKESPEARE MOBILE

Jan White as Volumnia and Kate Sullivan as Virgilia in a scene from Coriolanus.

The New York Shakespeare Festival produced by Joseph Papp in cooperation with the City of New York has pioneered in presenting various works of the Bard to a popular public, not only in Central Park but in other outdoor areas of Manhattan during the summers. Admission is free. In 1964 a handsome production of *A Midsummer Night's Dream* was performed in 39 open-air locations in five of the city's boroughs. Three big trailer trucks, unfolding to serve as a portable stage and dressing rooms, and an electronic power-wagon, comprised the Delacorte Mobile Theatre. In the 1964 production of *Dream* several Negro artists participated, including Ellen

Holly as Titania, Lynn Hamilton as the Queen of the Amazons, Gilbert Price as Snug and dancer Tana McClain as Cobweb. In a previous production James Earl Jones played Oberon.

Frank Silvera portrayed the leading role in 1962 in the Festival Theatre's presentation of *King Lear*, and Roscoe Lee Brown performed the part of Lear's Fool. P. Jay Sidney was also a member of the large cast. And in the 1963 production of *Antony and Cleopatra*, Ellen Holly, Robert Jackson, Bill Gunn and Clebert Ford participated. Donald McKayle directed the dances, William Hairston was theatre manager, and Negro essayist and Shakespearean authority Esther Jackson was

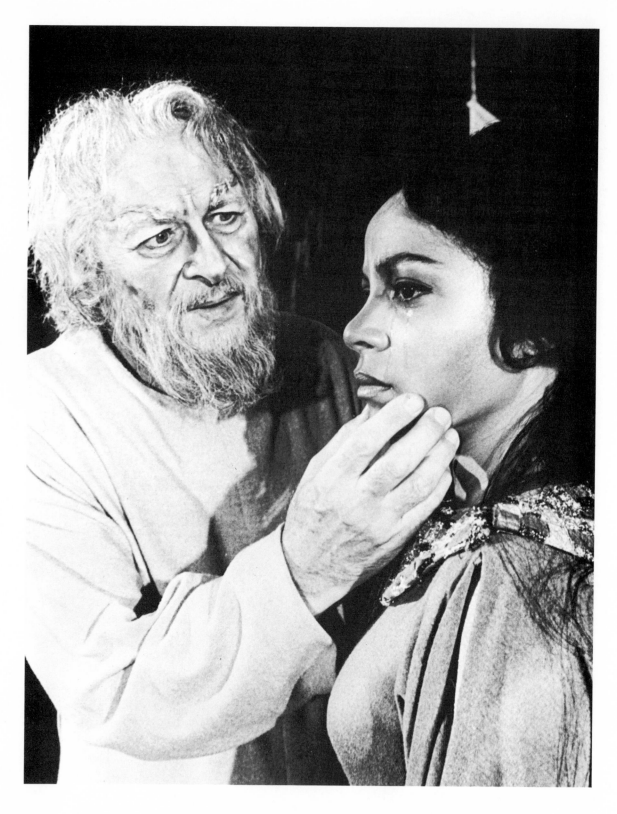

Ruby Dee as Cordelia, with Morris Carnovsky in the title role of King Lear, *presented by the Festival Theatre in Stratford, Conn.*

Henry V rules over New York streets in the Shakespeare Festival's outdoor summer productions. Here Robert Hooks raises his royal banner beneath tenement house windows.

assistant to the producer. In 1965 Jane White was Helen of Troy in *Troilus and Cressida.*

In the heat of mid-July 1964, Joseph Papp unveiled in Central Park so stunning a production that it caused critic Howard Taubman of the *Times* to exclaim in print: "The New York Shakespeare Festival, which does not condescend to its free clientele, has produced an *Othello* that would be a credit to the most illustrious companies. It is an *Othello* full of tempestuous passions and anguished tenderness . . . James Earl Jones, a young actor who has grown from strength to strength, assumes the biggest and toughest role of his career and meets the challenge impressively . . . Mr. Jones commands a full, resonant voice and a supple body, and his jealous rages and froth-

ing frenzy have not only size but also emotional credibility." So successful with the public was the Jones interpretation of *Othello* that it was booked into the Circle in the Square off Broadway in the autumn. Previously, in other Shakespeare Festival productions, Jones had played Oberon in *A Midsummer Night's Dream* and Caliban in *The Tempest.*

One of the most versatile of American actors, Earle Hyman, who previously played such varied roles as that of the Negro lieutenant in *No Time for Sergeants,* the bastard in Shaw's *St. Joan,* and the vagabond Didi, in *Waiting for Godot,* starred in 1957 in *Othello* for the American Shakespeare Festival's revival at Stratford, Connecticut. Alfred Drake was Iago. John Houseman directed. The

Roscoe Lee Brown as Lear's Fool, broods on the steps below the King, played by Frank Silvera in the 1962 production in New York's Central Park.

Othello, played by James Earl Jones, towers over dead Desdemona (Julianne Marie) and Emilia (Sada Thompson) in the 1964 production of the New York Shakespeare Festival.

New York Post hailed Hyman as "a great Othello." During the same season at Stratford, Hyman also played the soothsayer in *Julius Caesar,* and the Prince of Morocco in *The Merchant of Venice,* a role he had previously essayed at City Center in New York. In 1963, teamed with Miss Vinnie Burrows in an off-Broadway production, Hyman performed extracts from various plays woven into a montage called *The Worlds of Shakespeare.* With his interpretation of Shakespearean roles, Earle Hyman achieved great popularity in the Scandinavian countries, particularly in Norway where he performed in Norwegian, a language no previous American actor is known to have mastered.

At Stratford in the summer of 1965 Ruby Dee played Katharine in *The Taming of the Shrew.* In 1945 on Broadway the boxer-actor Canada Lee performed Caliban in *The Tempest,* sharing co-billing with Vera Zorina, and in summer theatres in 1948 he played Othello. College and tributary theatres over the years have engaged Negro actors in various Shakespearean roles throughout the country. Gordon Heath's performance in the Forties in a Hampton University campus production of *Hamlet* directed by Owen Dodson is credited with securing for Heath his first Broadway role in 1945, that of Lieutenant Brett in *Deep Are the Roots.* Aside from Shakespearean dramatic productions, Karamu Theatre in Cleveland, under Benno Frank's direction of its lyric activities, with Helmuth Wolfes, has been particularly successful in presenting interracial casts of singing actors in Benjamin Britten's musical adaptation of *A Midsummer Night's Dream* and Ernst Bloch's *Macbeth.*

For long-time devotion to a single Shakespearean role, William Marshall takes the prize with his consistent interpretation of Othello in various parts of the world. For more than a decade, Marshall has performed the Moor, first in a Harlem church with Lloyd Richards as Iago and a largely Negro cast. Then with the Brattle Shakespeare Players of Cambridge, and later with the same

William Marshall as Othello in the 1958 production. Ellen Holly played Desdemona.

Earle Hyman as Othello strangles Jacqueline Brookes as Desdemona in the American Shakespeare Festival's 1957 production at Stratford, Conn., directed by John Houseman.

group at New York City Center. In 1965 Mr. Marshall performed at the Shakespeare Festival in Central Park with Ellen Holly as Desdemona, and subsequently as guest artist for various groups in many parts of the United States. But it was at the Dublin Theatre Festival in 1962 that Marshall's Othello attracted world attention. The international public attending that Irish festival gave him such an ovation that the news services cabled his triumph to all the continents.

"William Marshall, the American actor who played the lead in *Othello* brought Dublin Theatre Festival first-nighters a memorable Shakespeare, coupled with a wonderful personal triumph," said one dispatch. "It is many a long day since we heard a reception such as that given Marshall." And Harold Hobson of the London *Sunday Times* wrote: "The American actor William Marshall is nobler than Tearle, more martial than Gielgud, more poetic than Valk. From his first entry, slender and magnificently tall, framed in a high byzantine arch, clad in white samite, mystic, wonderful, a figure of Arabian romance and grace, to his last plunging of the knife into his stomach, Mr. Marshall rode without faltering the play's enormous rhetoric, and at the end the house rose to him." So it is that *Othello*, portrayed frequently in our century by Negro performers, goes from the United States to the stages of the world.

A BROADWAY DECADE

Kenneth Manigault in the title role of Just a Little Simple *enjoys a beer with barkeeper Maxwell Glanville in the Alice Childress production at the Club Baron in Harlem.*

After 1947 there came a lull in problem plays on Broadway. In fact, there came several lean years for Negro actors, with little but maids' roles available. Except for the short-lived *Set My People Free* by Dorothy Heyward in which Juano Hernandez played the rebellious slave leader Denmark Vesey, there was nothing of any dramatic consequence on the boards other than *The Member of the Wedding* in which the only good Negro role was the lead played by Ethel Waters. Off Broadway, however, the Blackfriars Guild scored artistically with Father Nagle's *City of Kings* based on the life of Peru's black saint of the seventeenth century, Blessed Martin de Porres. In this Elwood Smith gave a moving performance as Martin the Dominican. Jacqueline Levy interpreted his mother.

In the Joshua Logan adaptation of Chekhov's *The Cherry Orchard* to a Louisiana milieu under the title of *The Wisteria Trees*, Ossie Davis, Georgia Burke and Alonzo Bosan played servants to the Dixie gentry. In Max Gordon's production of *The Small Hours*, John Marriott was also a manservant. In Lillian Hellman's *The Autumn Garden*, Maxwell Glanville portrayed the colored butler of a summer boarding house. P. Jay Sidney was a Pull-

Eartha Kitt plays the lead in Mrs. Patterson, *the 1953 Broadway production written by Charles Sebree with Greer Johnson.*

Alice Childress (standing at left) as the Defending Angel in the off-Broadway production of The World of Sholem Aleichem.

man porter in the Hecht-McArthur farce, *Twentieth Century,* and Ossie Davis played a handyman in the Kaufman-Ferber comedy, *The Royal Family.* Eulabelle Moore was the comic maid in *The Male Animal,* and Evelyn Davis supplied kitchen comedy in *Southern Exposure.* In *Four Twelves Are Forty-Eight* Rosetta LeNoire was a black servant with a Ph.D. degree! In *Fancy Meeting You Again* Earl Jones (the father of James Earl Jones) and Ellsworth Wright were deliverymen in the contemporary scenes and African slaves in the flashbacks. In Truman Capote's *The Grass Harp,* Georgia Burke played a cook who sat in a tree. Nine times out of ten in the theatre Negroes played servants.

Actor Frederick O'Neal once wrote: "Negroes could be—and, in rare instances have been—cast as military personnel, civil servants, lawyers, clerks, policemen and so on without altering the artistic intent or integrity of the production. In some cases, artistic values have been heightened. . . . When Negroes are seen only in the kitchens on television, in motion pictures and on the stage, the audience is subtly impressed that this is the Negro's so-called 'place' in American life. When he is shown only as a porter in a factory where only whites are shown as skilled workers, the impression is given that he is only capable of filling such menial jobs." There is, of course, nothing wrong in being a menial worker. Thousands of whites are. And from the viewpoint of those Negro actors who for many years made their living portraying such roles, Hattie McDaniels had a point when she said in Hollywood, "It is better to earn $7,000 a week playing a servant than to earn $7 a week *being* one."

Very few white playwrights presented Negroes in roles other than servants. Fortunately, during the first half of the Fifties, four young Negro playwrights enlivened the Broadway and off-Broadway scenes with plays depicting a broader range of Negro activities than those of just pots, pans and brooms. These newcomers to the theatre were Alice Childress, William Branch, Louis Peterson and Charles Sebree. In Harlem, Alice Childress directed her adaptation of the Langston Hughes Simple stories, *Just a Little Simple,* for The Committee for the Negro in the Arts at the Club Baron. Also at this former Lenox Avenue cabaret, her *Gold Through the Trees* was presented, as well as *A Medal For Willie* by William Branch. Ruth Jett was the Executive Director of The Committee for the Negro in the Arts, and among its actors were Kenneth Manigault, Clarice Taylor, Helen Martin, Julian Mayfield, Vinnie Burrows, Hilda Haynes and Maxwell Glanville.

On Broadway in 1953 Louis Peterson's *Take A Giant Step* opened. It introduced the teenage

Louis Gossett in the leading role of the adolescent protagonist, and presented (as successor to Dorothy Carter) the singer, Maxine Sullivan, in a rare dramatic appearance. Frederick O'Neal, Pauline Myers and Estelle Hemsley were also in the cast. The play, a critical although not a financial success, was later made into a motion picture with Johnny Nash as the boy. A few months after *Take A Giant Step, Mrs. Patterson* came to Manhattan with Eartha Kitt as its leading actress. This play also concerned an adolescent, a little girl with visions, and was the work originally of Negro artist and writer Charles Sebree. It reached Broadway with the aid of a white collaborator, Greer Johnson, and its cast included (since *Giant Step* had closed) the veteran Estelle Hemsley as well as

A scene from Alice Childress's Trouble in Mind, *presented at the Greenwich Mews, with Hilda Haynes.*

Vinnie Burrows, Helen Dowdy, Ruth Attaway, Jay Riley and Avon Long. The production became a Theatre Guild subscription play.

Off-Broadway, a fifth Negro playwright was represented in 1954 at the Greenwich Mews where William Branch's drama, *In Splendid Error,* was produced by Stella Holt. It concerned John Brown and Frederick Douglass, with William Marshall in the role of Douglass. That same season a play derived from the novel, *Shadows Move Among Them,* by the Negro Caribbean writer, Edgar Mittelholzer, appeared on Broadway in an adaptation by Moss Hart, and received serious critical attention. Earle Hyman and Jane White played Caribbean roles. It later became a Play-of-the-Week television production.

The latter half of the Fifties again brought to Broadway a drama by Lonnie Coleman with Eartha Kitt, this time in a Theatre Guild production of a play called *Jolly's Progress.* Its plot was not unlike Shaw's *Pygmalion.* Set in the South, it concerned the adoption of a wild little colored girl in a bigoted community by a wealthy white liberal who is, incidentally, a bachelor. Vinnette Carroll and Eulabelle Moore also took part in the production. The play did not last very long.

Still later in the Fifties, an all-Negro cast was brought to Broadway in a revival of Beckett's much discussed avant-garde fantasy, *Waiting for Godot.* Presented by Michael Myerberg, its cast of four consisted of Earle Hyman, Rex Ingram, Mantan Moreland and Geoffrey Holder. It did

Casting, regardless of color, was done by producer Stella Holt in her off-Broadway shows. Here Hilda Haynes plays a Jewish mother in Monday's Heroes.

Louis Gossett made his Broadway debut in 1953 as the adolescent in Take a Giant Step. *It was a first production, too, of Louis Peterson, a new Negro playwright. Dorothy Carter and Frederick O'Neal played the boy's parents.*

not have the success that the original all-white production had with Bert Lahr as star. Also short-lived was Alan Paton's beautifully mounted drama of South African apartheid, *Too Late The Phalarope.* In it Ellen Holly played a native colored girl pursued by a white Boer who loves her deeply, but who is prevented by Transvaal law and custom from possessing her. They loved not wisely —and not well. Off-Broadway, Alice Childress' *Trouble in Mind* about the plight of Negro actors faced with "darky" casting was a laugh success at the Greenwich Mews. The same theatre also presented Loften Mitchell's *A Land Beyond the River,* a problem play which the *Phylon* critic, Miles Jefferson, in 1956 termed "the best new play of serious purpose during the year." It concerned such contemporary racial problems as those of the ballot, equal schools and bus rights in the Deep South. A revival of *Take A Giant Step* at the Jan Hus Auditorium introduced new casting of quality tal-

ent—Bill Gunn as the boy, Bea Richards as the grandmother and Rosetta LeNoire as the maid.

The decade of the Fifties on Broadway and off produced a number of outstanding performances by single Negro actors in plays whose casts otherwise consisted of whites, or largely so. In some cases Negro performers were cast without regard to ethnic background in roles which white actors in former years would have played. Such a role was that of the Italian father in *A Hatful of Rain,* interpreted by Frank Silvera. In Tennessee Williams' *Camino Real,* Silvera played the non-racial part of a narrator (also it was not so titled), a role of great importance in holding the threads of the fantasy together. In the same playwright's *A Streetcar Named Desire,* the very brief but theatrically memorable moments of the Mexican Flower Woman were allotted to Edna Thomas. Previously, Muriel Rahn, stunning in a handsome evening gown, had an effective singing moment in the Clemence Dane play, *Come of Age.* Ruby Dee was the Defending Angel in *The World of Sholom Aleichem.* Clark Morgan played the featured role of the Ragpicker (not originally a Negro part) in a revival of *The Madwoman of Chaillot.*

In the Sixties the role of the narrator of the Albee adaptation of Carson McCuller's *The Ballad of the Sad Café* was played by Roscoe Lee Brown. Off-Broadway in the Indian fantasy, *King of the Dark Chamber,* by Rabindranath Tagore, Brock Peters performed the title role. In *Telemachus Clay* in 1963 an important part was handled by Clayton Corbin, who later on a national tour played the leading role, that of an Inca king, in *Royal Hunt of the Sun.* In 1965 Gloria Foster starred in *Medea* off-Broadway, and performed the leading role in Lorca's *Yerma* with the Repertory Theatre of Lincoln Center, whose several colored actors are used in various productions without regard to race. So a trend continues toward the integration of Negroes in roles other than those necessarily Negro—a trend which began in 1952 at the Greenwich Mews with the casting of Hilda Haynes as a Jewish mother in *Monday's Heroes*— with the blessings of Actors Equity, to open new avenues of achievement to colored thespians.

BITING THE DUST

Mr. Johnson was a Joyce Cary novel about colonial days in West Africa. Dramatized by Norman Rosten and presented in New York in the spring of 1956, it brought a great personal success to Earle Hyman in his first important Broadway role. Mr. Hyman played, as the program notes put it, "a native clerk working for the British government, who is more in tune with the bush than with the inexplicable taboo of civilization." In other words, having adopted the appellation *Mister,* Johnson is no longer tribal, but neither is he civilized in the conventional sense of the word. Hilariously funny yet sad happenings take place between his would-be decent employer and this Nigerian boy in a backwoods outpost of empire. The two men are friends, but the gulf between them is too great for genuine understanding. In the end the black boy is sentenced to hang for an unintentional crime. But rather than suffer the public indignity of the noose, he begs his white friend (who upholds the sentence) to shoot him. The white does. To paraphrase an old cliché of cowboy and Indian films, "Another Negro bites the dust."

Since the era of *Uncle Tom's Cabin,* many Broadway curtains have gone down on Negro characters completely done in in one way or another—in fact, often killed stone-cold dead as the play ends. Instances of Negroes biting the dust on Broadway during the last few minutes of playing time are indeed numerous. A few examples: the Pullman porter who made himself king in *The Emperor Jones,* the young black farmer lynched in *In Abraham's Bosom,* the Negro youth of *Never No More* who dies in flames, the half-caste in *Mulatto* who wants to use the front door of his white father's house and kills himself as the mob surrounds him; Bigger Thomas on his way to the death house in *Native Son;* Othello tricked into disemboweling himself over the body of Desdemona. Also, the execution for the slave leader, Denmark Vesey, in *Set My People Free;* the guns of the Union Army after Emancipation trained at sunset on a forlorn group of homesteaders facing eviction as *Our Lan'* ends; Black Absalom condemned to die in *Lost in the Stars;* Mr. Johnson begging to be shot. A few seasons later in *The Long Dream,* a bad young Mississippi Negro—who

215

Earle Hyman as the young West African clerk working for the British colonial government in Mr. Johnson, *the Norman Rosten play produced in 1956.*

would have been a Freedom Rider had he lived longer—was shot to death just before the final curtain.

In *The Cool World* the juvenile hero is head-whipped by the police and dragged away half-conscious. In the 1961 presentation of *Mandingo* concerning sex and slavery, a handsome buck slave, forced against his will, is bullet-riddled by his master. In *Black Monday* the good Negro is killed. That same season in *Tiger, Tiger Burning Bright* all the characters might as well have been annihilated, they are so utterly defeated by the time the play ends. At the final curtain in *Slow Dance on the Killing Ground*, the delinquent young black-amoor is on his way out into the darkness to be cut down in the wilds of Brooklyn. In James Baldwin's *Blues For Mister Charlie* the hero tumbles to his death, shot down in full view of the audience. In all these plays, triumphant whites are the killers, the Negroes the killed. Like the Indians of old in the Westerns, the blacks on stage must bite the dust.

It was not until 1965 when LeRoi Jones came along with *The Toilet* and *The Slave* that a leading Negro character on stage took a gun and shot a white man down. At last the theatrical tables had turned.

NEGRO PLAYWRIGHTS

Langston Hughes

In all its long theatrical history, the plays of only fourteen black dramatists have ever achieved legitimate productions on the Broadway stage. Over a period of forty years, only eighteen full-length dramatic plays by colored writers were produced in the commercial theatre. Of these eighteen, four were presented in collaboration with white playwrights who, with the exception of Paul Green, came into the picture in the capacity of play doctors after the original dramas were written. Thus only ten black dramatists with scripts *entirely* their own have ever seen a Broadway curtain rise on their work. Negro writers of musical comedies and revues have been more for-

tunate, and have made much more money from the commercial stage than the dramatists. Although a half dozen dramas achieved modest runs, only two plays by Negroes survived on the Great White Way for more than a year—*Mulatto* by Langston Hughes and *A Raisin in the Sun* by Lorraine Hansberry—and both made national tours of several months' duration, with various European productions following.

To black dramatists, the Federal Theatre during the Depression and the off-Broadway houses of the Fifties and Sixties proffered much greater opportunities than did Broadway. Under the Federal Theatre auspices in various cities, numerous plays

218

Lorraine Hansberry

The first Negro writer to achieve Broadway production was Garland Anderson. He had worked as a bellhop in San Francisco, and made a cross-country auto tour in 1925 to publicize his play en route to New York where he was greeted by the mayor in front of City Hall.

Ossie Davis

by Negroes were presented. The Harlem unit revived Frank Wilson's *Meek Mose* (retitled *Brother Mose*) and premiered his *Walk Together, Children*. It presented *The Conjur Man Dies* by Rudolph Fisher and *Turpentine* by J. A. Smith in collaboration with white Peter Morell. Off-Broadway, the Greenwich Mews of the Village Presbyterian Church and Brotherhood Synagogue, under the direction of Stella Holt, pioneered both in the integration of casts and the production of scripts by Negro authors. It was there that William Branch, Alice Childress, Loften Mitchell and William Hairston first received professional presentations. Stella Holt also presented *Simply Heavenly*

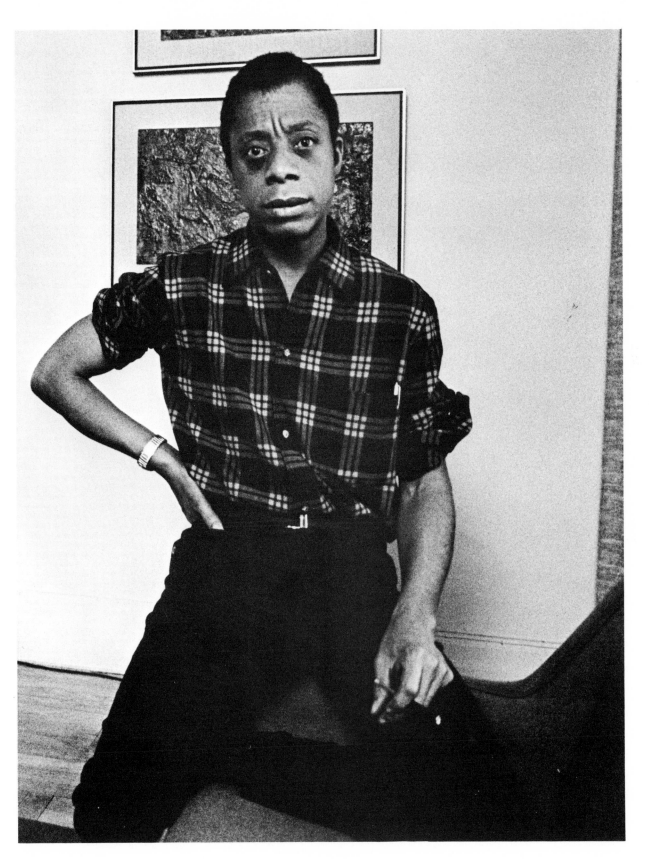

James Baldwin

221

Ronald Milner

LeRoi Jones

William Branch

Alice Childress

by Langston Hughes before it was installed at the Playhouse in midtown. And two of the same author's gospel song-plays were produced under Miss Holt's auspices, *Jerico Jim Crow* in the Sanctuary above the Mews, and *The Prodigal Son* in the theatre itself beneath the church. From the Mews in 1965 *The Prodigal Son* went to Paris.

In 1965 also, at the St. Mark's Playhouse in the East Village, two amusing satirical comedies by Douglas Turner Ward, *Day of Absence* and *Happy Ending,* opened to critical acclaim. This double bill received both the Vernon Rice and the Obie Awards, and after a year became off-Broadway's longest running dramatic offering. Ronald Milner's full-length drama, *Who's Got His Own,* was produced in 1966 at the American Place Theatre for a subscription run. But the most exciting Negro playright of the Sixties was LeRoi Jones. The violence of his story lines and the vileness of his language made him the most discussed young dramatist in Manhattan. His season in the sun is revealed in a succeeding chapter.

NEGRO PLAYWRIGHTS IN THE BROADWAY THEATRE

1925 *APPEARANCES* by Garland Anderson
1928 *MEEK MOSE* by Frank Wilson
1929 *HARLEM* by Wallace Thurman (with William Jordan Rapp)
1933 *LOUISIANA* by Augustus Smith
1933 *RUN LITTLE CHILLUN* by Hall Johnson (with Lew Cooper)
1934 *LEGAL MURDER* by Dennis Donoghue
1935 *MULATTO* by Langston Hughes
1941 *NATIVE SON* by Richard Wright (with Paul Green)
1947 *OUR LAN'* by Theodore Ward
1953 *TAKE A GIANT STEP* by Louis Peterson
1954 *MRS. PATTERSON* by Charles Sebree (with Greer Johnson)
1957 *SIMPLY HEAVENLY* by Langston Hughes
1959 *A RAISIN IN THE SUN* by Lorraine Hansberry
1961 *PURLIE VICTORIOUS* by Ossie Davis
1963 *TAMBOURINES TO GLORY* by Langston Hughes
1964 *BLUES FOR MISTER CHARLIE* by James Baldwin
1964 *THE SIGN IN SIDNEY BRUSTEIN'S WINDOW* by Lorraine Hansberry
1965 *THE AMEN CORNER* by James Baldwin

NEGRO PLAYWRIGHTS IN THE OFF-BROADWAY THEATRE

1937 *DON'T YOU WANT TO BE FREE?* by Langston Hughes
1938 *JOY EXCEEDING GLORY* by George Norford
1940 *BIG WHITE FOG* by Theodore Ward
1945 *ON STRIVERS ROW* by Abram Hill
1951 *A MEDAL FOR WILLIE* by William Branch
1952 *GOLD THROUGH THE TREES* by Alice Childress
1954 *IN SPLENDID ERROR* by William Branch
1955 *TROUBLE IN MIND* by Alice Childress
1956 *A LAND BEYOND THE RIVER* by Loften Mitchell
1960 *MARCUS IN THE HIGH GRASS* by Bill Gunn
1962 *MOON ON A RAINBOW SHAWL* by Errol John
1963 *WALK IN DARKNESS* by William Hairston
1964 *FUNNYHOUSE OF A NEGRO* by Adrienne Kennedy
1964 *DUTCHMAN* by LeRoi Jones
1964 *THE TOILET* and *THE SLAVE* by LeRoi Jones
1965 *HAPPY ENDING* and *DAY OF ABSENCE* by Douglas Turner Ward
1966 *WHO'S GOT HIS OWN* by Ronald Milner

BEFORE
JAMES BALDWIN

Diana Sands, co-starring with Alan Alda in The Owl and the Pussycat. *The comedy was a hit in both New York and London.*

Since there is no Negro theatre in Harlem or elsewhere to carry on a continuity of dramatic production, Negro actors who may get wonderful reviews in single Broadway shows usually have little chance to reap the benefits thereafter. Good parts in good plays for colored thespians are few and far between. So it was with Earle Hyman, declared in *Mr. Johnson* to be "a gifted Negro actor who at last has inherited a Broadway part worthy of his talents." In further laudation, *The New York Times* continued, "Mr. Hyman is superb." The *World-Telegram* found that he "played with magical insight, variety and sensitiveness." And Walter Kerr in the *Herald Tribune* said, "Mr. Hyman has an enormous emotional range." These reviews were written in 1956. In the decade that followed, Earle Hyman did not find another Broadway role of any sort in which to display his talents adequately.

Two expensive failures in 1960 of plays involving all-Negro casts further set back for a while the

Billy Dee Williams, the sailor in A Taste of Honey, *the Shelagh Delany play which enjoyed a long run on Broadway.*

224

opportunities of colored actors to be gainfully employed. Within the same week both *The Long Dream* and *The Cool World* closed after very short runs, which led Joel Schenker, producer of *The Long Dream,* to declare that he felt that it would be a long time before other dramas dealing with Negro problems were done on Broadway. He said, "I am now persuaded that a play that deals with a race problem awakens in the white auditor a sense of guilt and a sense of shame which keeps him away from the theatre . . . I am convinced Negroes, too, only go to the theatre to escape."

The Long Dream, adapted from a Richard Wright novel, concerned a Negro family in Mississippi trying to make their way against tidal waves of prejudice. Practically everyone in the play came to a bad end, although the Negro family of affluence in the community tried its best to get along with white folks. The *New Yorker* called *The Long Dream* "a trenchant exposure of the mutual degradation that ensues when the black man seeks wealth by crawling to the white and by aping his techniques of corruption." Its large cast was in charge of the Negro director, Lloyd Richards, and featured Lawrence Winters, Al Freeman, Jr. and Isabelle Cooley. It lasted five days. *The Cool World* had an even shorter run, although it was a beautifully mounted production with a great many talented actors, mostly teenagers. It dealt with "a few savage days in the life of a Harlem street gang." The *New Yorker* declared, "As a study in sociology it was probably true but terribly trite." By Warren Miller and Robert Rossen, it featured Billy Dee Williams, Calvin Lockhart, Hilda Simms, Roscoe Lee Browne and Harold Scott. *Variety* described it as a "sordid and brutal" melodrama "lacking characters that an audience is likely to care about." But its actors were praised, and the play contained amusing comic relief. One of the young hoodlums, on a visit to the apartment of a wealthy white homosexual, casually picked up an expensive antique vase. He was begged not to handle it so carelessly.

"It's two hundred years old," he was warned.

"I don't care if it's brand new," said the kid.

Four more expensive dramatic failures involving Negro actors in as many succeeding seasons—1961,

1962, 1963, 1964—proved Joel Schenker mistaken in his prediction that problem plays would not continue to be produced. All four of these dramas were given beautiful and well-acted productions, but did not catch the public fancy. *Mandingo,* starring Franchot Tone, had in it an adorable pair of little Negro twin boys whose naked backs Tone used for footstools for his gout. It also had the handsomest slave ever to appear on Broadway, naked to the waist, a Negro actor not heard of before or since, Rockne Tarkington. *Mandingo* failed. Likewise *Tiger, Tiger Burning Bright,* directed by Joshua Logan and starring Claudia McNeil, with Alvin Ailey, Diana Sands, Cicely Tyson, Roscoe Lee Browne and Ellen Holly. Miss McNeil and Miss Sands got excellent notices. *Tambourines to Glory,* adapted by Langston Hughes from his novel of the same title, with the gospel churches of Harlem as background, was produced in 1963 with Hilda Simms, Clara Ward, Louis Gossett, Anna English and Micki Grant. It lost $120,000. And the following year *Slow Dance on the Killing Ground,* in which Clarence Williams III attracted Broadway attention, closed after a very short run.

There were, however, in the first half of the Sixties, two successful critical as well as financial hits in which a Negro actor played an important role. In *A Taste of Honey* Billy Dee Williams acted the wandering sailor with, according to *Variety,* "finesse." Audiences liked him, and liked Angela Lansbury as the mother of the girl he loved, played by Joan Plowright. It had more than three hundred performances, although some critics were disturbed by the bittersweet aspects of its interracial misalliance. In the two-character comedy, *The Owl and the Pussy Cat,* which had a long Broadway run and later went to London, Diana Sands became a star. The piece was hilariously received. Like *A Taste of Honey,* it also concerned an interracial romance—but one played for fun, not problems. Although the casting of a colored girl and a white bachelor was hardly accidental, race did not figure in its farcical complications. Shortly before opening in this sprightly play, Diana Sands had made a big personal hit with a long dramatic monologue in the bitter *Blues for Mister Charlie,* the James Baldwin opus that aroused much discussion, pro and con. It featured Al Freeman, Jr., Rosetta Le Noire and John McCurry in a large cast.

An earlier play of Baldwin's, *The Amen Corner,* was not a problem play in the racial sense. It was produced and directed by Frank Silvera in California, and came to Broadway from the Coast in 1965. Laid in a Harlem store-front church, its leading role, that of a female pastor, was movingly played by Bea Richards. Frank Silvera was her sin-weak husband. A second production, directed by Lloyd Richards with Claudia McNeil starred, played various festivals on the Continent and enjoyed a London run, as well as appearances in Israel. There Miss McNeil stated she felt very much at home as she had lived part of her childhood with a Jewish family. Reuters reported that at the opening in Tel Aviv, "Following an ovation rarely rising to such intensity at Israel's National Theatre where the play was presented, the deeply moved star told the audience, 'I only wish my foster parents were here tonight. I am sure they are in spirit.' Miss McNeil was referring to the Jewish couple from Roumania who adopted her, a Negro girl of 12, thirty-six years ago. . . . At home the family maintained a kosher kitchen, she said, and to this day she cooks according to Jewish ritual law."

"A RAISIN IN THE SUN"

Lloyd Richards, director of the record-breaking Raisin in the Sun, *has piloted many productions on and off-Broadway, as well as on television.*

Although it opened in 1959, *A Raisin in the Sun* ran well into the Sixties and was the indisputable Negro hit of its era. It played to sold-out houses for many months and chalked up the longest run on Broadway of any work by a Negro playwright. Lorraine Hansberry's moving comedy-drama, which made a star of Claudia Mc-Neil, had a cast headed by Sidney Poitier and such other fine actors as Ruby Dee, Louis Gossett and Ivan Dixon. Star-to-be Diana Sands was also in the cast. *A Raisin in the Sun* was also done in London with Juanita Moore in the leading female role, and was translated into French and performed in Paris. It became a favorite in American sum-

mer theatres, and was made into a motion picture by David Susskind with most of the original cast intact. The play received the best-play-of-the-year citation from the New York Drama Critics Circle, winning out that season over *Sweet Bird of Youth* by Tennessee Williams and *J. B.* by Archibald MacLeish, runners-up for the award.

The early box-office success of *A Raisin in the Sun* was indicated by a *Variety* report during the summer of 1959: "Lorraine Hansberry is making a financial killing for herself and Uncle Sam in her debut as a Broadway playwright. She's thus far earned about $260,000 on her click drama. . . . Her royalty take thus far, covering 17 weeks on

228

In the original production of A Raisin in the Sun, *the leading roles were played by (from left) Claudia McNeil, Ruby Dee and Sidney Poitier.*

Broadway and seven pre-New York stanzas, totals about $80,000. Additional income of $180,000 is represented by her 60% author's share of the $300,000 sale of the film rights." The critics were unanimous in praise of the drama. "When the mother buys a house in a white neighborhood *A Raisin in the Sun* touches on the inflammatory topic of race relations," said Brooks Atkinson in *The Times.* "Miss Hansberry faces the issue frankly. . . . But she argues no causes. . . . *A Raisin in the Sun* is a lively and illuminating drama about people of great emotional vitality."

Walter Kerr called the play "an honest, intelligible, and moving experience." John Chapman in the *Sunday News* termed it "tender, funny and soundly wrought." And Richard Watts of the *Post* declared it "a notable work of dramatic art . . . *A Raisin in the Sun* is a victory for dramatic integrity." Of its leading actors he wrote, "There isn't a more enchanting portrayer of humorous and warm-hearted grandeur than Miss McNeil, who has all of Ethel Waters' richness of spirit in addi-tion to a quality of her own, and no finer young actor than Sidney Poitier." Said the *Herald Tribune,* "Lloyd Richards has directed Lorraine Hansberry's first play for the theatre with a fluid, elusive, quick-tempered grace that permits no moment and no shade of desperation to pass unexamined." The press in general hailed *A Raisin in the Sun* as a triumph of Negro production. But Harlem's *New York Age* admonished, "Don't go see this play only because a Negro wrote it, a Negro directed it, it's about Negroes, and Negroes act in it. Go see it because it is one of the most moving experiences you'll ever have in the theatre."

The Sign in Sidney Brustein's Window, Miss Hansberry's second play to reach Broadway, opened in the autumn of 1964. It concerned bohemian life in Greenwich Village where the author lived, and had a largely white cast. Its brief run closed on the eve of the author's funeral—Lorraine Hansberry died in early January 1965 at the age of 34. The American theatre had lost one of its most promising playwrights.

A scene from Lorraine Hansberry's last play, The Sign in Sidney Brustein's Window, *with Diana Sands in a leading role.*

DESIGNED FOR LAUGHTER

Melvin Stewart (right) as Simple gets some cautionary words from John Bouie (Watermelon Joe) as Claudia McNeil (Miss Mamie) looks on skeptically in this scene from Simply Heavenly.

Four comedies by Negro playwrights brought laughter to the New York theatre scene and sent audiences home happy: *Simply Heavenly, Purlie Victorious,* and the Douglas Turner Ward double bill, *Day of Absence* and *Happy Ending. Simply Heavenly,* with songs by David Martin, was a dramatization by Langston Hughes of his Simple stories that appeared for years in his weekly *Chicago Defender* column and later in the *New York Post.* A sort of Harlem Everyman, a sidewalk philosopher and genial commentator on the passing scene, Simple, as he is nicknamed, is in love with a girl who is a "fiend for culture" and whose hand he finally wins in marriage. Melvin Stewart played Simple, Anna English his glamorous "side gal," Marion Berry his fiancee, Alma Hubbard his landlady, and Claudia McNeil a singing Miss Mamie. In a Stella Holt production directed by Josh Shelly, the play in various productions went from off-Broadway to Broadway, California, London, and to television via the Play-of-the-Week series in 1957.

Purlie Victorious by Ossie Davis was a happy hit at the Cort Theatre in 1961, its leading roles

231

Ward's companion comedy, Happy Ending, *featured Robert Hooks (left), Frances Foster (center) and Esther Rolle (right). Ward is top man.*

Cap'n Cotchipee offers a little bullwhip homily in Purlie Victorious. *From left are Ossie Davis (star and author of the comedy), Helen Martin, Godfrey Cambridge, Ruby Dee, Bea Richards and Sorrell Booke.*

played by Ossie Davis, Ruby Dee and Godfrey Cambridge, directed by Howard da Silva. It was a farcical satire on certain aspects of Southern race relations, played against a rural background, with Davis as a kind of sepia Lil' Abner. Walter Kerr called it "A bucket full of bristling laughs and some of the sweetest strychnine we'll be tasting in a long time . . . a wild, nervy, outrageous fantasy . . . rich in its highly individual humor and most happily performed." The *Journal American* proclaimed it, "a gay and good humoured romp," and the *Mirror* said, "Heck, it's burlesque without the strippers." But according to the *Post*, what *Purlie Victorious* had to say behind the rich *gusto*

of laughter was that in the South "what the Negro needs is less fatback and more fight-back, less corn pone and more courage, less civil rights by the teaspoonful and more by the shovelful—and that the only way to get it is for the Negro to get up off his non-Caucasian rump and fight for it." In its uninhibited and jovial way, *Purlie Victorious* delivered its message, and Manhattan audiences revelled in it for months. "What Martin Luther King is doing with love," said its author, "I am trying to do with laughter."

A few years later in 1965 there came along another hilarious comedy, not written by a Negro but a play which happened to also have Ossie Davis in the cast. It, too, contained a message wrapped in laughter, written by Howard da Silva and Felix Leon, based on a story by Dan Jacobson. *The Zulu and the Zayda,* however, was not about the American South, but about the foibles and follies of apartheid in South Africa where life in Johannesburg, it seems, is not unlike Jackson, Mississippi. This comedy revolved around an elderly Jewish gentleman from London who retired to South Africa to die among relatives. But he makes friends with a young Zulu from the country, and both are most naïve concerning color lines. Their adventures on each side of the black-white fence prove hilarious, yet sometimes very sad. Louis Gossett played the Zulu and Menasha Skulnik the Zayda, complementing each other beautifully. Besides Gossett and Davis, other Negroes included Ed Hall, Christine Spencer, Charles Moore and Ella Thompson in the integrated cast of this non-integrated story.

Off-Broadway in late 1965 another evening of laughter rolled into an East Village theatre, the St. Marks Playhouse. Two comedies, with a guffaw a minute, brought to public acclaim a new Negro playwright who is also an actor, Douglas Turner Ward. The two comedies, *Day of Absence* and *Happy Ending,* spotlighted as well a new Negro producer who is also an actor, Robert Hooks. The plays were performed by an almost all-Negro cast including among others Hooks himself, the author Douglas Turner Ward, Moses Gunn, Frances Foster, Esther Rolle, Barbara Ann Teer, Lonne Elder and Hattie Winston, all directed by Philip Meister with Hal De Windt as assistant. *Day of Absence* and *Happy Ending* "supplement each other effectively," affirmed Richard Watts in the *Post.* "The first tells of a Negro family group in a Northern city cheerfully outsmarting their employers, while the second describes the chaos in a segregated Southern community when all the Negroes fail to show up for work one day. Shrewdly and entertainingly satirical as separate comedies, they combine to provide an evening of amused critical comment of a high order. . . . Douglas Turner Ward is a talented new dramatist who deserves attention." The Ward plays brightened the East Village for a long run and added a new glow to off-Broadway.

The Zayda (Menasha Skulnick) rests his weary feet on the Zulu (Louis Gossett) in the play about apartheid in South Africa.

Black actors don whiteface to play the roles of Southern townfolk abruptly deprived of "their" Negroes. In the center is the mayor, played by Douglas Turner Ward, in Day of Absence. *On the left—Barbara Ann Teer and Adolph Caesar. At right—Arthur French and Lonne Elder.*

OFF-BROADWAY SHINES

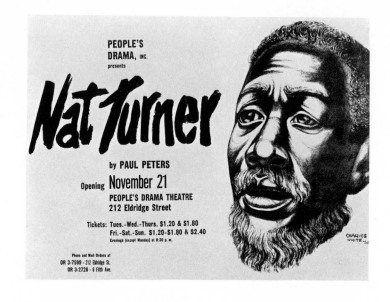

In 1950, Paul Peter's Nat Turner, *a drama of the Virginia slave revolt of 1831, was presented off-Broadway with Frank Silvera in the lead.*

Unlike the more commercial arena of Broadway, the little theatres in Greenwich Village and other outlying areas of Manhattan have for almost half a century been most hospitable to Negro playwrights and Negro actors. Off-Broadway is much more willing to take a chance on dramas dealing with racial themes or involving Negro actors than is the Main Stem itself. Eugene O'Neill's *Emperor Jones* with Charles Gilpin at the Provincetown began the trend, continuing from 1920 to *Happy Ending* 45 years later at the St. Marks Playhouse, with many other such productions between. There was *Roseanne* in 1924 with Charles Gilpin and Rose McClendon at the Greenwich Village Theatre and, that same year, Robeson in *All God's Chillun Got Wings*. There was Annie Nathan Meyer's *Black Souls* at the Provincetown; at the same theatre in 1926, *In Abraham's Bosom*; in 1928, a revival of *The Octoroon*. The socially conscious Thirties brought

236

A scene from the multi-level production of the Genet play, The Blacks, *which played almost four years in New York.*

Stevedore by the Theatre Union at the Civic Repertory Theatre. Later came the Blackfriars Guild's various productions—*A Young American* with Louis Peterson in the role of a sensitive Negro composer, *Trial by Fire,* and *City of Kings,* among others. Abram Hill's *Walk Hard* on the fiftieth floor of the Chanin Building. *The Fisherman* with Ruby Dee and Kenneth Manigault at Masters Auditorium. The *Phoenix '55* revue with Elton Warren, and at the same theatre that year, *Sandhog,* in which Negroes played effectively. Also at the Phoenix in 1955 there was a beautifully mounted production of Melville's *Moby Dick* in which Philip Hepburn gave a brilliant performance as Pip, the cabin boy. The Open Door's revival *Of Mice and Men* had as its leads Chuck Gordone and Clayton Corbin. Again Clayton Corbin in *The Ivory Branch* with Muriel Rahn at the Provincetown in 1956. The various productions of the Equity Library Theatre utilizing Negro actors included a revival of *The House of Connelly.* ANTA's Experimental Theatre shows included Euripides' *Hippolytus* with Muriel Smith and Osceola Archer, and Robert Glenn's *Shakespeare In Harlem* that began as one of the ANTA Matinee Series at the Theatre de Lys and then continued to run elsewhere. During the Sixties the Café La Mama, a tiny non-profit theatre club in the East Village operated by a dynamic young Negro woman, Ellen Stewart, presented highly experimental productions with interracial casts doing, said the *New York Post,* "more experiment with less resources than any other place in New York."

There was an all-Negro production of *The Egg and I* in 1958. And numerous plays over the years at the Greenwich Mews, with its regular policy of non-ethnic casting. In 1959 the Mews did an unusual production of *The Ballad of Jazz Street* with Avon Long, Lonnie and Tina Sattin, Helen Martin and Richard Ward. The following year a strange drama called *The Pretender,* directed by Herbert Machiz, opened at the Cherry Lane. James Earl Jones, Royce Wallace, Calvin Lockhart and Roscoe Lee Browne were in the cast. That same season Ernestine McClendon, Shauneille Perry and Josephine Woods appeared in *The Goose,* Bertice Reading played in *Valmouth* at the York, and Lincoln Kilpatrick was the leading man of *Deep Are the Roots* in a revival at the St. Marks. For several years thereafter this theatre was to house dramas by or about Negroes, each successful critically, financially, or both.

It was there that *The Blacks* chalked up a run of 1,408 performances, nearly four years in the same theatre. The Jean Genet fantasy opened May 4, 1961, and almost immediately became a favorite conversation piece among the cognoscenti from Park Avenue to the Village. *The Blacks,* an international sensation in its original French before it was translated into English, puzzled most yet pleased many who saw and nightly filled to capacity the little theatre in the semi-round where it played. Ingeniously staged against nothing but a winding ramp leading to a tiny balcony, and with half of its black actors in white face, *The Blacks* was an intriguing tour de force (not unlike *Waiting for Godot*) that challenged even the most sophisticated of playgoers. And it gave a large and varied assortment of actors work for many months since, due to its wage scale, it had a continually rotating cast—at off-Broadway salaries.

When an actor in *The Blacks* got a better paying Broadway part, he or she was free to take it, but could usually return to the cast of *The Blacks* at any time should Broadway not pan out—since there was almost always someone else leaving for an uptown venture. The result was that most of the cream of black actors appeared at one time or another in the Genet play. When nothing more artistically or financially profitable was in the wind, they effectively filled in for each other—which pumped new or revived blood into the play almost every week during its lengthy run. Such talents as Cicely Tyson and Barbara Ann Teer, Godfrey Cambridge and James Earl Jones, Abbey Lincoln and Duke Williams, Helen Martin and Lex Monson came in and out of the show interchangeably as freedom from roles elsewhere permitted. The company became a kind of actors' breadbasket where a good performer was almost always sure of finding an available role—though not always the part he had before. This permissive casting in repertory style kept the production exciting for its audiences since no spectator ever knew, on any given evening, whom he might see playing what.

On opening night the original cast in order of appearance was:

ARCHIBALD	Roscoe Lee Browne
VILLAGE	James Earl Jones
BOBO	Cynthia Belgrave
NEWPORT NEWS	Louis Gossett
SNOW	Ethel Ayler
FELICITY	Helen Martin
VIRTUE	Cicely Tyson
DIOUF	Godfrey M. Cambridge
MISSIONARY	Lex Monson
JUDGE	Raymond St. Jacques
GOVERNOR	Jay J. Riley
QUEEN	Maya Angelou Make
VALET	Charles Gordone
DRUMMER	Charles Campbell

But at various times and for varying periods during its long run, the following actors performed in *The Blacks*: Louis Gossett, Thelma Oliver, Lincoln Kilpatrick, Vinie Burrows, Harold Scott, Loretta Pauker, Bobby Dean Hooks, Lynn Hamilton, Brunetta Barnett, Moses Gunn, Louise Stubbs, Billy Dee Williams, and others. There was a Chicago company, a Los Angeles company, and a London company. And when the New York aggregation closed in late 1964, it went to Europe. *The Blacks* in English had a long consecutive performing life, creating a record for a non-musical production off-Broadway.

A kind of esoteric poem chopped up into seemingly haphazard dialogue, the play has no storyline as such. Its publicity man, Max Eisen, boldly stated to the press, "Nothing about *The Blacks* is conventional—which may explain the complete fascination and spell it casts over the audience and the actors." Certainly an unusual array of adjectives describing the play might be culled from the hundreds of reviews and commentaries it received: grotesque, debatable, bewildering, savage, taunting, terrifying, fascinating, stunning, hypnotic, witty, blunt, garish and compulsive, avantgarde. *The Blacks* was indeed more far-out than anything New York's Theatre of the Absurd had seen. And the novelty of observing Negro actors in so abstrusely-strange a production attracted a wide public. "It is a hot hothouse tense livid off-fag deep purple voodoo mon Doo production," wrote Norman Mailer in the *Village Voice*. "Fantasy, allegory and reality mingled," said *The Times*. "The performers were completely engrossing," stated the *World-Telegram*. And *Cue* declared, "The cast, all Negro, is masterly."

SPOTLIGHT
ON THE SIXTIES

Avon Long, the singing and dancing star, in Fly Blackbird.

The decade of the Sixties brought to off-Broadway a considerable number of productions with all-Negro casts or featuring colored performers—young performers—in important roles. Among these was Harold Scott who, in 1960, performed with an integrated company in three short dramas presented at the Gate Theatre. He was cast in non-Negro roles in each play, *Santa Claus* by e. e. cummings, *Calvary* by William Butler Yeats and *Escurial* by Michel De Ghelderode. *"Escurial,"* said *The New York Times,* "pro-

vides Harold Scott, as the King, with a gem of a role." That same year *The Pretender* brought forward the talents of the young Calvin Lockhart who went on to an important Broadway role a few months later in *The Cool World*. Clayton Corbin was featured in several good parts preceding and during the Sixties which led to such excellent

Gilbert Price singing in the Broadway musical, The Roar of the Greasepaint and the Smell of the Crowd.

240

The "God's Gonna Cut You Down Scene" from Jerico Jim Crow. In front, from left, threatening the Kluxer, are Joseph Attles, Rosalie King, Micki Grant and Gilbert Price.

Broadway roles as he later filled in Lillian Hellman's *Toys in the Attic* and the lavishly produced *Royal Hunt of the Sun.*

The musical revue, *Fly Blackbird*, brought from the West Coast in 1962 two talented young women, the singing comedienne Thelma Oliver and a young soprano, Mickey Grant. Miss Grant subsequently appeared in a revival of Marc Blitzstein's *The Cradle Will Rock*, in *Brecht on Brecht, Leonard Bernstein's Theatre Songs, The Blacks, Jerico-Jim Crow,* and *The Funny House of the Negro.* She made her Broadway debut in *Tambourines to Glory.* Thelma Oliver also went from *Fly Blackbirds* via *Cindy* to Broadway as one of the leading dance-hall hostesses, singing and dancing beside Gwen Verdon in *Sweet Charity. Fly Blackbird* also brought to attention a phenomenal 21-year-old baritone, Gilbert Price, who landed the leading role in *Jerico-Jim Crow*, and from there went directly into Anthony Newley's *The Roar of the Grease Paint*, and then into television as featured soloist on the *Merv Griffin Show.* In *Black Monday*, concerning the first day of school integration in a small Southern town, Billie Allen and Diana Sands had important roles. And Miss Sands in 1964 became a part of a new interracial troupe presenting an improvised revue in Bleecker Street called *The Living Premise.* Soon after she became a star in *The Owl and the Pussycat.*

Probably the busiest actor, white or colored, in the off-Broadway arena in the Sixties was James Earl Jones. He is the son of actor Robert Earl Jones who made his stage debut in 1936 in Harlem's *Don't You Want to Be Free?* and went from there to Broadway. James Earl Jones was born in Mississippi. He came to New York to join his father after discharge from the Army's Cold Weather Mountain Training Command in Colorado. His first acting role was in 1957, that of a soldier in *Wedding In Japan*, in which his love for a Japanese girl conflicted with that of a white GI from Georgia. In the decade since, Jones has played more than thirty roles, comprising almost the entire gamut of Shakespeare including parts in *Henry V, The Tempest, Measure for Measure, Richard III, The Merchant of Venice, A Midsum-*

Clayton Corbin, featured in Toys in the Attic *and* Royal Hunt of the Sun.

mer Night's Dream, and *Othello.* He starred at the Boston Arts Festival in *The Emperor Jones,* and since 1960 has had leading roles in *The Pretender, Clandestine on the Morning Line, The Blacks, Moon on a Rainbow Shawl* and *The Blood Knot,* besides appearing in lesser parts in *Next Time I'll Sing to You, The Last Minstrel, The Love Nest,* and Bertolt Brecht's *Baal,* all at off-Broadway theatres. For his performances during the 1961–1962 season he received the Daniel Blum *Theatre World* Award and an *Obie* as the best off-Broadway actor.

Another young man for whom off-Broadway served as a happy stepping-stone was Clarence Williams 3rd who first attracted attention in *Walk in Darkness* by Negro playwright William Hairston at the Greenwich Mews. Williams played the role of a young soldier in Germany during World War II. In 1963 at the Theatre de Lys he interpreted a jazz musician in *Sarah and the Sax.* (He seems to be one of the few young Negro actors

Vinette Carroll directing a scene in Black Nativity.

who did not ever appear in *The Blacks*.) In 1964 he went to Broadway in *Slow Dance on the Killing Ground*. A third highly individual talent, that of Cicely Tyson, received a further impetus from off-Broadway, after first having appeared in a Harlem production of *Dark of the Moon* directed by Vinnette Carroll. Miss Carroll later cast Miss Tyson in the leading role of the female preacher in *Trumpets of the Lord* adapted by Miss Carroll from the poems of James Weldon Johnson. The *Herald Tribune* termed Cicely Tyson "a marvel of foxy innocence" in the pulpit. With Al Freeman, Jr., Theresa Merritt and Lex Monson, *Trumpets* was an outstanding success at the Circle-in-the-Square during the 1963 season, and the following year was one of the entries in the Berlin Festival. Miss Tyson had previously appeared in *The Blue Boy In Black, Moon on a Rainbow Shawl* and, of course, *The Blacks*. Her first major motion picture was the Sammy Davis film, *A Man Called Adam*. Vinnette Carroll, both a director and an actress, appeared at the Phoenix in a revival of *The Octoroon* during the Sixties, and in the gospel song plays which she also directed off-Broadway, *Black Nativity* and *The Prodigal Son,* both of which toured abroad.

The Living Theatre, with its unusual scripts and avant-garde productions, enlivened the off-

Broadway scene for more than ten years, and utilized in three of its presentations a very talented Negro actor, James Anderson, sometimes programmed as Jim Anderson. He appeared in *The Apple.* He played Sam in the almost too real junkie drama, *The Connection,* in which the addicts invaded the audience. And he was one of the most sadistic of the Marine guards in *The Brig,* a horrifying portrayal of military brutality performed under the direction of Judith Malina who, with Julian Beck, founded the group. In commenting on *The Brig* in the *Village Voice,* Michael Smith wrote in 1963 that James Anderson and others in its cast "are privileged to be participants in the Living Theatre . . . our most original, profoundly adventurous, and persistently important theatre institution." However, the playhouse was closed shortly thereafter by the Federal Tax Bureau and other agencies of the government.

In the early Sixties less provocative productions than those of the Living Theatre in which Negroes appeared included a happy comedy about betting on the horses, *Clandestine on the Morning Line.* "Full of tender little moments, homely bits of wisdom and charming performances," said *The Times,* "but [it] just doesn't hang together as an exciting theatrical evening." James Earl Jones, Ed Cambridge and Rosetta LeNoire, among others, played it with warmth and sparkle. Miss LeNoire also appeared in a 1964 revival of *Cabin in the Sky* at the Mews with Kitty Lester, Tony Middleton and Joseph Attles. Mr. Attles at the same time doubled in another musical upstairs at the Sanctuary, *Jerico-Jim Crow.* At the Mayfair Theatre Irving Burgie's calypso musical, *Ballad for Bimshire,* with a story by Loften Mitchell, presented Ossie Davis, Jimmy Randolph, Miriam Burton, Alyce Webb

and other young thespians in a show that had several charming songs. Two teenage revues, *If We Grow Up* at Actors Playhouse and *Unfinished Business* (subtitled *Youth Sings Out, 1964*) at Theatre East, produced by The Next Stage, presented Negro and white youngsters in "exciting musical satire" which possessed, said the *World-Telegram,* "a great deal of charm." A Negro youth, Roscoe Orman, was among the featured singers.

At the Provincetown in 1964 Barbara Ann Teer and James Anderson appeared in *Home Movies.* Ruth Attaway and Harold Scott were in the Lincoln Center production of Arthur Miller's *After the Fall.* And in 1966 William Marshall starred in the Biblical play, *Javelin,* at the Actors Playhouse in the Village, while on Broadway Louis Gossett appeared in *My Sweet Charlie.* Actors Equity Theatre presented at Lincoln Center an adaptation by Woody King, Jr., of the poetry and prose of Langston Hughes, *The Weary Blues.* Pauline Myers performed a one-woman presentation of Negro poetry at the Greenwich Mews, *The World of My America.* And on Broadway an all-Negro cast under the direction of Roscoe Lee Browne presented a program of poetry and folk music, *A Hand Is On The Gate,* for a modest run. The previous season a Negro producer, Raymond A. League, presented at the Maidman Playhouse *A Sound of Silence,* a problem play of the Deep South by a white playwright, Harold Willis. Peter DeAnda and Evelyn Davis were in the cast. The *Post* called this play "a pile-driver, brilliantly written, brilliantly staged." Unfortunately, however, it failed. But it did indicate that off-Broadway continued to give brave and careful attention to serious dramas of merit by American playwrights in spite of box office hazards.

SMALL STAGES, BIG PLAYS

Her performance in In White America *earned Gloria Foster (above with Michael O'Sullivan) the 1963-64 "Obie" and the Vernon Rice-Drama Desk awards.*

Six productions involving Negroes on off-Broadway stages during the first half of the Sixties made sufficient impact on the American theatre to be remembered for some time to come. Two of the productions were of plays by new Negro playwrights, LeRoi Jones and Douglas Turner Ward, whose talents received enthusiastic critical acclaim. The dramas that from 1961 to 1966 attracted widespread attention of both press and public were, in order of production: Edward Albee's *The Death of Bessie Smith,* the Martin

Duberman documentary *In White America,* the three Jones one-acters performed on double bills, *Dutchman, The Toilet* and *The Slave,* the Robert Lowell adaption of Melville's *Benito Cereno,* and Ward's *Day of Absence* and *Happy Ending.* Three of these plays, those of Albee, Duberman and Lowell, were based on historical fact. The others were based on composite truths woven into moments of dramatic fantasy so real on stage that they could well be true in actuality. Their effect on audiences was memorable. People wept, or

Roscoe Lee Brown as Babu, the leader of the slave ship revolt, and Frank Langella as the ship's captain in Benito Cereno.

James Earl Jones (right) and J. D. Cannon in Blood Knot, *the South African play by Athol Fugard.*

cursed, or left the theatre midway. But seldom did any spectator remain unmoved by what he saw on the small stages of the Village where these big little plays were produced—*little* only in the sense that all of them were one-acters. None was a conventional full-length drama. The avant-garde theatre elided 8:30-to-11 curtain time into whatever span it chose.

The Death of Bessie Smith never presented its central character on stage. She was off-stage dying in front of a white hospital that would not admit her, which is in fact what happened to that famous blues singer in real life. Albee shows what might have happened inside the admittance room of the hospital were death and bigotry to meet. Clinton Wilder and Richard Barr presented the play, directed by Alan Schneider, with John McCurry and Harold Scott in the cast.

"Painfully vivid theatre," is what *The New York Times* called *In White America,* which was compiled from documents and from the mouths of various famous figures in American history. The material ranged from an actual account found in a slave-ship's log to a dialogue with Father Divine, and from the speeches of Thomas Jefferson to those of President Kennedy. The actors giving life to these segments of history were Gloria Foster, James Green, Moses Gunn, Claudette Nevins,

248

Michael O'Sullivan and Fred Pinkard. Three of these actors were white and three colored. Spirituals and folk songs were interwoven with the action. As a young Negro girl walking through a mob to enter Little Rock high school, Gloria Foster was superb in a narration taken from *The Long Shadow of Little Rock* by Daisy Bates. "This company has made something very special for the theatre," said the *Herald Tribune*. And *Cue* declared it "Off Broadway at its best."

Benito Cereno was the title of the Robert Lowell play based on the 1856 novella by Herman Melville, the story of a hair-raising revolt on a slave ship. It was brilliantly acted at the Theatre de Lys by a large cast including Roscoe Lee Browne and

a dozen rebellious slaves out to cut their captors down. Its gory climax was unforgettable. Originally a membership production at the American Place Theatre, demands for general admittance caused it to move where the public might buy tickets. Those spectators who were gripped by its tragedy are not likely ever to forget *Benito Cereno*.

The LeRoi Jones plays, and the two comedies by Douglas Turner Ward, with *Moon On A Rainbow Shawl* by Errol John and *Funny House of a Negro* by Adrienne Kennedy, brought to four the number of Negro playwrights shown in off-Broadway theatre during 1962–1965. *Moon on a Rainbow Shawl* by the Trinidadian playwright, Errol John, came to New York in a new production after

Gloria Foster in Medea, *adapted by Robinson Jeffers from Euripides' drama, and presented off-Broadway in 1965.*

having been seen in London and on English television. It depicted life in the Port-au-Spain courtyard of a poor tenement teeming with people and problems. The play "possessed force, directness and humor," said the *Post*. "The performances are fine . . . Vinnette Carroll is impressive . . . Cicely Tyson is a delight . . . James Earl Jones, who has become a kind of one-man stock company, brings his usual forcefulness to the role of a restless lover, and his father, Robert Earl Jones, is moving as the lost athlete."

As presented by Theatre 1964, Adrienne Kennedy's *Funny House of a Negro* lasted less than an hour on stage. But into it was "packed an overflowing portion of the hallucinated horrors that torment the last hours of a Negro girl," and which "give expression to her secret resentments and guilt," said Howard Taubman in *The Times*. "Miss Kennedy, herself a Negro, digs unsparingly into . . . the tortured mind of a Negro who cannot bear the burden of being a Negro." Visions of Queen Victoria, Jesus, and Patrice Lmumba figure in her mad fantasies which were ably ghosted by Cynthia Belgrave, Norman Bush and Gus Williams. Billie Allen was the self-tortured girl. "*Funny House of a Negro*," wrote Richard Watts, "is the compelling creation of a new playwright with a somberly original imagination." The play was a *succès d'estime*.

Blood Knot, a two-character drama by white South African Athol Fugard, treated in tortured fashion the plight of a couple of half-brothers, one half-white and the other African. Critics hailed it as a penetrating play depicting the abrasive anguish of South Africa's contemporary torment. James Earl Jones as the black brother and J. D. Cannon as the part-black one were praised for brilliant performances in which both were on stage together for most of the evening. Before the play closed, Louis Gossett and Nicholas Coster took over the two roles. And at one time the author himself played the part of the half-white brother.

In the spring of 1964 while *Blood Knot* was running, the *New Yorker* listed as then being performed nightly off-Broadway ten productions with all-Negro casts or featuring Negro actors. Aside from *Blood Knot*, there was simultaneously on the boards in New York *The Blacks, Jerico-Jim Crow, Trumpets of the Lord, In White America, Cabin in the Sky, Telemachus Clay* with Clayton Corbin, *The Trojan Women* with Jane White, *Cindy* featuring Thelma Oliver, and *Dutchman* by LeRoi Jones. Before the end of that year, two other plays by Jones, *The Toilet* and *The Slave,* had opened. Previously that season his *The Eighth Ditch* and *The Baptism* had been shown, all in the Village— so the year 1964 might well be called the Jones Year.

THE JONES YEAR

Robert Hooks and Jennifer West aboard the subway in LeRoi Jones's Dutchman.

J ones is great! . . . He's awful! . . . He's divine! . . . He's dirty! . . . He's talented! . . . He's terrible!" Over dinner tables and bars, across class lines and color, uptown and down, so it went anent LeRoi Jones. The Negro had achieved a controversial playwright, a black *enfant terrible*. During the 1964 season Jones became the most talked about dramatist in New York when he had five plays performed one after the other in four different houses. Each of his dramas depicted the moral and spiritual decay of

the United States. And these five one-acters attracted such attention pro and con that two of them were closed by orders of the police. The three not shuttered were hits. Overnight the spotlight fell on LeRoi Jones, who suddenly became the white-haired black boy of Negro culture, inheriting a large portion of the voluminous mantle of James Baldwin. Then Jones opened the Black Arts Theatre in a brownstone house in Harlem, refused whites admittance to his shows, and allegedly became a black nationalist. The police

251

raided the theatre, and darkness descended. His sun went into eclipse—but probably not for long since the stage is not his sole outlet. Jones writes not only plays, but poems, essays and fiction. He also makes speeches that shock the pants off many of his listeners, his basic theme being *Whites, drop dead!*

"LeRoi Jones' first play," the *Post* recorded, "happens to have a rhythm and a force unusual on the stage." But Jerry Tallmer observed in his review that he would not be surprised if the police closed it—"since their representatives have been around at the New Bowery the past couple of evenings taking diligent plainclothes notes." *The Eighth Ditch,* concerning a homosexual rape in an army tent, was closed. It had been presented by the Poets' Theatre in early March 1964. Before the end of the month another one-acter by Jones, *The Baptism,* was presented at the Writers Stage Theatre. Set in a store-front church, it portrayed a black priest, a white acolyte in red tights, a boy who cannot pray without getting sexually excited, and a chorus of pregnant virgins. "I cannot possibly convey the extent of the outrage it commits," wrote Michael Smith, reviewer for *The Village Voice,* "the unrestrained blasphemous travesty it perpetrates on a whole flock of sacred subjects. . . . And it has the further temerity not to take its outrages seriously, but persists in being outrageously funny all the while. . . . Jones has, in addition to his strength as a playwright, a wildly satirical sense of humor." *The Baptism* too closed under duress.

By the time *Dutchman* was presented that spring by Theatre 1964, word had gotten around concerning the startling talents of the amazing new playwright. Lines formed at the box office at the Cherry Lane and the play was a hit almost before it began. Laid in a New York subway car in motion, the story concerned a white floozie across the aisle who so teases and baits an unknown Ivy League black boy she had never seen before, that he explodes, cusses out the floozie, and receives a knife in his belly as a result. The boy is thrown onto the tracks between the subway cars, and the train roars on. This play, coupled with a revival of Albee's *American Dream* as a curtain raiser, had a highly successful run with Robert Hooks as the boy and Jennifer West as the girl, and in 1966 was filmed in England with Al Freeman, Jr. and Shirley Knight.

The first complete theatre evening which Jones had all to himself came in December 1964, when his *The Toilet* and *The Slave* opened a double bill at the St. Marks Playhouse. These two violent shockers, almost worthy of the old Grand Guignol in Paris, nearly shook the critics and the public as well out of their seats. Over the reviews the next day *The Times* headline proclaimed: AN ANGRY MAN. The *World-Telegram* declared: RACE HATRED PERVADES 2 LEROI JONES PLAYS. In bold black type the *News* announced: 'THE TOILET' IS SEVERAL THOUSAND DIRTY WORDS. The mildest of all was the *Journal American* which merely labelled the dramas: CONTROVERSIAL THEATRE, but then in the first line of its text called the production "the most controversial and terrifying evening in the theatre this season, or any other for that matter." The review concluded, "It's certainly something you won't forget, much as you wouldn't forget an attack of cholera."

For LeRoi Jones in most of the reviews of *The Toilet* and *The Slave,* both praise and damnation were mixed. Admire Jones or not, it was obvious he was a playwright who could never be ignored. "One of the angriest writers to storm the theatre—and one of the most gifted," wrote Taubman in *The Times.* And *Variety,* that "Bible of show business" usually more concerned with box office than quality, affirmed, "Playgoers who want a glimpse into the mind of a playwright with a terrifying vision may find *The Toilet* and *The Slave* unforgettable." From then on it was clear that LeRoi Jones had made a big black mark on the American theatre.

BIG, BRIGHT
AND BEAUTIFUL

Featured in Blue Holiday, *a 1945 production, were Ethel Waters and Josh White.*

Beautiful all-Negro musicals and lively revues such as were prevalent in the first third of the century—from the Williams and Walker shows to *Blackbirds* and *The Hot Mikado*—became quite scarce on Broadway following the Depression. In the Forties there were only three major musicals with all-Negro casts—*Cabin in the Sky, Carmen Jones* (considered a Broadway opera) and *St. Louis Woman.* Ed Sullivan's *Harlem Cavalcade, Caribbean Carnival* and *Carib Song* were frail entries of short duration. The first two were vaudeville revues, and the last a con-

trived continuity for Katherine Dunham's dancers.

There were a half dozen musicals in which a few Negro performers (in otherwise white casts) had bit roles, or sometimes a featured part with perhaps one or two good songs to sing. The most outstanding individual in this category was Juanita Hall as Bloody Mary singing "Bali H'ai" in *South Pacific* in 1943, and Dooley Wilson, Richard Huey and Hubert Dillworth the following year with the "Railroad Song" in *Bloomer Girl.* Mildred Smith had a featured role opposite Alfred Drake in *Beggar's Holiday,* the Duke Ellington version of *The*

Juanita Hall, the Bloody Mary of South Pacific.

254

Bill Robinson is the center of attention in The Hot Mikado, *the all-Negro version of the Gilbert and Sullivan work.*

Beggar's Opera with lyrics by John La Touche. Dolores Martin made a hit song of "Necessity" in *Finian's Rainbow*. In *Kiss Me, Kate* Lorenzo Fuller sang the show stopper, "Too Darn Hot," and Annabelle Hill led the opening number. In *Arms and the Girl* Pearl Bailey was one of the most *soigné* maids ever seen. There were singers or dancers, mostly chorus girls or boys in several other musicals. *Sing Out Sweet Land* had eleven Negroes in the cast, *This Is the Army* had ten, *On The Town* six, *Call Me Mister* had four, *Street Scene* four, and *Annie Get Your Gun* three. In most cases they were members of the ensemble like the other actors, without racial tags.

The outstanding all-Negro musicals of the Forties were *Cabin in the Sky* and *St. Louis Woman* —omitting *Carmen Jones* previously considered as a converted opera. A sparkling fantasy harboring in its make-believe cabin such scintillating females as Ethel Waters and Katherine Dunham, along with Rex Ingram as Lucifer, Jr., Todd Duncan as The Lawd's General, and Dooley Wilson as Little Joe, *Cabin in the Sky* had a happy run and a long cross-country tour. It ended as a Hollywood motion picture with Louis Armstrong as the Trumpeter and Lena Horne as Georgia Brown. Staged by George Balanchine with a score by Vernon Duke and John La Touche, and introducing "Taking a

255

Louis Armstrong as Puck and Maxine Sullivan as Titania in Swingin' the Dream, *the jazz adaptation of Shakespeare's* Midsummer Night's Dream.

Chance on Love," "Cabin in the Sky" and "Honey in the Honeycomb"—with the addition of Harold Arlen's "Happiness Is a Thing Called Joe" in the picture—the show had radio and record listeners whistling its tunes for a very long time after it left Broadway. Calling Ethel Waters "an astonishing actress," John Mason Brown wrote, "Miss Waters is one of the irresistible personalities of our stage."

St. Louis Woman five years later produced as tantalizing a score as *Cabin,* with songs like "Come Rain, Come Shine," "Anyplace I Hang My Hat Is Home" and "Ridin' on the Moon" by Harold Arlen and Johnny Mercer. The show had a book by the Negro poets Arna Bontemps and Countee Cullen, based on Bontemps' novel, *God Sends Sunday.* And it was this musical that brought Pearl Bailey to stardom as one of the drollest singing comediennes of our time, but with an eventual preference for nightclubs and the variety stage rather than the theatre. Her singing of "Legalize My Name" and "A Woman's Prerogative" were high points of *St. Louis Woman*. A charming young singer, Ruby Hill, had the lead in the show, supported by such stalwarts as Juanita Hall, Rex Ingram and the dancing-since-childhood Nicholas Brothers. The story, laid in St. Louis in the Nineties, the heyday of Negro jockeys and the big diamonds and big bets, was stunningly set and costumed by Lemuel Ayers, directed by Rouben

Mamoulian of *Porgy* fame, and enchantingly performed by a large cast of fine voices and nimble feet. Chapman of the *News* called *St. Louis Woman* "The best Negro musical in many seasons," and *Life* predicted, "Its place in stage history is assured by Pearl Bailey, the best Negro singer of show tunes since Ethel Waters." Unfortunately, not all the critics were so enthusiastic. The show had only a modest run.

This was also true of *House of Flowers* in 1955, a handsome production laid in Haiti, which pleased a few critics but not others. And so, as

A shooting scene from St. Louis Woman, *with (from left), Harold Nicholas, Ruby Hill, Fayard Nicholas and Pearl Bailey.*

257

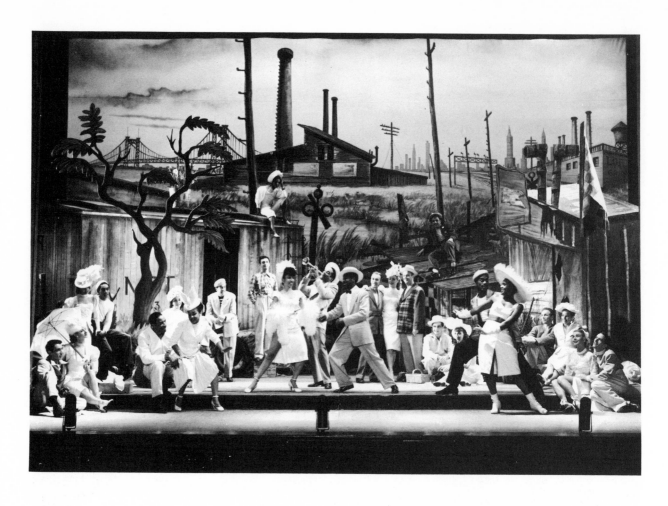

St. Louis Woman, *the musical version of Arna Bontemps' novel of Negro jockeys.*

happens often on Broadway, it did not make its investment back, although it too had in its cast the talented Misses Pearl Bailey and Juanita Hall, plus Diahann Carroll, such excellent voices as Miriam Burton and Rawn Spearman, dancers Alvin Ailey and Carmen de Lavallade, and an entire West Indian steel band. The book was a tropical fable by Truman Capote set to Broadway music by Harold Arlen. Richard Watts termed it "a beautiful and likable show," but *The Times* called it "commonplace." Nevertheless, it served to launch Diahann Carroll as a pretty singer to watch. "A great find," said the *World-Telegram*. "She has a rich, lovely, easy voice, and a rare freshness of personality." And Kerr called her, "a plaintive and extraordinarily appealing ingenue." So from two big, bright, beautiful musicals that did not quite make it, came two stars who did make it, Miss Carroll and Miss Bailey.

ESPECIALLY FOR STARS

Hirschfeld's sketch of the action in Jamaica, *with Lena Horne in center, Josephine Premice at left, and Ricardo Montalban at right.*

Sammy Davis, Eartha Kitt, Lena Horne and Diahann Carroll were the colored stars who had musicals especially fashioned for them on Broadway. Their names shone in lights over the marquees. Other Negro performers, not starred but sharing billing with white artists in musical productions during the Fifties and Sixties, were Mae Barnes in *By the Beautiful Sea* with Shirley Booth; Harry Belafonte with Marge and Gower Champion in *3 for Tonight*; comedienne Ann Henry and guitar-playing Tiger Haynes in *New Faces of '56*; Jane White as the Queen Mother in *Once Upon a Mattress*; Juanita Hall as Madam Liang in Rodgers and Hammerstein's *Flower Drum Song*, and Rosetta LeNoire in *Sophie*. In vivid bit parts there was beautiful Myrna White in *A Funny Thing Happened on the Way to the Forum*; Royce Wallace in *Funny Girl*; Lavinia Hamilton and Nat Horne in *What Makes Sammy Run*; dancer William Louther in *Miracle on 34th Street*, and ten-year-old Terrin Miles in *Here's Love*. Ellis Larkins was in the

259

Sammy Davis as the boxer in Golden Boy, *and Paula Wayne as his girl friend in the musical version of the Clifford Odets play.*

quickly closed Duke Ellington musical, *Pousse Café*. And the short lived *Kwamina*, laid in Africa, had in its cast Brock Peters, Terry Carter, Ethel Ayler and Rex Ingram.

Sammy Davis, Jr. was the bright and shining star of his own *Mr. Wonderful*, which opened March 22, 1956, at the Broadway Theatre. This versatile entertainer sang, danced, played a trum-

Diahann Carroll stepped from the supper club circuit into stardom when Richard Rodgers chose her for the lead in his No Strings.

pet, acted and drummed the evening through, then repeated all the high spots of his nightclub act just before the finale, including his hilarious impersonations of other performers. *Mr. Wonderful* came near being a one-man show, but due largely to its star, it was a continuously entertaining one. "An unusually talented and versatile performer, with a notable gift for assured showmanship," wrote the *Post*, reporting that there was also in the show, "Jack Carter, a brisk and alert comedian, Pat Marshall who is a bouncy and dynamic soubrette, Chita Rivera, a pert and humorous dancing comedienne, and Olga James, a nice ingenue who sings the attractive title song pleasantly. But the evening is chiefly Sammy Davis, Jr., an indefatigable entertainer." The show was billed as "A New Musical Comedy with the Will Mastin Trio starring Sammy Davis, Jr." The Trio, with whom Sammy had been associated theatrically since his birth and which had developed his varied talents, consisted of his father, an uncle and an old family friend. This association was dissolved shortly after the close of *Mr. Wonderful*, and the "Jr." disappeared from Sammy's name. Quite on his own in show business eight years later he opened simply as "Sammy Davis in *Golden Boy*" at the Majestic Theatre in 1964.

Golden Boy had one of the most successful runs of any musical in recent history. Forty weeks after its premiere, in the middle of a very hot summer, it was still selling standing room only. Never during its run did box office receipts fall under $11,000 a day. One week its intake was $94,000. There were always uniformed guards backstage, since it had once been rumored that Sammy Davis might be kidnapped. Based on the drama *Golden Boy* by Clifford Odets, with the racial identity of its troubled boxer changed to Negro, with a dozen songs added, and breathtaking choreography by Donald McKayle, it proved a stunning show in which Sammy Davis demonstrated his acting ability as no less effective than his talents as a song-and-dance man. The show had a long try-out period on the road, doctored and re-doctored so reports said, and the leading role most carefully tailored to suit its star. This paid off in public response to what had become a moving musical drama. Choreographically, it possessed one of the most exciting openings and closings ever seen on Broadway—the ins and outs of prize fighting done in brutally surrealistic dance.

The second of the Broadway musicals slanted to suit the talents of a star (it followed *Mr. Wonderful*) was *Shinbone Alley* in 1957. Here Eartha

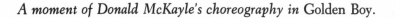

A moment of Donald McKayle's choreography in Golden Boy.

Kitt played a cat—the famous feline, mehitabel (with a small *m*) of the Don Marquis stories about the romance of a lady alley cat and a cockroach. Eddie Bracken was archy, the roach of this stage version of *archy and mehitabel*. The score was by George Kleinsinger, who "improvised an animal and insect world out of music with humor, drollery, street tunes and juke-box pandemonium," and Atkinson described Miss Kitt as a "sleek, torrid cat who . . . dances with animal grace and sings with mocking plausibility." But he continued, "Too bad *Shinbone Alley* does not really come alive as a stage composition." Blaming the transition from book to footlights for its theatrical defects, while finding many good things in the musical, most of the critics agreed in essence with Walter Kerr who said, "archy and mehitabel remain locked in the author's dusty desk." This brave try at whimsy did not last on Broadway. Miss Kitt returned to a more intimate ambience—like the Persian Room at the Plaza.

One of the most successful musicals ever to star a Negro artist was *Jamaica*. Conceived by those old pros of Broadway, Harold Arlen, E. Y. Harburg and Fred Saidy, and directed by Robert Lewis, it starred Lena Horne and Ricardo Montalban with Adelaide Hall, Josephine Premice and Ossie Davis in the large cast, Alvin Ailey and Christine Lawson as its leading dancers, and choreography by Jack Cole. It was a highly professional production, presented by David Merrick, with sets designed by Oliver Smith. Under the musical direction of Lehman Engel, Lena Horne approached the footlights in *Jamaica* supported in all departments by a dozen of the top names in show business. In spite of the fact that some critics thought *Jamaica* a dull show—except when the scintillating Miss Horne was on stage—it ran for many months and grossed a very large amount of money at the box office. LENA IS RADIANT IN A VOID headlined Walter Kerr, adding, "there can't be a handsomer creature on the face of the earth." Miss Horne's beauty and ability were praised by everyone, and audiences did not seem to care that the show itself was only a "jovial, old-fashioned musical comedy"

as Atkinson described it—but with approval, since everyone in it, he said, "is the master of his genre and does not feel under the necessity of proving it."

Certainly *Jamaica* was a triumph for Lena Horne with "an exciting ability to give a song style and distinction." *The Post* further proclaimed her, "probably the most beautiful woman in the world. . . . With her grace, her lithe dignity, her quiet humor, her curious combination of sullenness and sweetness . . . she is one of the incomparable performers of our time." *Time* magazine, in describing previous nightclub appearances, had already called her a "chocolate cream chanteuse" who "seethes her songs with the air of a bashful volcano." After *Jamaica* opened, critic John Chapman's *amen* to all her former praise was simply, "Miss Horne is splendid."

During the eight years between *House of Flowers* in which she was "discovered" and *No Strings* in which she starred, Diahann Carroll did not appear in any theatres on Broadway or off. She was too busy singing in smart supper clubs from the Waldorf in New York to the Hilton in Cairo, or appearing in motion pictures—*Carmen Jones, Porgy and Bess, Paris Blues*—and on television shows such as Red Skelton's and Jack Paar's. When Richard Rodgers, who wrote the score and produced *No Strings,* chose Diahann Carroll for its female star, he declared her to be an artist of singing charm and great chic. The role is that of a high-fashion model in Paris, and the entire action of the libretto occurs in such stylish places as Monte Carlo, Deauville and St. Tropez. Being a very personable young lady of great charm, Miss Carroll filled her part well, and filled the Broadhurst Theatre, too, for quite a while, with Richard Kiley as her co-star. The only colored performer in the musical, Miss Carroll was gowned in the most glamorous of haute couture.

Diahann Carroll, Lena Horne, Eartha Kitt and Sammy Davis star in their own right on Broadway with top billing—their names "over the show"—which is the highest honor the commercial theatre can give to an artist.

DANCERS AND DANCING

Avon Long and Katherine Dunham sketched by Hirschfeld in Carib Song, *a 1945 production.*

The first serious Negro dance recital in America, according to the program, was presented at the Theatre-in-the-Clouds atop the Chanin Building in New York on April 29, 1931, by the New Negro Art Theatre. Ruth St. Denis was one of the patrons, and Felicia Sorel, Gluck Sandor and Grace Hooper aided in the production. Its moving spirit was Hemsley Winfield, pioneer Negro dancer in the interpretive field. This initial concert featured Winfield, Edna Guy and Ollie Burgoyne. Randolph Sawyer, later a part of various Broadway musicals, was among the eighteen dancers. Besides a suite based on African themes and another based on spirituals of the Negro South, there were interpretive vignettes like "A Figure From Angkor'vat," "Life and Death," and "Song Without Words." When Lawrence Tibbett in blackface interpreted *The Emperor Jones* in opera at the Metropolitan, the Hemsley Winfield Ballet incarnated the "Little Foolish Fears." In 1935 Eugene Von Grona organized the American Negro Ballet Group, who were later featured in Lew Leslie's *Blackbirds*.

In his book, *100 Years of the Negro in Show Business,* Tom Fletcher reports that about 1910, Ada Overton Walker, the brownskin leading lady

Katherine Dunham with her dancers in "Rora Tonga," a number in Tropical Revue.

Katherine Dunham

of the Williams and Walker musicals, made an excursion into serious dance at Hammerstein's Theatre, following Gertrude Hoffman in a solo interpretation of *Salome*. White Miss Hoffman and Ruth St. Denis both had been acclaimed for their rhythmic representation of the Biblical seductress. Hammerstein, Fletcher said, "was one of the four big white producers of that time who regularly ignored consideration of race in engaging performers."

At the Chicago World's Fair in 1893, a troupe of Dahomey dancers helped make Americans conscious of the rhythmic excitement of African dancing, and attracted Negro performers in the United States to its entertainment values. But attempts to derive interpretive elements from the purely ethnic patterns of the African dance developed only in the Thirties and came to public attention with the production in New York of Asadata Dafora's dance-opera, *Kykunkor,* in which Dafora performed. In the same period a young Liberian dancer, Toniea Massaquoi, who appeared at Radio City and with the Creative Dance Unit of Hampton Institute, was credited by the editor of *Theatre Arts,* Edith Isaacs, with bringing to both old ritualistic and modern dance forms his "own free African character and clear sense of beauty."

In love with African dancing as a hobby, Pearl Primus, a young 1940 graduate of Hunter College in New York, had prepared to teach biology as a means toward earning money for medical school. Instead she won an unexpected scholarship from the New Dance Group and at its studio created a solo sequence called *Ceremonial,* utilizing African motifs. Miss Primus also took an interest in the possibilities of the spirituals and the blues as backgrounds for interpretive movement. Shortly she gave a concert at the Y.M.H.A. which drew praise from critic John Martin. Thus encouraged, she formed a small group of her own and in 1944 performed in concert for ten days at the Belasco Theatre, dancing to both spoken poetry and music, with blues guitarist Josh White accompanying her and Gordon Heath as narrator. "Vital and always deeply moving," said the *Post.* "Her personality hits you between the eyes." Concert programs across America over the years followed and with dancing partner Percival Borde, many New York appearances as well. As both performer and researcher, Pearl Primus also made a long tour of the West African coast, and spent considerable time in Liberia helping the government organize its African Performing Arts Center.

The most distinguished pioneer in the transition of folk and popular dances from the ethnic into the interpretive was a student of anthropology at the University of Chicago, Katherine Dunham. She went to both library and living sources for her materials before bringing them to the stage. On a Rosenwald fellowship she travelled far afield in search of Afro-Caribbean and American Negro rituals, rhythms and patterns of movement. Both as a choreographer and dancer, Miss Dunham left her mark, and a very distinct mark at that, on the national dance scene. For more than twenty years she kept together a dance company that performed in most major cities of the world, and periodically returned to Broadway in a variety of dance presentations.

Miss Dunham's first New York appearance in 1940 was a concert of American and Caribbean dance forms which, said Arthur Todd in *The Times*, in exhibiting "her sense of rhythm, theatre and costuming and her wonderful performers—as well as her choreography and dancing—put serious Negro dance on the map once and for all." Katherine Dunham's *Tropical Revue* at the Martin Beck in 1943 "shows that there is nothing arch about a hot style, that its expression is serious and sometimes angry," said the *Herald Tribune*. "Her dance conceptions offer color, variety, as well as an unusual human warmth," said the *Post*. And the Negro press approved. The *Afro-American* reported, "Nothing in the *Tropical Revue* makes you ashamed of your people. There is no Uncle Toming, vulgar cavorting, or humorous attention called to racial differences. . . . Every scene is like a painting by Orozco or Rivera or the Brazilian artist, Portinari. The stage is actually a canvas upon which Miss Dunham painted." Her next Broadway excursion, *Carib Song*, was spoiled by a plot. But in 1946 *Bal Negre* arrived at the Belasco and, according to the critics, "Miss Dunham and her company danced wonderfully." The troupe at that time included Eartha Kitt, Vanoye Aikens, Lucille Ellis, Lenwood Morris and Jean Leon Destine. And Robert Sylvester in the *News* avowed, "Katherine Dunham is the best dancer in America today." Some years later when Sol Hurok presented her at the Broadway Theatre after one of her European tours, John Martin in *The Times* observed, "Playing in Europe has apparently given the company a sense of being exotic, which it never could have acquired here, and this constitutes a kind of objective style, a basis for comment, a framework in which to present the material with the emphasis of an artist. . . . John Pratt has done wonders with the simple decor and the beautiful costumes."

For *Bamboche*, the title of the Dunham dance fete on Broadway in 1962, her company was augmented by a large number of musicians and dancers from the Royal Troupe of Morocco and, in contrast, a group of Negro gospel singers. Both additions seemed not really needed. Miss Dunham and her own dancers still made the show, although *Variety* lauded the Moroccans as being "exciting and colorful," and an act-long ballet pantomime, *The Diamond Thief*, was praised. At various times outstanding dancers in Miss Dunham's companies, including non-Negro dancers, have been Syvilla Fort, Noelle Adam, Ricardo Avalos, Hope Clarke, Roger Chardieno, Tommy Gomez, Lavinia Williams, Laverne French, Talley Beatty, Clifford Fears and Claude Marchant. Katherine Dunham has directed the dances in various productions at home and abroad for stage, motion pictures and television, in which she herself did not appear. And she became the first Negro choreographer at the Metropolitan Opera House in charge of the ballet for a new production of *Aïda* which opened the 1963–1964 season. In 1966 Miss Dunham was in residence for several months at Dakar where she was Artistic Advisor to Senegal's *First World Festival of Negro Arts*.

Pearl Primus

BALLET TAKES WINGS

Clive Thompson in Martha Graham's "Secular Games."

A leading American dance impresario once made a private statement to the effect that Negro dancers with their (as he put it) "natural" body movement could not fit into white companies with more disciplined patterns and trained modes of expression. Happily, some years later, he revised his opinion and the companies that came under his aegis—which included one of the most stable and continuing aggregations on the American dance scene—incorporated Negroes. One of them is now a featured soloist. Preconceived notions regarding race die hard in the United States—but they die less hard in the arts than in many other areas. Every great American dance group now has Negroes on its roster. Mary Hinkson, Matt Turner and Clive Thompson are soloists with Martha Graham. John Jones is with the Joffrey Ballet. Louis Johnson danced in Jerome Robbins' *Ballade* with the New York City Ballet. Carmen de Lavallade stars with the Ballet Theatre and at the Harkness Dance Festival. Alvin Ailey and others from his group have participated in Harkness-sponsored ballets in Paris, London and New York. For years Jamie Bower danced with the

Janet Collins, prima ballerina, in La Gioconda *at the Metropolitan Opera House.*

Mary Hinkson in "Diversion of Angels," with choreography by Martha Graham.

Dunham dancer, Donald McKayle, Eleo Pomare, Ernest Parham, Louis Johnson, Alvin Ailey, Sevilla Fort, Lester Wilson and, known largely on the West Coast for her programs of primitive dance, Ruth Beckford. Under a grant from the Lena Robbins Foundation in 1959, Talley Beatty created a balletic work since repeated over the years, *The Route of the Phoebe Snow,* laid along the tracks over which that famous train ran. To music by Duke Ellington and Billy Strayhorn, the thirty-minute work "seems to be virtually a suite of related dances," wrote John Martin, "almost like some Negro folk *Sylphides* . . . until at the close we find ourselves suddenly in the midst of a highly dramatic situation. . . . The total effect is stunning." To music by Dizzy Gillespie, Charlie Mingus and Gil Evans, Beatty's *Come and Get the Beauty of It Hot* excited the dance world in 1962. Its chief roles were performed by Mabel Robinson and Herman Howell. The following year the Talley Beatty Dance Company presented *Migration* to music by Margaret Bonds.

Matt Turney in "Seraphic Dialogue."

Roland Petit *Ballets de Paris,* and Billy Williams with the Netherlands Ballet. Numerous Negro dancers have performed at Spoleto's Festival of Two Worlds. Janet Collins was the first colored prima ballerina at the Metropolitan, but since then Miss De Lavallade and Geoffrey Holder, among others, have been a part of its corps de ballet. And Mercedes Ellington, the granddaughter of Duke, dances at Radio City. Contemporary ballet and the modern dance take wings to fly over the color line.

Most modern dance companies are integrated, including those that formerly were all-Negro. In the course of integration the troupes usually change their names. The New York Negro Ballet became the Ballet Americana shortly before the group danced a charming program under the auspices of Coffee Concerts in Harlem and at the Y.M.H.A. in 1959, with Anthony Bass as principal dancer and choreographer.

Aside from Katherine Dunham, leading Negro choreographers include Talley Beatty, a former

Geoffrey Holder dancing in the Metropolitan's production of Aïda.

Carmen de Lavallade, solo dancer at the Metro-politan.

bow *Round My Shoulder* won critical kudos. His full-length dance work in twelve parts, *Reflections in the Park,* to a score by jazz composer Gary McFarland, was presented at Hunter College in 1964. McKayle choreographed the Sammy Davis hit, *Golden Boy,* and the first of Harry Belafonte's television productions, *The Strollin' Twenties.*

Alvin Ailey as both dancer and choreographer has had wide acclaim. Beginning as a disciple of dance master Lester Horton in California, he came East to perform in *House of Flowers* and *Jamaica.* He then began forming his own groups based at the Clark Center for the Performing Arts in New York. Since 1960 the Alvin Ailey Dance Theatre has appeared on every continent around the world, and in 1966 broke all box office records during the World Festival of Negro Arts at Dakar. Arthur Todd, American correspondent for London's *Dance and Dancers,* has called Ailey "the greatest male dancer in his field today and a choreographer of enormous talent." His assistant is James Truitt, an excellent dancer and dance director. At various times the Ailey company has included besides its former star, Carmen de Lavallade, "who dances the way birds sing," such vivid personalities as Loretta Abbott, Morton Winston, Georgia Collins, Minnie Marshall, Ronald Platts, Thelma Hill, Altovise Gore, and Dudley Williams. Among Ailey's outstanding creations are *Roots of the Blues* and *Revelations* performed against a background of Southern Negro songs, and his *Creation of the World* in which Ailey dances man newly born from the earth. "The very best in American Negro dancing . . . such fun and feeling, such vivacity and virtuosity, such wit and wizardry," is the way a London paper characterized Ailey's presentations. Another called the ten Negroes in the cast, "exceptionally sensitive and vivacious artists." The ethnic elements in this American Dance Theatre triumphed abroad although the word *Negro* appeared nowhere in its title. *The New York Times* contended that in considering artistic exchanges our government should not overlook "the tremendous cultural bond that we might build with other countries by exporting one of our major and most authentic and most vital treasures, an American Negro dance company."

Donald McKayle's integrated dance company, besides its Negro artists, included in the 1962 programs Takako Asakawa, Alfred De Sio, Louis Falco, Mariko Sanjo and Jaimi Rogers. Mary Hinkson, Jacqueline Walcott, Charles Moore, Pearl Reynolds and Thelma Oliver were among the excellent colored dancers. Dorothea Freitag, long associated with Katherine Dunham, contributed original music as well as arranging traditional jazz material for the highly diverting *District Storyville* about the New Orleans of redlight and music days. McKayle's famous *Games* of earlier seasons has become a classic, and his colorful *Rain-*

The Alvin Ailey Dance Theatre.

Alvin Ailey and his dancers.

In contrast to Alvin Ailey's commendable accent on ethnic values, there is Arthur Mitchell who dances, as *The New York Times* puts it, "without regard for color" in either the form or content of his work. Allen Hughes writes that, "As a principal dancer and longtime member of the New York City Ballet, he is a star of international reputation in the rarefied stratosphere of classical ballet. He is the first Negro to have attained that distinction. Mr. Mitchell is not, of course, the first or only great Negro dance artist, nor even the first to venture successfully into the classical ballet field. To date, however, he has been the *only* Negro to establish himself as a leading dancer of one of the world's great ballet companies. . . . He won his place in the New York City Ballet because he is a superior dancer, and the company has used him freely in its repertory without regard for the color of his skin." For more than six years Arthur Mitchell has danced the *pas de deux* in *Agon* with

Barbara Wright, Louis Johnson and Georgia Collins in "Variations."

In addition to his accomplishments with the New York City Ballet, Arthur Mitchell has danced and choreographed in many of the major cities of Europe and Canada, and for television and Broadway.

One of the leading dancers of the New York City Ballet, Arthur Mitchell first came to attention when he won the Dance Award as a student at New York City's High School of Performing Arts.

either Diana Adams or Allegra Kent, a role especially created for him by George Balanchine to a commissioned score by Igor Stravinsky. In writing about *Agon* in the Tenth Anniversary booklet on the company, Edwin Denby observed that the fact that his partner is white "and Mr. Mitchell Negro is neither stressed nor hidden; it adds to the interest."

Arthur Mitchell is a lithe, quite dark and handsome young man who, by contrast, stands out strikingly in the company. There is no mistaking that Mitchell is Negro. He has made a 15,000 mile tour of Europe and the Middle East with the company, dancing at Covent Garden in London the Scala in Milan, the Paris Opera, and in major

cities from Athens to Tel Aviv. At the Bolshoi in Moscow, the Associated Press reported, "Most applause went to Arthur Mitchell. . . . When Mitchell danced in a cowboy suit, he brought them up to the footlights in droves." *Western Symphony*—beloved of the Russians—*Allegro Brillante, Orpheus, A Midsummer Night's Dream, Bakuko* and *The Nutcracker* are other ballets in which Arthur Mitchell has participated with the New York company. Abroad as a soloist he danced the role of Mercutio in *Romeo and Juliet* in Stuttgart, and that of the Moor in *Othello* at the Munich Opera. His dancing feet have taken him almost all around the world, but his base is Lincoln Center in Manhattan.

Mary Hinkson and Scott Douglas, who have long been with Martha Graham's company.

Carmen de Lavallade with Glen Tetley in his "Pierrot Lunaire," with music by Arnold Schonberg.

BOULDERS IN THE WAY

*Roland Hayes: beaten in his home town in Georgia
because he sat in the wrong seat in a shoe store.*

Concerning Arthur Mitchell and his duet in the ballet *Agon* with Allegra Kent, who is white, dance critic Allen Hughes of the Sunday *Times* wrote, "Mr. Mitchell and Miss Kent can dance this duet on theatre stages around the world, but they cannot dance together on television in this country, at least not on commercially sponsored shows, which includes virtually all shows of major significance. Why? Television stations in the South would refuse to carry the shows, and advertisers would not like that. . . . Why does he not perform on television with other Negro

dancers? He can, and he has, but this does not allow him to show the television public what he is famous for—his roles in the New York City Ballet. . . . If he appears on television at all, then, it must be outside the repertory he has worked for a decade to master."

The general public is not often aware of such boulders in the paths of Negro performers. For example, in former years an actor might be a Bert Williams or a Claudia McNeil yet, following thunderous applause in the theatre, find it almost impossible after the show to find a restaurant to

Ethel Waters: forced out of Atlanta because she didn't like the way the piano was tuned.

Bessie Smith: died after an auto accident in Mississippi because she was refused medical attention at a hospital.

Cab Calloway: "I can't stand that split audience policy."

get a midnight snack or a hotel room in which to sleep. Happily, such problems in most major Northern cities no longer exist. Another boulder of heartbreaking proportions was that of audience segregation, or the total barring of Negroes from hundreds of American theatres. Colored artists on road tours often had to perform in playhouses where Negroes were shunted to the top gallery or, as at the National Theatre in Washington, not admitted at all to any part of the house. Marian Anderson and Ethel Waters on tour often had to look out at audiences where Negroes were only a very small segregated segment at the very back or the very top of the auditorium. In performances on stage, integration of white and Negro artists was forbidden in most Southern communities. Mixed casts could not play. Colored concert artists were not allowed to use their regular accompanist if the pianist happened to be white (as was Kosti

Vehannen with Marian Anderson), or else the pianist must be placed out of sight behind a screen.

In his home town of Birmingham, appearing before a segregated audience in 1956, Nat King Cole made a concession to Southern custom by putting his integrated orchestra backstage behind a scrim, well hidden. He appeared on the stage alone. Neverthless, in the middle of a song, he was attacked in full view of the audience by three white ruffians who knocked Cole to the floor and attempted to drag him off the stage before they were stopped. Singer Dinah Washington, when she heard of the incident, said, "I'm from Alabama —but I'm gonna *stay* from there." Cab Calloway declared, "As for me, I've been out of the South for a long, long time. I couldn't stand that split audience policy so I quit going there years ago." In 1955 Lena Horne called off a Miami Beach engagement on account of hotel discrimination,

Hazel Scott: "I can't give a concert before an audience that represents the exact opposite of things I stand for."

before the policies became more liberal there. The hotel in which she was to sing would not register her for a room. Hazel Scott, in cancelling a concert contract at the University of Texas where she had thought the audience would be unsegregated, said, "I couldn't walk out on that stage and give a concert before an audience that represents the direct opposite of things I stand for." Most of the younger Negro nightclub entertainers refuse to perform in the South, except at Miami Beach where, because of its Northern clientele and the changing racial climate, they may get a non-segregation clause in contracts.

In the early days of his career, tenor Roland Hayes performed behind a scrim in a Louisville movie house. At the height of his fame in 1942, in a shoe store in his home community in Georgia, Hayes was beaten because he happened to sit down on the wrong seat not knowing those at the front of the shop were for whites. After his triumphs in London and Paris and Berlin, perhaps

Hayes had forgotten the ways of his birthplace. At any rate, he moved to Boston.

Almost all the autobiographies of show people of color relate examples of discrimination, not on the part of white performers themselves, but of the citizens of cities in which they performed. Billie Holiday in *Lady Sings the Blues* describes her long bus tour with the Artie Shaw band. Many of the restrooms along the highways were labeled FOR WHITE ONLY. "It got to the place where I hardly ever ate, slept, or went to the bathroom without having a major NAACP-type production. . . . I got so tired of scenes in crummy roadside restaurants over getting served. . . . Some places they wouldn't even let me eat in the kitchen. Some places they would. Sometimes it was a choice between me eating and the whole band starving. I got tired of having a federal case over breakfast, lunch, and dinner. . . . But the biggest drag of all was a simple thing like finding a place to go to the bathroom."

Ethel Waters in *His Eye Is on the Sparrow* records some harrowing incidents experienced on Southern tours. In Macon, Georgia, the body of a lynched boy was thrown into the lobby of the colored theatre as a warning to other Negroes not to be "uppity." In Atlanta, Miss Waters herself had to leave town under cover of darkness, spirited off in an old horse cart to a country railway station because, after a dispute over the tuning of a piano for her act, the white theatre owner had her followed by police and gave orders not to allow her to purchase a ticket to leave town. This theatre owner had once physically assaulted Bessie Smith. The great blues singer did not write an autobiography, nor did Bessie Smith live to tell anyone about the gravest incident of discrimination in her career —that of refusal of hospital attention because of color after she was seriously injured in an auto accident on a road in Mississippi. That night she died. Though acts of bigotry and prejudice may beset the paths of Negro stars and non-stars outside the theatre, in the profession itself it is generally agreed that there is less intolerance among performers than in any other field of American endeavor. Actors had their own civil rights bills in their hearts long before Washington began to make laws about it.

Lena Horne: refused a room in a hotel that booked her as a star.

MEMOIRS
AND MEMORIES

Surprisingly little has been written on the overall history of the Negro in the American theatre, and prior to World War II nobody kept a very detailed record of what was going on. A pioneer volume, and a beautiful one, is that of Edith J. R. Isaacs, *The Negro in the American Theatre,* which covers the period up to 1946. Replete with memories of the old days, particularly the first quarter of the 1900's, is Tom Fletcher's *100 Years of the Negro in Show Business.* And there are some very valuable segments of research and contemporary history up to the Depression in James Weldon Johnson's *Black Manhattan,* as well as in Abbe Niles' foreword to W. C. Handy's *A Treasury of the Blues.* Fascinating biographies are those by Herbert Marshall and Mildred Stock, *Ira Aldridge, The Negro Tragedian,* and by John Jay Daly, *A Song in His Heart: The Life and Times of James A. Bland* whose background was the minstrels. In the 1928 edition of *The Official Theatrical World of Colored Artists*

there is a portion of the memoirs of William Foster, *Pioneers of the Stage,* edited from his manuscript by Theophilus Lewis. And in the annual bound volumes of *Phylon,* the Atlanta University Quarterly issues dated from 1945 to 1958, there is excellent running commentary covering each season under the title, "The Negro on Broadway." Fred Weldon Bond's *The Negro and the Drama* is valuable, as is Dr. Alain Locke's *The Negro and His Music* and Sterling Brown's *Negro Poetry and Drama* in the Bronze Booklet Series, and Loften Mitchell's *Black Drama.*

Arna Bontemps tells the story of the famous Fisk Jubilee Singers of Reconstruction times in his volume *Chariot in the Sky.* Mezz Mezzrow and Bernard Wolfe touch on numerous show business personalities, especially those of jazz, in their *Really the Blues. Famous Negro Music Makers* by Langston Hughes contains eighteen sketches on both concert and popular performers from Jelly Roll Morton to Lena Horne. And the small volumes in the excellent London series, *Kings of Jazz*, range from King Oliver to Bessie Smith and Duke Ellington. There are, of course, a great many excellent books on jazz and its practitioners, too many to list adequately here, but whose titles are easily found in public libraries. In the serious music field there are McKinley Helm's *Angel Mo' and Her Son Roland Hayes*, Marian Anderson's *My Lord, What a Morning*, Marie Seaton's *Paul Robeson* which treats of both his concert and stage careers, and *Paul Robeson, Negro* by his wife, Eslanda Goode Robeson.

Among the most interesting and revealing autobiographies (or as-told-to books) which touch on many personalities other than themselves are W. C. Handy's *Father of the Blues*, Taylor Gordon's *Born to Be*, Louis Armstrong's *Satchmo—My Life in New Orleans*, Ethel Waters' *His Eye Is on the Sparrow*, Eartha Kitt's *Thursday's Child*, Lena Horne's *Lena*, Sammy Davis' *Yes, I Can*, and one of the frankest and most moving of American autobiographies, Billie Holliday's *Lady Sings the Blues*. For a wider knowledge and greater understanding of the Negro in American entertainment, these are some of the books one might read. The stories of the Negro in the theatre are about so much more than merely the theatre. And most of their narratives would make wonderful plays.

ACTORS EQUITY

Frederick O'Neal presiding over an Actors Equity meeting.

Many of the happiest moments in the American musical theatre have been those created by its Negro performers: Bert Williams singing "Nobody," George Walker's "Bon-Bon Buddy," Dora Deane dancing the cakewalk, Bojangles tapping up and down the stairs, Florence Mills in *Blackbirds*, Ethel Waters, Pearl Bailey, Lena Horne, Louis Armstrong swinging out, Eartha Kitt crooning "Santa, Baby," Sammy Davis drumming and jiving in *Mr. Wonderful*, Thelma Oliver go-go-going in *Sweet Charity* and, a while back, Juanita Hall singing "Happy Talk": "If you don't have a dream, how you gonna' have a dream come true?"

"Yes, I can," dreamed Sammy Davis—and became a Broadway star. "There's no business like show business," is an old saw on which the song hopefully embroiders, "Yesterday they told you you would not go far. That night you open—and there you are! Next day on your dressing room they've hung a star." Young performers look forward to that happy day—but for Negro performers, since their road is a bit more thorny than that of others, extra efforts for progress have to be exerted, both

Frederick O'Neal, distinguished actor of stage, screen and television, was first Negro performer to be elected to the presidency of Actors Equity. He was re-elected at the end of his first term.

Josephine Baker never suffered discrimination silently. Here an NAACP picket-line protests Stork Club anti-Negro policy, with Walter White, Laura Z. Hobson and Mrs. Bessie Buchanan in demonstration.

by themselves and others who care. The Actors Equity Association has made a very great contribution toward the democratization of every area of American entertainment—from that of the stage itself to non-segregated seating in theatres to hotel accommodations for touring performers. This association of actors has spurred other unions, and producers as well, to liberalize their policies. The 54-year-old Equity, with about 12,000 members, resolved in 1947 that no actors belonging to the Association would perform in the National Theatre in Washington after May 31, 1948 unless its

policy of not admitting Negroes were dropped. At that time no legitimate theatres in Washington admitted colored spectators. Clarence Derwent, then president of Equity, said, "It is preposterous that this situation should exist in the nation's capital."

It was Ingrid Bergman, Swedish star of stage and films, who brought the Jim Crow theatre situation in Washington to a head. In 1946 an interracial group of World War II members of the American Veterans Committee attempted to attend a performance of *Blithe Spirit* at George Washington University's Lister Auditorium. The Negro veterans in the group were turned away at the door. The Committee for Racial Democracy then picketed the theater. When Miss Bergman, scheduled to play there the following week in the Playwrights Company's *Joan of Lorraine,* learned of what she felt was an incredible situation, it was too late for her to get out of contractual obligations to perform. But the author of the play, Maxwell Anderson, Miss Bergman, and members of the all-white cast, petitioned Actors Equity to issue a ruling forbidding its members to participate in future productions in Washington theatres. Backing Equity, 33 members of the Dramatists Guild, including most of America's leading playwrights, pledged to allow none of their plays to be performed there until the color ban was lifted. In 1947 George Washington University announced that Negroes would be admitted to Lister Auditorium.

The National Theatre, however, still persisted in barring colored playgoers. African dignitaries like the Ambassador of Liberia or non-white members of the United Nations were unwelcome—even when all-Negro casts such as *The Green Pastures* or *Porgy and Bess* were playing there. Court action and picketing were ineffective. It was not until the members of Equity voted overwhelmingly to forbid its members to perform there that the policy was broken. Still stubborn, however, the theatre then decided to show motion pictures only. But after four years it submitted to Equity's edict, restored stage shows in 1952 and opened its doors to the public in general. Equity rulings later achieved similar victories in cities elsewhere, for the example set by the Association in relation to the legitimate stage spread to other segments of the entertainment industry. In 1951 the Metropolitan Opera Association cancelled a week's performance of *Die Fledermaus* at Washington's Capitol Theatre which refused to sell seats to Negroes. And in 1962 the Metropolitan stated that it would no longer be a part of the Atlanta and Birmingham seasons unless discriminatory seating customs were abolished. In the jazz field, the Birdland Stars refused to accept engagements in cities where there was such discrimination. Since the Equity rulings, many theatres all over the country, except where state laws expressly forbid racial mixing in auditoriums, have dropped their segregated customs. Actors Equity is considered the most democratic of America's major unions. In 1964 veteran Negro actor Frederick O'Neal was elected its president, and presides over its governing council.

PROS AND CONS

When *Simply Heavenly* opened at the 85th Street Playhouse in May 1957, it followed other plays that had been done there without incident. But no sooner had this all-Negro show opened, than the Fire Department began almost daily inspections of this off-Broadway house, each time finding in the building some hitherto undiscovered violation which had not been uncovered during the runs of other attractions. The steps to the women's dressing room were declared too narrow. The dressing room was closed, so the women of the cast had to costume themselves in the toilet. Then the stairs to the balcony were pronounced too narrow and the balcony had to be closed, thus cutting off a portion of the box office revenue. Since the show was a hit and the main floor crowded nightly, the management was then called upon to limit the number of folding chairs in the auditorium. Each time the orders relative to the alleged violations were complied with by the management. Finally the Fire Department stated that the building, a fraternal lodge hall, should have had (in the years before) a ten thousand gallon water tank on the roof for fire prevention. The astonished owners of the building were ordered to install one forthwith. They thereupon gave up and asked the *Simply Heavenly* company to vacate the premises, since the landlords could not afford so expensive an installation simply to accommodate a new theatrical tenant.

Since tickets were selling well uptown, the show was invited by the owners of the Playhouse on West 48th Street to attempt a Broadway run during the summer when that house was otherwise vacant. *Simply Heavenly* moved to Broadway in August. The critics reviewed it favorably for a second time. But the summer was unduly hot. Also an incipient flu epidemic cut down attendance. After 41 performances the show fell under the required weekly box office gross that a production must make to remain in a Broadway theatre, so it closed—only to reopen again off-Broadway, this time in the Renata Theatre in the Village. At Village prices the small theatre was filled and tickets were selling for several weeks ahead when Actors Equity stepped in to declare that once a production had been on Broadway paying Equity salaries, it could not transfer to off-Broadway at the pay scale

allowed smaller theatres. Playing to packed houses as it was, the show nevertheless had to close by orders of Equity. It did.

When preparations for the production of *Simply Heavenly* first began, a little theatre in the basement of a hotel in the midtown area (classed as off-Broadway because of its limited seating capacity) was sought. There had previously been a play there with only one colored performer in the cast. But when the owner learned that there were to be eighteen Negro actors in *Simply Heavenly,* he refused permission for the play to be done, stating that hotel guests would be dismayed to see so many colored people passing nightly through the lobby. The lovely auditorium of a newly built community house was then secured and a contract was on the verge of being signed the day after the call for auditions was issued. It happened that the first auditions were held on the night of the monthly board meeting of the trustees of the community house. The board members had never seen colored people coming in their building before, so they demanded to know what was happening. When told that their auditorium was soon to be rented for the presentation of a Negro play, they immediately voted against allowing this to happen. So many Negroes, no! Finally the 85th Street Playhouse was secured. However, after so many vicissitudes, when the show was forced to close at the Renata, it was difficult to convince the colored members of the company that the various trials and tribulations of *Simply Heavenly* were not in some way connected with Jim Crow.

A controversy about the show developed among Negro playgoers that expressed a division in Negro thought. Some said its difficulties served *Simply Heavenly* right—that there was no longer a place for an all-Negro company in these days of integration. Others contended that with the few roles available in the commercial theatre for Negroes, productions giving black actors and playwrights a chance to further develop their talents were desirable. The East Side Yiddish theatres were given as examples of ethnic playhouses producing such fine performers as Luther Adler, Molly Picon, Paul Muni, Menasha Skulnik, Herschel Bernardi and Gertrude Berg. And from the Hebrew Actors Union on the East Side, Actors Equity had evolved. As to whether or not there should be in Harlem another American Negro Theatre, some said *yes,* some said *no,* especially since there are Negro actors in City Center and the Lincoln Repertory Company. Others said these actors constitute less than a handful, therefore Negroes should have their *own* center and their *own* repertory companies—ethnic arts must preserve themselves, and this can be done only in ethnic centers. Genuine integration in the theatre or elsewhere is a long way off, some contend. Yet there are a few colored actors who refuse to appear in all-Negro plays, and one Negro director has stated that he does not want to direct Negro plays since his wish is to "not be typed." LeRoi Jones, on the other hand, contends that directors, actors, plays and playgoers should *all* be black. So the controversy goes, pro and con, with those who take the middle ground believing there is no good reason why there should not be both ethnic theatres and integrated theatres in the United States.

DREAMS COME TRUE

Theophilus Lewis, dramatic critic of American *magazine.*

During the Fifties the Actors Equity Committee on Ethnic Minorities, the Negro Actors Guild, and the Co-ordinating Council for Negro Performers all worked toward increasing job opportunities in theatre, radio and television, and the changing of racist concepts in casting. Frederick O'Neal recorded, "The Council discovered through a survey in 1953 that Negro actors constituted less than one-half of one percent of the total number of performers shown on the television screens in a single week. This was at a time when four networks were in operation. . . . During this same period it was estimated that there were between 350,000 and 400,000 Negro television set owners in the New York area alone. . . . Negro actors contend that they are the only ones whose employment is limited to racial casting patterns. White actors can play and are cast as Indians, Japanese, Arabs, and even Negroes, but the Negro artist is limited to so-called 'Negro parts.' The Negro actor feels that the refusal of employers to consider them simply as actors, as is done with other groups, and not as 'Negro actors' constitutes discrimination and even more, but perhaps unwittingly, an adverse form of propaganda having a damaging effect. The absence of Negroes in any

Long the director of CBS-TV's graphic arts department, Georg Olden won many awards for his creativity.

but an occasional menial role gives a distorted picture of one-tenth of the nation's population, which in turn prejudices the struggle of the Negro for full citizenship. So the point at issue is more than just jobs for Negro actors, but one of the principal forces that can help or hinder the drive towards the realization of full democracy."

Actors Equity in conjunction with the Dramatists Guild and the League of New York Theatres issued a statement calling "on all responsible elements in the allied entertainment arts to join" towards "the integration of Negro and other non-Caucasian artists in all media of the performing arts." This resolution in the decade since its inscription has produced some positive results. In

1959 Equity, with the blessings of the Theatre Guild, John Shubert, Kermit Bloomgarden and other Broadway powers, presented at the Majestic Theatre an *Integration Showcase* in which top Negro and white performers appeared together in expertly staged portions of well-known plays—*Volpone, Tea and Sympathy, Room Service,* and the *Caine Mutiny Court Martial.* There were musical and dance sequences as well, new and old. More than 1,500 producers, directors and authors watched this presentation. Succeeding seasons indicated definite advancement. Employment increased. Of the 59 Broadway shows during 1962–1963, 21 of them had Negroes in the cast. In twelve of these shows they played non-ethnic roles. For example, Frank Silvera had a prominent part in *Camille*, the old Parisian romance presented as *The Lady of the Camellias*. Carmen de Lavallade was a featured dancer in *Hot Spot*.

In areas other than acting during the Sixties, Lloyd Richards directed several non-Negro shows in succeeding seasons. Charles Blackwell stage-managed some of the biggest musicals. Perry Watkins continued to design sets. In television Fred Lights, formerly floor manager for the Dave Garroway programs, became stage manager for leading shows on NBC-TV. Sidney Vassal is also a stage manager there. Arthur Johnson is an ABC-TV camera man, Morgan Smith a sound technician on the same network, George Corrin a set designer and Edward Gaines a program administrator. Gene Whitlock is a unit manager at NBC, and John Thomas a sound engineer for the CBS-TV network. In Philadelphia Herman Murray is a master control audio technician at KYW-TV.

In areas other than technical, Howard Robert has an important musical post at the Records Division of CBS, Bob Teague is an NBC-TV newscaster, Dave Hepburn is a director of Public Relations for WNEW-TV and George Norford a general executive of Group "W" at the Westing-

More and more non-performing jobs are being filled by Negroes in television, such as boom mike operator.

house Broadcasting Company. Lovely Joan Murray is an on-the-screen news reporter at WCBS-TV in New York, and beautiful colored models are occasionally seen on television commercials. "It isn't a matter of idealism," said one of the heads of a top advertising agency. "It is just that some people are beginning to get the idea that there's a whale of a Negro market." Realizing this, some of the big industrial shows started to employ Negro entertainers and demonstrators, and high fashion emporiums have started to utilize a few Negro mannequins to display their wares.

Negro booking agents and managers handling talent in the various entertainment fields without regard to race include John Levy, Andrew Stroud, Bob Redcross, and Ernestine McClendon. In both jazz and serious music, new integrated musical groups came into being, including the Symphony of the New World. These amiable happenings in the amusement world over the years have been ably recorded by Jesse Walker, entertainment editor of Harlem's *Amsterdam News* and leading uptown drama critic. Besides Walker, among the few widely read Negro writers on the theatre for many years is Theophilus Lewis, who also once reviewed plays for the *Amsterdam News*. He then became drama critic of *America*, the first Negro to serve in such a capacity on a white periodical. As Juanita Hall sang in *South Pacific*, "If you don't have a dream, how you gonna' have a dream come true?"

A wardrobe mistress backstage in television.

296

Jesse H. Walker is drama critic as well as managing editor of the New York Amsterdam News.

Dave Hepburn is public information officer for Metromedia.

George Norford, reporter, columnist, editor and film writer, is a general executive of Westinghouse Broadcasting Company, coordinating the Broadcast Skills Bank designed to expand job opportunities for minority group members.

Negroes are appearing in front of the television cameras not only as entertainers but as staff reporters. Here Robert Teague covers a civil rights demonstration for NBC-TV.

THE NEGRO IN FILMS

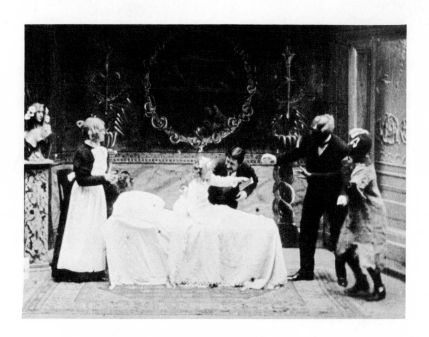

Little Eva's deathbed scene in the first film version of Uncle Tom's Cabin, *directed in 1909 by Edwin S. Porter. A white actor in blackface played Tom as the stereotype of the old faithful slave. The next film production of Mrs. Stowe's novel, four years later, had the veteran Negro actor Sam Lucas in the title role.*

I t has been a long journey to this moment," said Sidney Poitier in Hollywood as he was presented with an Oscar for his performance in *Lilies of the Field*. He was the first Negro to achieve this award, although in 1939 Hattie McDaniel was chosen Best Supporting Actress for *Gone with the Wind*. The long journey for Negro actors of which Poitier spoke began in silent films when the stereotypes were firmly set from which Negro actors have not yet been completely freed. Typical films of this period were the two series *Rastus* (around 1910) and *Sambo* (1909–1911), which pictured their characters as humorous, lazy, shiftless and stupid.

With the advent of talkies, the range of stereotypes widened to embrace the humble and loyal Mammy, who seemed not only to cook well but to sing jubilantly. From such early musical films as *Hallelujah* and *Hearts in Dixie* in 1929, which were beautifully performed by Negro casts, the path led to *The Green Pastures* (1936) and eventually to *Porgy and Bess* (1959). Talented players

Sidney Poitier, first Negro actor to achieve film stardom solely through acting. He won the Academy award in 1963 for the best performance of the year.

There was a third version of Uncle Tom's Cabin *in 1918, with the same white actress playing both Eva and Topsy. In 1927 Universal filmed the novel, casting the Negro actor James Lowe (above) in the lead, with Virginia Grey as Eva. Lowe, who replaced Charles Gilpin when that actor quit in protest over the director's sentimental interpretation of the role, gave Tom a more militant reading.*

whose names flashed across the screen in the early days included Clarence Muse, Stepin Fetchit, Daniel Haynes, Nina Mae McKinney, Paul Robeson, Frank Wilson, Rex Ingram, Eddie "Rochester" Anderson, Bill "Bojangles" Robinson, Butterfly McQueen and finally Hattie McDaniel, the great Mammy of *Gone with the Wind*.

While Hollywood was busy pouring the wealth of Negro talent into limited molds, a handful of independent "colored" film companies (owned by whites but catering to a Negro public), sprang up to give such fine actresses as Louise Beavers a chance to change from traditional bandana or maid's uniform into such fashionable creations as her Hollywood salary permitted her to buy, and to play roles closer to her own life. There were Ralph Cooper's Million Dollar Productions which presented *The Duke Is Tops* starring Lena Horne and himself; the Oscar Micheaux creations made from his own scripts; the Goldberg productions of *Mystery in Swing* (1938) and others; and the first all-Negro cowboy film, *Harlem on the Prairie* (1939).

Following World War II, a rash of all-Negro films came out including *Cabin in the Sky* (1943) with Ethel Waters, Lena Horne, Eddie "Rochester"

The Birth of a Nation was an historic picture for two reasons. Through it the Southern director, David Wark Griffith, made many contributions to film art. At the same time, his racist bias made it a gross distortion of the historical facts and a vicious libel on the Negro people. In the scene below, the "heroic" Ku Klux Klan terrorizes one of the Negroes presented as a murderous bully out to desecrate pure white Southern womanhood. There was a storm of protest against the showing of the film.

Darktown Follies, *one of the films made by small companies catering to Negro audiences. For one such company Nobel Johnson, a Negro actor, became a producer and director in 1919, after some years of playing Indians in Western serials.*

Anderson, Rex Ingram, Butterfly McQueen; and *Stormy Weather* (1943) starring Miss Horne again. Three films on "passing for white" appeared: *Imitation of Life* (1943) with Louise Beavers and Fredi Washington; *Pinky* (1949) with Ethel Waters; and *Lost Boundaries* (1949).

Some outstanding Negro performances in films have been Leigh Whipper in *The Ox Bow Incident* (1943), Canada Lee in *Body and Soul* (1947), James Edwards in *Home of the Brave* (1949), Juano Hernandez in *Intruder in the Dust* (1949), Ethel Waters in *The Member of the*

Wedding (1953), Marpessa Dawn in the French *Black Orpheus* (1959), Brock Peters in *To Kill A Mockingbird* and *The L-Shaped Room* (1963), Ruby Dee in *The Balcony* (1963), Brock Peters and Thelma Oliver in *The Pawnbroker* (1965), and Ivan Dixon, Abby Lincoln and Gloria Foster in *Nothing But A Man* (1965), which received the top film award at the First World Festival of Negro Arts in Dakar, Senegal in 1966.

Samuel Goldwyn in 1959 brought to the screen in color his $7 million production of *Porgy and Bess* with Sidney Poitier, Dorothy Dandridge,

In 1922, seven years after his Birth of a Nation, D. W. Griffith launched the movie cliché of the cowardly but funny Negro frightened to death by ghosts. A white actor in blackface depicted the scared Negro. The formula of Negroes running scared persisted in films until quite recently.

Hal Roach's "Our Gang" comedies began in the silent era and always featured a Negro child as part of the neighborhood bunch that played together naturally. The popular series was criticized for sometimes making the Negro child the butt of the humor.

The "dear old Southland" beloved by Hollywood was the setting for the pioneer all-Negro film, Hearts in Dixie, *made by Fox in 1929. Stepin Fetchit was featured in his lazy, shuffling, no-account Negro routine. Vivian Smith, Clarence Muse and Eugene Jackson held the principal roles.*

MGM swiftly followed Hearts in Dixie *with King Vidor's* Hallelujah, *another all-Negro film. It gave Daniel Haynes and Nina Mae McKinney major roles, but it did not break with the cliché of the childish, irresistibly funny, laughing-dancing-singing Negro.*

Pearl Bailey, Sammy Davis, Brock Peters, Diahann Carroll, Clarence Muse, Leslie Scott and Ruth Attaway among the players. Robert McFerrin and Adele Addison dubbed the songs for Porgy and for Bess. The screenplay was by N. Richard Nash. Otto Preminger directed. There were no Negroes listed on the production staff, nor among its technical or artistic advisors. Negroes have very infrequently participated in these areas of film making, or in those of cinema writing or producing. Exceptions in writing are *Way Down South* (1942) with a screenplay by Langston Hughes and Clarence Muse; *Bright Road* (1953) based on

Mary Elizabeth Vroman's story *See How They Run; Odds Against Tomorrow* (1959) from a screenplay by John Oliver Killens produced by Harry Belafonte; *Take A Giant Step* based on the drama by Louis Peterson; *Raisin in the Sun* (1961) with play and script by Lorraine Hansberry; *Gone Are the Days* (1963) which later reverted to its stage title, *Purlie Victorious,* from a play by Ossie Davis.

Although many fine performances have been turned in by Negro performers in films, only one actor in the *dramatic* sense alone has achieved stardom. Lena Horne came up by way of singing,

Dorothy Dandridge caught the public fancy in the musical *Carmen Jones* (1954), and Harry Belafonte first became a name through the medium of the folk song. It was Sidney Poitier who achieved stardom as a straight actor, neither singing nor dancing. Climaxing a dozen roles including those in *No Way Out* (1950), *The Blackboard Jungle* (1955), *The Defiant Ones* (1958), *Paris Blues* (1960), and *Raisin in the Sun* (1961), Sidney Poitier in 1963 following the success of *Lilies of the Field*, received Hollywood's top award, the Oscar as the year's Best Actor. In 1966 he starred in *The Slender Thread, A Patch of Blue* and *Duel At Diablo*. His name now receives top billing on movie marquees around the world.

Half-a-dozen years passed before Hollywood tried another all-Negro film, The Green Pastures. *Warner Bros. put the Marc Connelly play on the screen with Rex Ingram as De Lawd, advertising it as "a delightful and daring portrayal of Negro religion." Eddie Anderson played Noah, and Ernest Whitman, Pharaoh, with Clinton Rosemond and Oscar Polk showing their talent in other roles.*

Rex Ingram played the runaway slave, Jim, in MGM's 1939 version of Huckle-berry Finn. Mickey Rooney was Huck. Ingram, born in 1895, had entered the Hollywood film jungle in 1920 through a role in Tarzan of the Apes.

308

The boxing champion, Archie Moore, played Jim when another version of Mark Twain's masterpiece was put on the screen in 1960. This time Eddie Hodges was Huck.

309

A maid's, butler's, or stableman's uniform for a long time was the standard costume when Negroes appeared in movies. At lower right is Clinton Rosemond in Jezebel *with Bette Davis and Donald Crisp.* Above, with Vivien Leigh, star of Gone With the Wind, *is Hattie McDaniel in the role that won her an Oscar for the best supporting actress of 1939. At top right Hattie McDaniel lords it over the other maids in* Maryland (1940).

311

In the film adaptation of the Ellen Glasgow novel, In This Our Life (1942), Ernest Anderson played a Negro law student whom whites try—but fail—to frame for the killing of a child by a car. The Warner film, directed by John Huston, dealt boldly with the racial issue.

The screen musical, Carmen Jones, starred Harry Belafonte and Dorothy Dandridge.

Bill Robinson and Lena Horne co-starred in Stormy Weather, *which also included Katherine Dunham, Cab Calloway, Fats Waller, the Nicholas Brothers
and Dooley Wilson. The all-Negro musicals of the 1940s were not commercial
hits; the South banned them. Memphis censors even snipped Lena Horne out
of* Ziegfeld Follies *and banned another film because in it the white star tipped
his hat to a Negro.*

Cabin in the Sky *gave Lena Horne her first film chance and let Eddie Anderson get out of his "Rochester" groove to show how he could act. Kenneth Spencer, Buck and Bubbles, Louis Armstrong, Mantan Moreland and Duke Ellington displayed their talents in the night club sequences.*

In the wartime film Crash Dive (1943), *Ben Carter played a part modelled on Dorie Miller, the Navy messman on the battleship* Arizona *who shot down four Japanese planes in the attack on Pearl Harbor and became one of World War II's early heroes.*

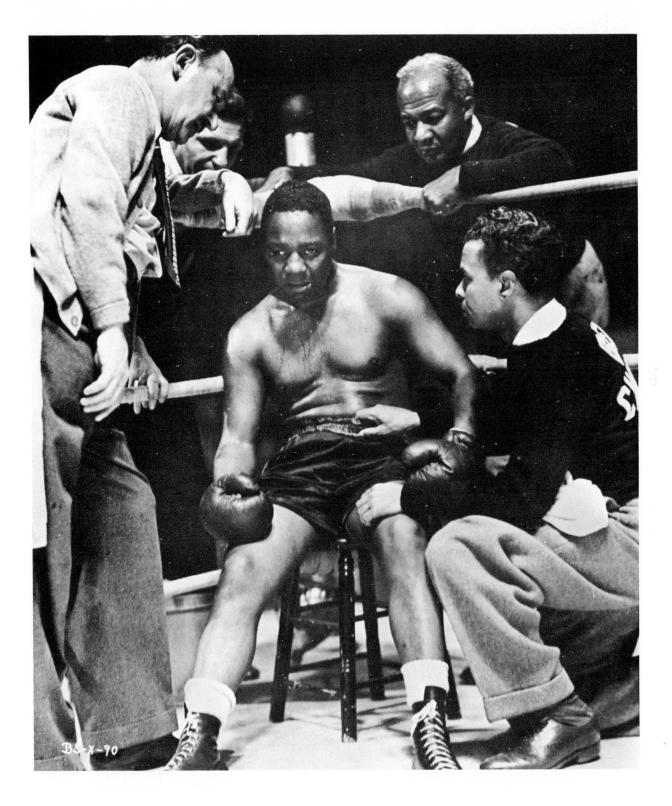

Canada Lee's screen performances were usually superb. The Kentuckian was a successful boxer who turned to acting and won a great reputation on Broadway before going to Hollywood. Here he is the fighter in *Body and Soul*.

In Cry, the Beloved Country, *a film about South Africa, the veteran Canada Lee played alongside the newcomer Sidney Poitier.*

Canada Lee in Alfred Hitchcock's Lifeboat.

Pinky, *one of the postwar films with "passing for white" as a theme, featured* Ethel Waters *and* Frederick O'Neal (*later the first Negro to be elected president of Actors Equity*). Jeanne Crain—*white—played the Negro girl trying to pass.*

James Edwards in Home of the Brave. Originally a Broadway play about anti-Semitism, it was converted into one of the early postwar films against anti-Negro prejudice.

Paul Robeson appeared in several films in the 1930s, all of them made in England. His best was The Proud Valley, in which he played a miner in a Welsh village. In 1943, after his great success as Othello on Broadway, he made Tales of Manhattan in Hollywood, with Ethel Waters and Eddie Anderson (above). Disappointed in the stereotyped outcome, he refused all offers to make additional American films of that kind.

Dotts Johnson was featured in Roberto Rossellini's Paisan, one of the early postwar Italian films in the neorealist style. Johnson stayed abroad playing roles in many films shot in Italy.

Dooley Wilson as Humphrey Bogart's friend ("play it, Sam") in Casablanca, provides the lyric notes for a love scene with Ingrid Bergman. Wilson was a bandleader in Europe for many years, became an actor in the Federal Theatre, and then mixed Broadway with Hollywood for several years.

In The Ox-Bow Incident *(1943), a strong attack on lynch law, Leigh Whipper played a Negro preacher who tries to stop a mob murder. The 20th-Century-Fox film, directed by William Wellman, ranked with* Fury *and* Grapes of Wrath *as a powerful social document.*

319

In A Patch of Blue *(1966), Sidney Poitier tries to teach blind Elizabeth Hartman how to be self-sufficient.*

One of the earliest postwar films to present a Negro not as an entertainer or menial was No Way Out, *in which Sidney Poitier played a doctor.*

A shot taken during the filming in Chicago of A Raisin in the Sun, *made from Lorraine Hansberry's hit play. Sidney Poitier is in the booth and Claudia Mc-Neil, playing his mother, stands by. They did the same roles on Broadway.*

One of the most discussed films of its year was the prize-winning Nothing But a Man, *co-starring the young Ivan Dixon with Abbey Lincoln, the singer turned actress. It was the story of a Negro railroad worker in a Southern town.*

'A PATCH OF BLUE' DRAWS IN SOUTH

NYT 4/766

Movie Makers Find Signs of Changing Atmosphere

By VINCENT CANBY

"A Patch of Blue," Metro-Goldwyn-Mayer's sentimental film about the relationship between a blind white girl and a Negro office worker, is proving to be as big a box-office hit in the South as it is in the North.

Southern audiences, however, are seeing the film minus a short scene in which Elizabeth Hartman, who has won an Oscar nomination for her performance as the blind girl, kisses Sidney Poitier, who plays the office worker. The kissing scene, said by one Metro executive to represent about eight seconds of running time, has been eliminated only from prints shown in the Southern market.

A subject for film industry debate currently is whether or not the success of the film in such cities as Atlanta, Miami, Dallas, Houston and Charlotte signifies any important change in Southern attitudes towards films dealing — even indirectly — with the racial issue.

Mr. Poitier, who was awarded an Oscar for "Lilies of the Field," has played in several films that have done well in the South, particularly "Lilies." However, "Path of Blue" is the first Poitier film to hint at a contemporary Negro-white romance, even in the most restrained terms.

In the film Miss Hartman, the blind daughter of parents who are as disreputable as they are poor, is befriended by Mr. Poitier, who is instrumental in her spiritual rehabilitation while spurning her tentative romantic advances. One film executive interprets white Southern reaction to the film as meaning:

"He [Mr. Poitier] should be noble, as he is in the film, to make up for the fact that he's a

RADIO AND ITS PAST

Eddie "Rochester" Anderson, radio's most popular Negro performer, with Jack Benny, on whose program he was featured for many years.

In 1928 the white team of *Amos 'n' Andy* made its national debut on radio in blackface. Almost instantly it became a top rated show. Its characters were created by two white comedians, Freeman Gosden and Charles Correll, who in 1925 began broadcasting on a local Chicago radio station a show called *Sam 'n' Henry,* the prototype and forerunner of *Amos 'n' Andy.* Negroes were eventually used in supporting roles on the national radio hookup as the cast increased, but nevertheless many claimed the show presented the old stereotypes, and, even though it was generally agreed it was amusing, it served to perpetu-

ate a graven image. Such well-known personalities as Hattie McDaniel and Amanda Randolph were criticized for their participation in the show. Nevertheless, *Amos 'n' Andy* endured for forty years from radio popularity into television.

There were other highly popular shows including *Duffy's Tavern* which featured the former vaudeville comedian, Eddie Green. Butterfly McQueen once presided weekly on the *Danny Kaye Show* as the president of his one-woman fan club. Lillian Randolph was Birdie on *The Great Gildersleeve Show.* Thelma Carpenter was billed on Eddie Cantor's weekly variety hour as his "singing

Betty Grainger

George Goodman

Jack Walker

Nora Holt

discovery." *Beulah,* with Hattie McDaniel in the title role, was a long-run series, with Butterfly McQueen as Oriole. But the most popular of all the Negro performers in radio was Eddie "Rochester" Anderson, who became a permanent fixture on the *Jack Benny* program.

Negro actors on radio, however, remained scarce. But Negro singers had more representation, especially during the Forties. Groups rather than individual singers were the rage then, and The Charioteers, The Delta Rhythm Boys, The Southern Harmonizers, The Inkspots, Wings Over Jordan, and The Four Vagabonds (considered radio's best beer salesmen), were often guests and sometimes featured as regular members on programs. The Four Vagabonds were members of the American Broadcasting Company's *Breakfast Club,* were regulars on ABC's *Club Matinee,* and on weekends did guest appearances on NBC.

During the big-band era Ethel Waters and Billie Holiday were singers who appeared frequently on dance band shows as soloists and were usually backed by white bands. But none of the big popular colored bands such as Duke Ellington, Lionel Hampton and Count Basie were able to get a foothold in radio as regulars. They were relegated to occasional guest appearances only. For a time songstress Midge Williams had a solo program on the Blue Network. And the singing pianist, Una Mae Carlisle, in 1951 was given her own show on an American Broadcasting Company network, aired over more than one hundred stations and reaching a Saturday evening audience of some 7,000,000 listeners.

Least impressive of all was Negro participation as announcers, newscasters or scriptwriters. There were and still are not any coast-to-coast network persons of color in these categories. In 1946, a

Lillian Randolph as Birdie on The Great Gildersleeve.

local New York station, WMCA, seems to have been the first station to hire a Negro as a staff announcer. He was Roi Ottley. Another local New York station in the 1960's sponsored the jazz pianist, Billy Taylor, in his own show. But customarily only those stations in various cities having programs beamed primarily at Negro listeners employed more than token Negroes in any staff capacities, or as disc jockeys, commentators or newscasters.

WLIB in New York employed a large colored staff including George Goodman, Clarence Rock and several others on news, Evelyn Cunningham and Betty Grainger handling interview programs, with Jack Walker and Dr. Jive jockeying rock and roll, Nora Holt conducting classical programs, and Joe Bostic in charge of *The Gospel Train*. In Cleveland, Mary Holt and Valena Williams have been pioneer women commentators, as has Alma John in New York and Bernice Bass in Newark.

Top Negro disc jockeys have included Don Barksdale in San Francisco, Ollie McLaughlin in Ann Arbor, Cane Cole in Memphis, Daddy-O Dailey in Chicago, and Hall Jackson and Larry Fuller in New York, where Doc Wheeler is also a popular gospel announcer.

Script writers include William Branch in educational radio, George Norford, Langston Hughes and Chicago's Richard Durham who did an extended series on Negro history for the *Chicago Defender*. Durham also wrote a popular soap opera series, *Here Comes Tomorrow*. Atlanta and a few other cities have Negro-owned radio stations presenting varied programs, but with the accent on music, news and comment appealing primarily to colored listeners. Popular as guest artists (but seldom with their own regular shows) have been top Negro singers: Sammy Davis, Lena Horne, Leslie Uggams, Nancy Wilson and Gilbert Price as well as numerous folk and rock-and-roll artists.

"The Charioteers," one of radio's many popular vocal groups.

Negroes have played a part in radio away from the mike, too: as sound effects technician, publicity man, music clearance supervisor.

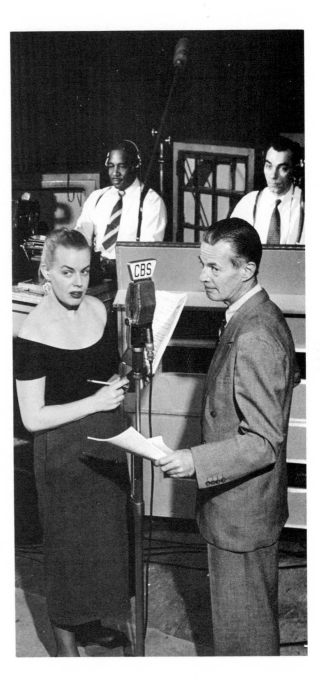

327

TELEVISION
OPENS DOORS

The Philco TV Playhouse, one of the major dramatic series in early days, featured Sidney Poitier in The Parole Officer.

From the very beginning of television, in contrast to radio, Negro performers were more or less employed with dignity, if not with regularity, as on the *Ed Sullivan* show. Sullivan was always an outspoken critic of segregation and a pioneer in using Negroes as performers not consigned to stereotypes. On his first show in 1948, against the opposition of southern salesmen for sponsored products, he upheld his right to present colored guests. Sullivan's is the oldest variety show on television. Essentially the same argument against the use of Negro performers prevailed in television as in radio—that the southern market would violently object. However, in 1951 *Amos 'n' Andy* came to TV with an all-Negro cast, featuring Tim Moore in the role of Kingfish. The new show enjoyed almost as much popularity on TV as it did on radio, until 1966 when it was retired by CBS after more than forty years on the airwaves.

In TV's infancy, Negroes were mainly seen on variety shows. Their participation in dramatic presentations was almost nil until the late 1950's when major changes in our society began to occur on the racial front. Many half-hour dramatic shows then initiated Negroes as guest performers. Diahann Carroll appeared on *The Peter Gunn* series. Eartha

One of TV's first stars, Sid Caesar, included the Billy Williams Quartet on his long-run program.

The first major show produced by a Negro for TV was Harry Belafonte's Strolling Twenties. The CBS program was presented in 1966.

Kitt acted in shows such as *Burke's Law*. Miss Kitt was also one of the first Negro performers to appear in a dramatic show without regard to a racial designation. She starred in the role of Salome in *Omnibus*. With an all-Negro cast, *The Green Pastures* received a major production with William Warfield as De Lawd. Claudia McNeil starred in *A Member of the Wedding*.

In 1957 in the musical realm, Nat "King" Cole was given his own show by NBC. It ran for several months but failed to attract commercial sponsors. However, on all the major variety programs in the 1950's Negroes were frequent guests. Pearl Bailey, Lena Horne, Louis Armstrong and Harry Bela-

fonte became favorite artists. It was not until 1966 that a Negro finally got his own show with important commercial sponsors. But the Sammy Davis NBC variety hour did not last long. Before that, Davis, like many other Negro stars, went to Canada and England and did spectaculars (hour-long telecasts) which were eventually shown over local stations in America, but never over a national hookup.

Harry Belafonte was the first Negro performer in the United States to have an hour-long spectacular on TV. One of his two spectaculars won an Emmy award for its excellence. Belafonte was also the first Negro to produce a major show for tele-

Lloyd Richards, director of Broadway shows, was the first Negro to direct major TV productions.

vision. His 1966 *Strollin' Twenties* with a script by Langston Hughes and Sidney Poitier as narrator, starred Sammy Davis, Diahann Carroll and Nipsey Russell.

Bill Cosby, a nightclub comic, became the first Negro to co-star in a continuing series with a white actor. *I Spy,* an hour's thriller, lost no sponsors for the network in any of its markets, and the show became a favorite of television audiences. Cosby won an Emmy award as the best dramatic actor in a TV series for 1965. A significant breakthrough for Negroes in television (as in radio) came through opera. Leontyne Price sang the taxing title role of *Tosca* for the *NBC Opera Theatre,* gathering unanimous praise. And the airwaves have hosted numerous Negro voices from the Metropolitan. Such religious programs as *Lamp Unto My Feet* have consistently employed Negroes in a variety of ways as actors, singers and ballet dancers, and they have also used scripts by colored writers.

Simply Heavenly was the first all-Negro musical presented on *Play of the Week,* which also introduced Eartha Kitt in Maxwell Anderson's *Winged Victory.* Sammy Davis was featured in *Ben Casey*

and Hilda Simms appeared often in *The Nurses,* as did Claudia McNeil and Ruby Dee. Perry Como and his *Kraft Music Hall* presented Lena Horne as a frequent guest, while Leslie Uggams, often on the *Mitch Miller Show,* and the Supremes in various spot appearances, were popular. Ossie Davis, Ruby Dee, James Earl Jones and Diana Sands interpreted Negro poetry on the video screen. Nipsey Russell co-hosted a nighttime show with Les Crane, and comics Godfrey Cambridge and Dick Gregory have often had happy innings as television guests. In 1967 Harry Belafonte presented a spectacular of Negro comedy.

East Side, West Side, a CBS drama series built around a social worker, featured several Negroes weekly, including Cicely Tyson.

331

The I Spy thriller series on NBC-TV won national attention for presenting Bill Cosby as co-star with Robert Culp.

Often the guest star on other programs, Sammy Davis ran his own show over NBC-TV in 1966.

Louis Armstrong joins Carol Channing on a Du Pont special over CBS-TV.

333

Claudia McNeil starred in Member of the Wedding *on Du Pont's Show of the Month.*

The oldest variety show on television, The Ed Sullivan Show *has always presented Negro guests. Louis Armstrong plays amid an integrated chorus.*

The Dean Martin Show *has often played host to such Negro stars as Ella Fitzgerald (below) and Pearl Bailey (opposite).*

335

THE GOLDEN DOZENS

Of the all-time greats among Negroes in the various fields of entertainment, there can be little argument concerning the place of such names as Ira Aldridge, Buddy Bolden, Black Patti, Ernest Hogan, Bert Williams, Florence Mills or Bojangles, whose talent and popularity history confirms, or whose sparks of personality still light the memories of living spectators old enough to have once seen or heard any of them—excluding, of course, Aldridge. Concerning contemporary artists there may well be differences of opinion. But measured by audience appeal and box office grosses, those listed below can certainly compete with any newcomers who might be named. They may well be headlined members of the Golden Dozens.

CONCERT SINGERS

Marie Selika
Elizabeth T. Greenfield
Sissieretta Jones
Roland Hayes
Marian Anderson
Dorothy Maynor
Muriel Rahn
Camilla Williams
William Warfield
Leontyne Price
Mattiwilda Dobbs
Adele Addison

GOSPEL SINGERS

Mahalia Jackson
Marion Williams
Alex Bradford
Edna Galmon Cooke
Brother John Sellers
James Cleveland
Sister Tharpe
The Caravans
The Ward Singers
The Nightingales
The Martin Singers
The Staples Singers

ACTORS

Ira Aldridge
Charles Gilpin
Hattie McDaniel
Rose McClendon
Paul Robeson
Canada Lee
Claudia McNeil
Sidney Poitier
Ruby Dee
Ossie Davis
Diana Sands
Gloria Foster

COMICS

Sam Lucas
Ernest Hogan
Bert Williams
Billy King
Billy Higgins
Eddie "Rochester"
   Anderson
Dusty Fletcher
Jackie "Moms" Mabley
Pigmeat Markham
Nipsey Russell
Godfrey Cambridge
Dick Gregory

POPULAR SINGERS

Ma Rainey
Bessie Smith
Florence Mills
Ella Fitzgerald
Jimmy Rushing
Billie Holiday
Mabel Mercer
Nat "King" Cole
Lena Horne
Harry Belafonte
Ray Charles
Nina Simone

FOLK MUSICIANS

Jelly Roll Morton
Blind Lemon Jefferson
Leroy Carr
Pinetop Smith
Lonnie Johnson
Memphis Slim
Bertha "Chippie" Hill
Big Bill Broonzy
Memphis Minnie
Brownie McGhee
Sonny Terry
Josh White

DANCERS

Ida Forsyne
Bill "Bojangles" Robinson
Johnny Huggins
Janet Collins
Bill Bailey
Nicholas Brothers
Katherine Dunham
Pearl Primus
Mary Hinkson
Arthur Mitchell
Carmen de Lavallade
Alvin Ailey

JAZZ PERSONALITIES

King Oliver
Buddy Bolden
Louis Armstrong
Duke Ellington
Fats Waller
Count Basie
Lionel Hampton
Charlie Parker
Thelonious Monk
Dizzie Gillespie
Charlie Mingus
Miles Davis

A Golden Dozen of very versatile artists who can hardly be classed correctly in any single category would include the singing-composer-minstrel man, James Bland; the dancer-actor-singer-comedian, George Walker; the musical and dramatic artists, Abbie Mitchell, Ethel Waters, and Juanita Hall; and the all-around performers, Cab Calloway, Josephine Baker, Pearl Bailey, Eartha Kitt, Marpessa Dawn, Thelma Oliver and multi-talented Sammy Davis who impersonates, sings, dances, acts, drums, blows a horn and stands on his head. If he were asked could he do anything else in the performing field, he would probably say, "Yes, I can!"

MANHATTAN MILESTONES

Taking the long view back into the past as a prelude to the present, there are certain milestones to remember in relation to the Negro's participation in American entertainment. New York City is the center of the nation's entertainment industry, exercising an influence on the entire country. Negro performers have been appearing on the stage in Manhattan for almost a century and a half. A chronology of some of the major events in this regard follows:

1821   THE AFRICAN GROVE performs Shakespeare.
1882   CALLENDER'S CONSOLIDATED SPECTACULAR COLORED MINSTRELS open.
1892   SISSIERETTA JONES (Black Patti) sings at Madison Square Garden.
1894   THE CREOLE SHOW, first Negro company to use singing and dancing girls.
1896   WILLIAMS AND WALKER introduce the cakewalk to the stage.
1898   CLORINDY, a musical by Will Marion Cook and Paul Laurence Dunbar.
1902   IN DAHOMEY opens in Times Square with Williams and Walker.
1905   MEMPHIS STUDENTS, first Negro jazz band, open at Proctor's.
1910   BERT WILLIAMS becomes a star in the Ziegfeld Follies.
1912   CLEF CLUB CONCERT at Carnegie Hall presents a symphonic jazz orchestra of 125.
1914   LAFAYETTE STOCK COMPANY opens in Harlem.
1917   THREE PLAYS FOR A NEGRO THEATRE at the Garden Theatre.
1920   THE EMPEROR JONES with Charles Gilpin at the Provincetown.
1921   SHUFFLE ALONG introduces Sissle and Blake, Miller and Lyles.
1923   ROLAND HAYES makes his debut at Carnegie Hall.
1924   DIXIE TO BROADWAY starring Florence Mills in first Negro revue.
1927   PORGY with Frank Wilson and Rose McClendon.
1929   APPEARANCES by Garland Anderson, first play on Broadway by a Negro.

338

1929 HARLEM by Wallace Thurman, second Negro playwright on Broadway.

1930 THE GREEN PASTURES introduces the creative use of Negro folklore in drama.

1935 PORGY AND BESS, destined to have many revivals over the years.

1936 MACBETH directed by Orson Welles for the Federal Theatre in Harlem.

1936 DON'T YOU WANT TO BE FREE? begins a record Harlem run.

1939 MAMBA'S DAUGHTERS introduces Ethel Waters to the dramatic stage.

1943 OTHELLO with Paul Robeson begins longest American Shakespearean run.

1943 KATHERINE DUNHAM in *Tropical Revue* consolidates her long-lasting dance company.

1944 ANNA LUCASTA begins record run of nearly a thousand performances.

1946 TODD DUNCAN and CAMILLA WILLIAMS, first Negroes with New York City Opera.

1952 GREENWICH MEWS THEATRE introduces non-ethnic casting to off-Broadway.

1955 MARIAN ANDERSON's debut at the Metropolitan Opera House.

1956 MR. WONDERFUL, the first Sammy Davis musical.

1957 JAMAICA starring Lena Horne is a Broadway success.

1959 A RAISIN IN THE SUN by Lorraine Hansberry begins record run.

1961 PURLIE VICTORIOUS by Ossie Davis becomes the first Negro hit comedy.

1961 THE BLACKS, first avant-garde success with all-Negro cast.

1966 LEONTYNE PRICE opens the new Metropolitan Opera House at Lincoln Center.

MILLION-DOLLAR EXPORT

America's most famous theatrical export for over forty years has been Josephine Baker. She went to Paris in 1925 as a teenager featured in the chorus of *La Revue Nègre*. Within a year she was a star. After her European triumphs —including her name in lights twenty feet tall (and her name alone) for several seasons over the *Folies Bèrgere*—she returned to New York in 1936 for an engagement in the *Ziegfeld Follies*. But she was coldly received by both press and public. American audiences, before the days of Eartha Kitt, were not accustomed to seeing a Negro in Fath or Patou gowns singing French songs in French, or American songs with a French accent. After a very brief engagement, Miss Baker went back to Paris and did not return to Broadway for fifteen years. This time she broke all box office records at the Strand, doing two shows a day between films with lines outside stretching around the corner. The papers declared nothing like Josephine had ever before been seen on stage in a motion picture presentation theatre—such elegance, charm, sparkle, warmth and personality! The enthusiasm of her 1951 reception indicated that times

had changed. She was declared one of the most beautiful, talented and best-dressed women on the musical stage.

She had left home in St. Louis at the age of fifteen to dance with a Bessie Smith show, and before going to Europe she had been in the chorus lines of *Shuffle Along, Chocolate Dandies,* and at the Plantation Club in New York. At the Champs Elysées Theatre in Paris she was allowed to do a specialty number or two which so enthused the French that she was hailed as the personification of *le jazz hot,* and ever since, Josephine Baker has been credited with creating the continued vogue for jazz music in France. Within a year she was a star at the world's most famous music hall, the *Folies Bèrgere*. During her first long run there she is said to have received some 40,000 love letters and more than 2,000 proposals of marriage even before she had celebrated her twenty-first birthday. In 1930 after her return to France from a world tour of 28 countries, the Casino de Paris created a show around her as a singing and dancing comedienne. Her excursions into motion pictures during that period included the lead in *Zouzou* opposite Jean

Joséphine Baker

Gabin. And during her first five years in Paris she is said to have brought more than a million dollars into Parisian box offices.

During World War II Josephine Baker engaged in underground activities for the Resistance movement before she escaped from Nazi-occupied territory to North Africa where she became a sub-lieutenant in the women's division of the Free French forces. Later in Red Cross clubs and in other allied military installations, she entertained troops all over North Africa and the Middle East. After the liberation of Paris in 1944, she returned to the French capital to appear at the Theatre aux Armees. For her services to the armed forces, the French Republic awarded Josephine Baker the Legion of Honor and the Rosette of the Resistance. In 1956 the President of the Municipal Counsel of Paris presented her with the rarely bestowed Medallion of the City of Paris. At her home in the village of Les Millandes in the Dordogne valley, she and her husband have adopted fourteen children of various nationalities and colors which she calls her "rainbow family." In her stage and night-club appearances around the world, Miss Baker consistently refused to accept engagements in any theatres or clubs that practiced racial discrimination. Offered a large fee for a nightclub appearance in Miami Beach in the Fifties, she declined stating, "I have been told that Negroes cannot go to night-clubs in Miami. I cannot work where my people cannot go. It's as simple as that." The Copa City Club in Miami, desirous of obtaining Miss Baker, thereupon changed its policy, as did other clubs subsequently. Josephine Baker, with a non-discrimination clause in her contract, is credited with breaking the color bar for audiences in Miami.

Genet, whose famous letters from Paris to the *New Yorker* date from the year when Miss Baker made her debut there, wrote in 1949, "Josephine Baker has returned to the *Folies Bèrgere* as its leading lady. She is still excellent star material. Her voice continues to be as sweet and reedy as a woodwind instrument." In 1956 Genet wrote from Paris, "On the Olympia stage, wearing a gorgeous white silk confection *de la haute couture*, with a jewelled white headdress outlining her well-shaped skull, with diamond sequins pasted on her lips so that her laughter, her speech and her singing all seemed to sparkle with refined savagery, she was a dazzling and inexhaustible spectacle."

Concerning her 1951 American appearances, *Ebony* said, "The legend named Josephine Baker has come home again to her native land to score an artistic triumph that show business historians will probably call the most remarkable of our times. The fabled Negro star of the *Folies Bèrgere* of Paris has at the age of 44 achieved the one great success that ironically eluded her in the 26 years of her remarkable career: a smash hit in her own U.S.A."

When Miss Baker, nearing 60 but looking as youthful as ever on stage, performed in New York in 1964 wearing gowns designed by Dior, Balmain, Balenciaga and Lanvin, the *Journal American* described her as appearing in "the most lavish wardrobe and fantastic coiffure since the invention of money." The Associated Press reported her "a champion show queen still." And Manhattan newspapers employed all their superlatives, as random quotes from various reviewers indicate: "She was gorgeous. . . . A superb singing actress. . . . French, English, Spanish and Italian songs don't faze Miss Baker, a crystal-clear enunciator in any language. . . . At times you hear a swinging Edith Piaf, then for a moment the intensity of Lena Horne, then a touch of the lament of Mahalia Jackson. . . . An eyeful and an earful. . . . One of the century's most durable and inimitable stars. . . . The electricity of a superb artist sending waves of excitement across the footlights . . . that voice, that youth and that figure that have made a fool of time."

INTERNATIONAL EXCHANGE

Miriam Makeba, Xosa singer from South Africa.

Among the most gratefully received of African imports to American shores was the talented Miriam Makeba, a Xhosa singer from South Africa, whom *The New York Times* describes as "rolling her remarkably bright, large eyes and clicking like a field of beetles. Miss Makeba sings and pantomimes a large and constantly increasing repertory of Xhosa, Zulu, Calypso, Jewish and English-language songs—each in a style at once indigenous and personal. . . . She is a piquant combination of the exotic, the primitive and the sophisticated." Also from South Africa came Hugh Masekela, jazz trumpeter, and his combo. The Capetown pianist and jazz composer, Dollar Brand, made solo appearances at New York jazz clubs, as did pop singer Sonny Pillay. And in April 1964, a large company of Johannesburg actors associated with the Union Artists Center for Black Africans, opened in New York in an Alan Paton drama, *Sponono,* supervised by the Indian director, Krishna Shah, with a choir of Zulu chanters, and movingly acted by Cocky Tlohothalemaje, Ruth Nkonyeni, Philemon Hou and others. A dozen of the performers remained in New York to perform as the Zulu Dancers at the World's Fair for two seasons.

Michael Olatunji, Nigerian drummer who has stayed in the U.S. to lead a group of African performers.

A long time resident in Manhattan, Michael Olatunji, came to the United States from Nigeria as a student and remained as a drummer and the organizer of a popular troupe of African singers and dancers. Also from Nigeria came Fela Sowande, the first serious African composer to be heard in New York, "gaunt and clad in a brown figured tribal tunic" when he conducted the Philharmonic at Carnegie in 1962 in a program of his own work. Actor John Akar from Sierra Leone played an African role on Broadway in *Mr. Johnson*. And in 1964 Harry Belafonte brought from Guinea to Lincoln Center an amazing tenor, Kandia Conte Fode, with a Gueckedou Orchestra. On more than one visit to America the *Ballets Africains,* also from French-speaking West Africa, delighted Broadway with their "sizzling dances from the jungle." In exchange, although not a conscious one, a troupe of twenty Americans directed by Bob Destiny and starring Liza Donzell, Miss Harlem of 1958, opened in Dakar, Senegal, to begin a tour of French West African capitals.

From Brazil to Broadway's musicals and nightclubs came the mulatto enchantress, Carmen Miranda, the exotic Chiquita Banana of the commercials; from Puerto Rico the singer, Celia Cruz; from Havana the voodoo dance team of Marta and Alexander imported for Sonja Henie's Ice Revue of 1953; also from Cuba the actress and *recitadora* of Caribbean poetry, Eusebia Cosme, and from Martinique the tropical entertainer, Moune de Rivel. Alphonse Cimber, the Haitian drummer, settled in New York, as did Jean Leon Destine, dancer-choreographer, heading his own troupe of Haitian dancers. From Trinidad came dancers Belle Rosette and brothers Bosco and Geoffrey Holder, and from Jamaica the folk singer and comedian, Louis Bennett. Excellent steel bands and Calypso singers like the Mighty Sparrow and the Duke of Iron have contributed their songs and their rhythms to American entertainment over the years. In return many American Negro entertainers and jazz men have appeared in Caribbean and South American cities. Exchange of performers is an unplanned two-way traffic from South to North, North to South, to the delight of all.

THE WORLD'S A STAGE

A poster for the Peters Sisters, entertaining in Paris.

In the Far East during the decade preceding World War II, Teddy Weatherford's aggregation of colored musicians was the favorite jazz band with British colonists from Shanghai and Hong Kong through Siam and Burma to Calcutta and Bombay. Periodically the band made long tours through the Malay States and wherever else the Union Jack flew over British compounds. Other popular Negro jazz combinations in the East were those of Bob Hill, Jimmie Carsona and Jack Carter. Buck Clayton, star soloist, played with various bands, and Bill Hagemon was cocktail pianist at the Cathay in Shanghai. During that period Chicago's Nora Holt was a smart chanteuse at Shanghai's Little Club performing in both English and French, the Drinkards were adagio dancers at the Canidrome Gardens, Midge Williams and her brothers were singing and dancing at various clubs, as was Valaida Snow, and the Mackey Twins tapped their way throughout the Orient. Numerous Negro entertainers received hearty welcomes in Australia. Tap dancer U. S. Thompson toured down under for a year. Comedian Pigmeat Markham recently regaled the

Nora Holt was one of the many American Negro performers popular in Shanghai in the early 1930s.

Aussies. *Black Nativity* with Alex Bradford toured there and in New Zealand during the Sixties, while the Alvin Ailey Dancers came back to Sydney and Melbourne twice for return engagements. In Tokyo the singing comedian, Billy Banks, who was formerly at Billy Rose's Diamond Horseshoe in New York, became a revue and television star to the delight of the Japanese public.

Since the turn of the century when James Bland, other minstrel men, and Williams and Walker delighted Britishers, colored entertainers have been warmly received in England. There they have especially enjoyed singing teams like Creamer and Layton, Hatch and Carpenter, and Rosamond Johnson and Taylor Gordon, as well as quartets like the Four Harmony Kings, the Southernaires and the Delta Rhythm Boys. Florence Mills was loved in Britain, also Muriel Smith who created the role of Lady Thiang in the London production of *The King and I*. Comedy stars Greenlee and Drayton, pianist Leslie Hutchinson and singing pianist Zaidee Jackson were hits there, as were entertainers Fats Waller, Elizabeth Welch, Adelaide Hall and tap dancer Teddy Hall. Paul Robeson was a great favorite in England both on stage and in concert. Bertice Reading was a hit in *The Jazz Train*. Gospel singer Mahalia Jackson had S.R.O. crowds at London's Albert Hall. Lena Horne, Sammy Davis and Eartha Kitt were frequent nightclub headliners. In return, England sent to America song stylist Mabel Mercer of New York's fashionable East Side night spots, and Shirley Bassey who popularized the song *Goldfinger*. In the theatre Claudia McNeil captured English hearts in *The Amen Corner*.

In Paris, Eartha Kitt first came to fame, and pretty Marpessa Dawn from Washington became a star, giving more than one thousand performances in French in the comedy *Cherie Noire*, and in Brazil she made the motion picture *Black Orpheus*. Lorraine Hansberry's *A Raisin in the Sun* (*Un Raisin au Soleil*) was performed by a colored French-speaking company at the Comedie Caumartin, and Adrienne Kennedy's *The Rats' Mass* was done in Rome. Folk singer Gordon Heath of the Club Abbaye in Paris, who is an executive of the Studio Theatre there, directed *In White*

Billy Banks, singing comedian, a star in Japan.

America, Telemachus Clay, and Arthur Miller's *After the Fall*. Donald Cardwell does sets for Parisian plays including *Topaze*, a 1966 hit. Jimmy Davis, co-composer of *Lover Man* and long-time resident of France, wrote the score for Nicolas Bataille's *Paris 1900-24*, and appeared in the first Alain Delon film. Babe Wallace starred at the *Folies Bèrgere* and toured the continent.

Colored entertainers have long been popular in the French capital—the dancing Berry Brothers, the Nicholas Brothers, the Peters Sisters, Hazel Scott. Louis Armstrong, Lionel Hampton, Clara Ward, Nancy Holloway and Dionne Warwick have headlined at the Olympia. And in jazz Sidney Bechet, Bud Powell, Memphis Slim, Jack Dupree,

Featured among the American artists at the African Festival of the Arts in Dakar, Senegal in 1966 was the Alvin Ailey dance company.

348

In New Delhi, Duke Ellington chats with members of the orchestra at the Bharatiya Kala Kendra school following a performance given in his honor.

Art Taylor, Joe Turner who sings in nine languages at the Calvados, Kenny Clarke at the Blue Note, and pianists Art Simmons and Aaron Bridges who are long-time fixtures at the Living Room. In the Soviet Union before the war, Wayland Rudd was a popular performer in both films and theatre. In Italy John Kitzmiller, Dots Johnson and Leo Coleman had excellent film roles, and William Demby and Ben Johnson have written for movies there. *Mulatto* with Italian actors in blackface was a part of the repertoire of the Compagnia del Teatro Italiano in Rome and Milan. And a small group of colored artists who remained in Rome after the filming of *Cleopatra* formed an acting

company under the direction of Jay J. Riley which presented *Shakespeare in Harlem, Trumpets of the Lord,* and other American works in Italy.

Scandinavia has given a warm welcome to colored performers in recent years, particularly to exponents of the modern dance and its choreographers, including Talley Beatty, George Mills and Sylvester Campbell. Singer Anne Wiggins Brown, the original Bess of *Porgy and Bess,* lives in Oslo, as does contralto Ruth Reese, known throughout the North Countries as "The Black Rose." Soprano Mattiwilda Dobbs has settled in Stockholm and concertizes throughout Europe. Set and costume designer Ves Harper resides in Copen-

In the 1700-year-old Roman coliseum in Tunis, Leonard de Paur (right) presents a souvenir album of songs by the De Paur Chorus to Kheled Kallala. In background is a group of Tunisian singers who presented traditional music for the American chorus.

After her concert at the Charter Hall in Lusaka, Zambia, the American pianist, Armenta Adams, receives a Barotse tray from a government official.

*At the Cheshire Home for Crippled Children in Addis Ababa, Ethiopia, Dennis
Perren of the Phoenix Singers gets a young chorus under way.*

hagen. The Tivoli Gardens in that city frequently
has Negro stars from America topping its variety
bills. The Howard University Players were applauded in Scandinavia for their performances of
Ibsen in English. And Earle Hyman is a favorite
Othello there.

The Cultural Division of the State Department
has sponsored numerous tours abroad of Negro
artists and jazz men—the Leonard DePaur Chorus,
Marion Williams, Randy Weston, Louis Armstrong, Cozy Cole and others in Africa, and Dizzy
Gillespie in Turkey and the Near East. To the
First World Festival of Negro Arts in Senegal in
1966, the government sent Duke Ellington and
his band, opera star Martina Arroya, pianist Armenta Adams, the Alvin Ailey Dancers and others.

Hundreds of Negro entertainers toured the
U.S.O. clubs and army installations during World
War II, from Europe to the South Pacific, and
later to Korea and Vietnam where they entertained not only the military personnel but the native people as well. The warmest international re-
ceptions ever accorded any large group of travelling
performers were those tendered the *Porgy and
Bess* company on its two-year State Department
tour of four continents. Louis Armstrong and Duke
Ellington have been hailed just about everywhere,
too, from the Congo to Calcutta. From Bamako
to Bombay the basic beat throbs. Its black magic
is welcomed around the world. Where live performers do not go, records and video tapes travel.
Telestar transmits—just as Duke Ellington wrote

it—"It don't mean a thing if it ain't got that swing." For over a century, Negro performers have been the joyous ambassadors of an important phase of American cultural life.

Predictions are onerous, but the past speaks for itself. Certainly, the Negro performer has had a large and appreciative audience over the years, with great salvos of applause for his success. There have been changes in styles and fashions of entertainment, from the minstrels to the theater of the absurd. To all of these changes the Negro has adjusted and contributed the unique aspects of his talent. As the last quarter of the twentieth century approaches, the Negro performer awaits ever greater participation in the mainstream of American expression. He awaits, as well, his own great

playwrights to express the various as yet untouched nuances of Negro life. He awaits the return to Broadway of singing musicals to utilize the rich voices seldom heard in the theatre since the days of Williams and Walker. And he awaits a Negro theatre center in the heart of Harlem or elsewhere for the implementation of his folk arts as well as the extension of all forms of modern expression, oriented toward the needs of the Negro people but for the enjoyment of all. America has a wealth of Negro talent recognized today at home and abroad. When additional means are found to use its still only partially tapped reservoirs of expression, outer space may throb to basic beat and the moon may be its stage.

The Phoenix Singers perform at the University of Khartoum in the Sudan.

PICTURE CREDITS

Key to picture position: t—top; c—center; b—bottom; l—left; r—right. Combinations: br—bottom right, etc. The following are abbreviations used for picture sources:

American Shakespeare Festival Theatre	ASF
Authors' Collection	AC
Chicago Historical Society	CHS
Columbia Broadcasting System	CBS
Columbia Records	CR
Culver Service	Culver
Greenwich Mews Theatre	GMT
Harvard College Library, Theatre Collection	HTC
Hurok Attractions	HA
Metro-Goldwyn-Mayer, Inc.	MGM
Metropolitan Opera Association	MO
Museum of the City of New York	MCNY
Museum of Modern Art, Film Library	MMA
National Broadcasting Co.	NBC
New York City Ballet	NYCB
New York Public Library:	
Dance Collection	NYPL(DC)
Music Collection	NYPL(MC)
Picture Collection	NYPL(PC)
Schomburg Collection	NYPL(SC)
Theatre Collection	NYPL(TC)
New York Shakespeare Festival	NYSF
RCA Victor Record Division	RCA
Twentieth Century Fox	TCF
United States Information Service	USIS
Village Gate, Art D'Lugoff	VG
Warner Bros. Pictures Inc.	WB
Yale University Library, James Weldon Johnson Collection	YJ

INDEX

B

Baal, 243
Bailey, Bill, 96, 337
Bailey, Buster, 181
Bailey, Pearl, 170, 182, 186, 255, 256-257, 258, 286, 306, 330, 335, 337
Bailey, Therman, 147
Bainter, Fay, 35
Baker, Josephine, 4, 91, 97, 98, 101, 170, 288, 337, 340-342
Baker, LaVern, 170, 186
Bal Negre, 267
Balanchine, George, 255, 276
The Balcony, 302
Baldwin, James, 217, 221, 223, 227, 251
Ballad for Bimshire, 245
The Ballad of Jazz Street, 238
The Ballad of the Sad Café, 214
Ballet, 268-276; see also Dancing
Ballet Americana, 270
Ballets Africains, 345
Bamboche, 267
Bandana Land, 46, 54
Banks, Billy, 348
The Baptism, 250, 252
Barber, Samuel, 156
Barksdale, Don, 326
Barnes, Irving, 160
Barnes, Mae, 182, 259
Barnett, Brunetta, 239
Barnum, P. T., 61, 62, 63
Barr, Fred, 170
Barr, Richard, 248
The Barrier, 128, 144, 163
Barrymore, Ethel, 196
Basie, Count, 77, 79, 84, 170, 325, 337
Basket, Jimmy, 172
Bass, Anthony, 270
Bass, Bernice, 326
Bassey, Shirley, 348
Bates, Daisy, 249
Bates, Peg Leg, 63
Beatles, 4
Beatty, Talley, 267, 270, 350
Beavers, Louise, 301, 302
Bechet, Sidney, 73, 75, 348
Beck, Julian, 245
Beckford, Ruth, 270
The Beggar's Opera, 255
Bel Geddes, Barbara, 199
Belafonte, Harry, 84, 125, 126, 185, 186, 259, 277, 306, 307, 312, 330-331, 336, 345
Belgrave, Cynthia, 239, 250
Bell, Nolan, 189, 191
Bell, Service, 120
Benito Cereno, 246, 247, 249
Benjamin, Bennie, 88
Bennett, Louis, 345
Bennett, Robert Russell, 160
Benny, Jack, 323

Berg, Gertrude, 292
Bergman, Ingrid, 288-289, 318
Bernard, Annabel, 147
Bernardi, Herschel, 292
Berry Brothers, 69, 96, 348
Berry, Marion, 231
Bibb, Leon, 63, 130, 131
Big George, 63
Big Maybelle, 61
Big White Fog, 124, 223
Bigard, Barney, 75
Billy Williams Quartet, 329
Birdland Stars, 289
The Birth of a Nation, 301, 303
Bishop, Andrew, 123
Bishop, Walter, 88
Black Arts Theatre, 251-252
Black Diamonds, 69
Black Drama, 284
Black Manhattan, 106, 284
Black Monday, 217, 243
Black Nativity, 168, 169, 244, 348
Black Orpheus, 302, 348
Black Patti's Troubadours, 48
Black Souls, 196, 236
Blackbirds, 103, 253, 264, 286
Blackbirds of 1928, 103, 105
The Blackboard Jungle, 307
Blackfriar's Guild, 199, 209, 238
Blackmon, Teddy, 123
The Blacks, 237-239, 243, 244, 250, 339
Blackwell, Charles, 295
Blackwell, Otis, 88
Blair, Mary, 110, 113
Blake, Eubie, 69, 71, 88, 97, 99, 101, 338
Bland, James A., 7, 26, 28-29, 85, 284, 337, 348
Bledsoe, Jules, 113
Blind Tom, 6, 14
Bliss, Helena, 147
Blithe Spirit, 288
Bloch, Ernst, 207
Blood Knot, 243, 248, 250
Blood Stream, 113, 196
Bloomer Girl, 253
Bloomgarden, Kermit, 294
The Blue Boy in Black, 244
Blue Holiday, 253
Blues, 80-84, 97, 284
Blues for Mister Charlie, 217, 223, 226
Boatner, Adelaide, 142
Boatner, William, 128
Body and Soul, 302, 315, 317
Bogart, Humphrey, 318
Bohee Brothers, 27
Bolden, Buddy, 73, 336, 337
Bond, Fred Weldon, 284
Bonds, Margaret, 128, 132, 135, 270
Bontemps, Arna, 256, 258, 284
Booke, Sorrell, 233
Booth, Shirley, 259
Borde, Percival, 266
Born to Be, 285
Bosan, Alonzo, 163, 209

E

F

Fairbanks, Mabel, 64
Falco, Louis, 272
Falls, Mildred, 166
Famous Negro Music Makers, 284
Fancy Meeting You Again!, 211
Father of the Blues, 285
Fears, Clifford, 267
Federal Theatre, 117-120, 121, 218, 220, 318, 339
Female impersonators, 64
Ferrer, Jose, 200
Fetchit, Stepin, 301, 305
Fields, W. C., on Bert Williams, 54
Ferguson, Helen, 161
Films, Negroes in: 298-307
Finian's Rainbow, 255
The Fire in the Flint, 194
First World Festival of Negro Arts, 267, 272, 302, 349, 352
Fisher, Rudolph, 220
The Fisherman, 238
Fisk Jubilee Singers, 126, 128, 284
Fitzgerald, Ella, 79, 88, 170, 172, 186, 335, 336
Flavin, Martin, 196
Fletcher, Dusty, 69, 170, 336
Fletcher, Tom, 67, 70, 264, 266, 284
Flower Drum Song, 259
Flowers, Martha, 158, 160
Fly Blackbird, 240, 243
Fode, Kandia Conte, 345
Folies Bèrgere, 98, 340, 342, 348
Folk Musicians, "Golden Dozen," 336
Ford, Clebert, 203
Forsyne, Ida, 75, 92, 96, 337
Fort, Syvilla, 267, 270
The Forty Whites and Thirty Blacks, first integrated minstrel company, 27
Foster, Frances, 232, 234
Foster, Gloria, 214, 246, 248, 249, 302, 336
Foster, Leesa, 160, 191
Foster, William, 284
Four Blind Boys, 168
Four Harmony Kings, 69, 348
Four Prophets, 69
Four Saints in Three Acts, 158, 159
Four Step Brothers, 96
Four Twelves Are Forty-Eight, 211
The Four Vagabonds, 325
Frank, Benno D., 191, 207
Franklin, Aretha, 168
Franklin, Marion, 168
Franzell, Carlotta, 160
Free Southern Theatre, 195
Freeman, Al Jr., 226, 227, 244, 252
Freeman, J. Lawrence, 63
Freitag, Dorothea, 272
Frierson, Andrew, 160
Frisco, dancer, 91
The Frogs, 60

Frohman, Charles, 36
Frohman, Gustave, 36
Front Porch, 189
Fugard, Athol, 248, 250
Fuller, Larry, 326
Fuller, Lorenzo, 255
Funny Girl, 259
A Funny Thing Happened on the Way to the Forum, 259
Funnyhouse of a Negro, 223, 243, 250

G

Gabin, Jean, 342
Gaillard, Slim, 88
Gaines, Edward, 295
Gardella, Tess, 29
Garner, Errol, 79, 88, 180
Garroway, Dave, 295
Gee, Lottie, 99
Genet, 342
Genet, Jean, 237, 238-239
George, Zelma, 161, 163
Georgia Jubilee Singers, 37
Georgia Minstrels, 27
Gershwin, George, 84, 135, 158
Gilbert, Mercedes, 196
Gillespie, Dizzy, 79, 88, 182, 270, 337, 352
Gilliat, Sy, 14
Gilmore, Buddy, 75
Gilpin, Charles, 110, 123, 124, 236, 300, 336, 338
Gilpin Players, 189
Glanville, Maxwell, 125, 209, 212
Glen and Jenkins, 99
Glenn, Robert, 191, 238
Gold Through the Trees, 212
Golden Boy, 261, 262, 272
The "Golden Dozens," 336-337
Golden Gate Quartet, 69, 131
Goldwyn, Samuel, 302
Gomez, Tommy, 267
Gone Are the Days, 306
Gone With the Wind, 298, 301, 310
Gonzales, Babs, 63, 88
Goodman, Benny, 90
Goodman, George, 324, 326
Goodman Theatre, 194
The Goose, 238
Gordon, Max, 209
Gordon, Taylor, 53, 128, 285, 348
Gordone, Charles, 238, 239
Gore, Altovise, 272
Gorky, Maxim, 199
Gosden, Freeman, 323
Gospel music, 164-168
Gospel singers, 164-168, "Golden Dozens," 336
Gospel songwriters, 168
Gospel Train, 168
Gospel TV Time, 168
Gossett, Louis, 212, 214, 226, 228, 234, 239, 245, 250

373

Y

Z